Advanced Persistent Threat
Understanding the Danger and How to Protect Your Organization

Advanced Persistent Threat

Understanding the Danger and How to Protect Your Organization

Dr. Eric Cole

AMSTERDAM • BOSTON • HEIDELBERG • LONDON
NEW YORK • OXFORD • PARIS • SAN DIEGO
SAN FRANCISCO • SINGAPORE • SYDNEY • TOKYO

Syngress is an Imprint of Elsevier

Acquiring Editor:	Chris Katsaropoulos
Development Editor:	Benjamin Rearick
Project Manager:	Malathi Samayan
Designer:	Matthew Limbert

Syngress is an imprint of Elsevier
225 Wyman Street, Waltham, MA 02451, USA

Notices
Knowledge and best practice in this field are constantly changing. As new research and experience broaden our understanding, changes in research methods or professional practices, may become necessary. Practitioners and researchers must always rely on their own experience and knowledge in evaluating and using any information or methods described herein. In using such information or methods they should be mindful of their own safety and the safety of others, including parties for whom they have a professional responsibility.

To the fullest extent of the law, neither the Publisher nor the authors, contributors, or editors, assume any liability for any injury and/or damage to persons or property as a matter of products liability, negligence or otherwise, or from any use or operation of any methods, products, instructions, or ideas contained in the material herein.

Library of Congress Cataloging-in-Publication Data
Cole, Eric.
   Advanced persistent threat: understanding the danger and how to protect your organization/ Dr. Eric Cole.
      pages cm
   Includes bibliographical references and index.
   ISBN 978-1-59749-949-1 (alk. paper)
 1. Computer networks–Security measures. 2. Computer security. 3. Data protection. 4. Computer crimes –Prevention. I. Title.
   QA76.9.A25C5966 2012
   005.8–dc23

                                                              2012043183

British Library Cataloguing-in-Publication Data
A catalogue record for this book is available from the British Library

ISBN: 978-1-59749-949-1

Transferred to Digital Printing in 2013

Working together to grow
libraries in developing countries

www.elsevier.com | www.bookaid.org | www.sabre.org

ELSEVIER   BOOK AID International   Sabre Foundation

For information on all Syngress publications, visit our werbsite at *www.syngress.com*

Dedication

At the end of your life there is really only one thing that matters—family and friends. While this book is dedicated to everyone who has encouraged me along the way, God has blessed me with one of the most wonderful wives anyone could ask for. She has been with me through ups and downs and has always been a shoulder to cry on and a person to celebrate with. She has blessed me with three wonderful children that provide constant joy and truly define the meaning of happiness.

This book is dedicated to my wonderful wife and three amazing children.

Contents

SECTION I UNDERSTANDING THE PROBLEM

SECTION II EMERGING TRENDS

Author Biography

Dr. Eric Cole is an industry-recognized security expert with over 20 years of hands-on experience. Dr. Cole has experience in information technology with a focus on helping customers identify the right areas of security by building out dynamic defense solutions that protect organizations from advanced threats. Dr. Cole has a master's degree in computer science from NYIT and a doctorate from Pace University, with a concentration in information security. Dr. Cole is the author of several books, including *Hackers Beware*, *Hiding in Plain Site*, *Network Security Bible*, and *Insider Threat*. He is the inventor of over 20 patents and is a researcher, writer, and speaker. He is also a member of the Commission on Cyber Security for the 44th President and several executive advisory boards. Dr. Cole is founder of Secure Anchor Consulting, in which he provides state of the art security services and expert witness work. He also served as CTO of McAfee and Chief Scientist for Lockheed Martin. Dr. Cole is actively involved with the SANS Technology Institute (STI) and SANS working with students, teaching, and maintaining and developing courseware. He is a SANS faculty Fellow and course author. Dr. Cole is an executive leader in the industry, where he provides cutting-edge cyber security consulting services and leads research and development initiatives to advance the state of the art in information systems security.

Preface

Security is a challenging area in which to work because there are always adversaries that are trying to defeat the measures that are put in place to secure an organization. The threat is typically in direct proportion to the amount and worth of the assets the adversaries are after. If an entity has assets that are worth very little with little value, the type of threat will be smaller than if an organization has high worth assets. The advanced persistent threat is a natural evolution of organizations' increased reliance on networks. As more and more information became available in electronic form via the Internet, the concept of having an advanced adversary target this information in a persistent manner with the goal of stealthy data acquisition was inevitable. The only question was when - with the answer being now.

Having worked in cyber security for over 20 years, it has been an exciting journey because every day is a new adventure. There are always new offensive techniques being discovered and as soon as a new defensive measure was deployed the adversary will try to find a new way to exploit it. Since the invention of networks and electronic records, there have always been cyber-attacks, but in recent years a new level of sophistication has evolved. We have moved from fighting the cyber common cold to cyber cancer. The new threat has moved from static, visible, distributive attacks to stealthy, targeted, data focused attacks known as the advanced persistent threat.

Attackers have always adapted to increase the sophistication of their attack methods; however, it has always been a linear progression in terms of the advances. Therefore the security that organizations deploy could naturally evolve, building on the previous security blueprints that have been created. With the advanced persistent threat, there is now an exponential enhancement in how the adversary works. This means the old way of doing security is no longer going to scale against a game-changing adversary, the APT.

There will always be some organizations that get compromised by threats, but typically it is organizations that have not performed proper security or had the proper resources to defend their intellectual property. With various exploitation techniques, viruses and worms, we would analyze the compromised organizations and it was obvious that something was lacking in security. These vulnerabilities in organizations still exist, and core, fundamental security methods are still valid today. However, looking at the recent advanced, next generation threats that changed all of the rules, many organizations that would have received an A in security five years ago are now being compromised. What organizations typically do to protect themselves is no longer scaling, and we have to look at security differently.

After talking with many organizations, executives, and working on many compromise incidents, it has become evident that a paradigm shift is upon us. We need to change the vantage point from which we look at security. Organizations need new methods, techniques, and solutions. After much analysis, research, and verification on what techniques actually work against APT, I decided to write this book. One of the driving themes of my career is a desire to help people. Nothing is a better feeling than giving people who are struggling with a problem advice that actually works and can help them solve it. In the spirit of helping organizations better defend against APT, I began to document an effective game plan and create a playbook for dealing with the next generation of threats—the APT.

The goal of this book is to focus in on building a defensible network and cover the gaps that need to be addressed to deal with APT. There are many solid references for performing forensic analysis with regards to APT. This is not a forensic book. This book is about meeting APT head on and employing an environment that minimizes the impact of the adversary and increases the chances of detection. Organizations are losing the war on APT. This book is a battle plan of how to start winning the war. Based on the persistent nature of the adversary, some attacks will always occur. The goal of this book is to enable organizations to be battle ready to minimize the damage and impact of the APT. Organizations are still going to lose a few battles, but with proper understanding and focus they can still win the war.

Many organizations feel very defeated and have lost hope in dealing with the APT. No matter what we do we are going to get compromised. Some organizations state that we should just give up, since any technique that we focus resources on is not going to be effective. Any exploit, no matter how advanced, has to take advantages of vulnerabilities to break in. Any exploit, no matter how advanced, has to perform some actions that are different than normal users. Any exploit, no matter how advanced, can be managed from a security perspective to minimize the risk to an acceptable level. This book is about changing the rules and giving power back to the defense. By re-thinking how we approach security, effective preventive and defensive measures can be deployed against the APT. This book is about strategy. This book is about approach. This book is about solutions that work, and, most importantly, this book is about giving organizations hope. It will not be easy, but you can win the fight—just do not give up!

Understanding the Problem

Organizations recognize that cyber security is a concern and resources need to be allocated to protect an organization. However, there are many different types of threats from worms/viruses, hacktivists to the APT. Many organizations understand how to defend against many of the traditional threats and treat the current advanced threats in the same manner they have always dealt with security. The problem is this approach does not work. The APT is a completely different problem and until an organization understands the problem, they will not be able to fix it.

The first section of this book will lay out the problem and show how an organization needs to take an integrated, adaptive approach to dealing with the APT. The following are the chapters that will be covered:

Chapter 1: The Changing Threat
Chapter 2: Why Are Organizations Being Compromised?
Chapter 3: How Are Organizations Being Compromised?
Chapter 4: Risk Based Approach to Security

In the first chapter, The Changing Threat, organizations will understand that dealing with the APT is a completely different problem in which most organizations are not properly prepared to handle. In order to be able to deal with a threat, organizations have to understand what they are up against. The initial response from many executives is that they have already invested significant money into cyber security and this should be sufficient for dealing with the APT. Chapter 2, Why Organizations are Compromised, will explain why this is not the case. The APT is able to bypass much of the security that organizations use today. In order to be able to fix the problem, an organization needs to understand why it is happening. After understanding why it is happening, Chapter 3 cover How Organizations are Compromised? Knowing how an organization is being broken into will allow an organization to understand what needs to be done to fix the problem. Chapter 4, covers the Risk Based Approach to Security that organizations need to follow in order to be successful.

The traditional method that most organizations deploy today is to ignore the threat, get compromised, after notification by law enforcement, perform hunting and forensics to find and clean up the compromise after the fact. Based on the stealthy nature of the APT hunting and forensics will always play a key role, but this book is about creating an integrated solution that will prevent, detect and minimize the exposure of an organization. The book is about deploying an effective defensive stance to protect organization from today's advanced persistent threat and tomorrows next generation of threats. The APT is a cyber-adversary displaying advanced logistical and operational capability for long-term intrusion campaigns. Its current goal is to maintain access to victim networks and exfiltrate intellectual property data as well as information that is economically and politically advantageous. The APT is not a bot-net. It is not malware. It is the DNA of an adversarial group. This book will help an organization protect against the APT.

The Changing Threat

INTRODUCTION

Organizations continue to spend significant amount of money on security but today an interesting trend is happening. In the past spending money on security led to less compromises and increased protection. Today, organizations are increasing their security budgets but still getting compromised. What is being done today no longer seems to work.

The problem is that the threat has changed but organization's approach to security has not changed. While traditional threats are still a concern and cannot be ignored, organizations now have a new challenge dealing with the Advanced Persistent Threat known as the APT. The APT is well funded, organized groups that are systematically compromising government and commercial entities. The term originally was developed as a code name for Chinese-related intrusions against US military organizations. The term has evolved to refer to advanced adversaries that are focused on critical data with the goal of exploiting information in a covert manner. APTs are highly sophisticated and bypass virtually all "best practice" cyber security programs to try and establish a long-term network presence. The APT is attacks that are stealthy, targeted, and data focused which is quite different than traditional worms or viruses. The APT are very well-organized entities (typically foreign adversaries) that are targeting an organization to gather a specific piece of information today and ultimately maintain long-term access so information can be extracted at will in the future. APT breaks all of the rules of attackers by typically adapting their techniques on the file, targeting users as the entry point, and hiding their tracks very carefully; therefore many traditional security measures are not effective at dealing with this threat.

Today, the term APT has evolved and different people refer to it as different things. Some people only refer to attacks from China, while others include all attacks as being part of the APT. The goal of this book is not to debate a definition but to provide a guide of how to implement effective security that actually works against the advanced threats that are bypassing and rendering traditional security measures to be less effectively than they previously were against traditional viruses and worms. While the focus of this book is on APT, the real focus is implemented effective security that secures an organization from all threats up to and including the APT. The ultimate goal is raising awareness so organizations can have effective security against the APTv2 and the next generation of threats. A mistake that we have seen organizations make is they focus all their effort on the APT, forgetting about traditional threats and still get compromised.

THE CURRENT LANDSCAPE

Today, one cannot open up a newspaper, read a magazine, or turn on the news without hearing about another organization being compromised. It seems that organizations of all shapes and sizes have been compromised and there is no end in sight. Government, commercial, non-profit, universities, national, and international organizations have all had data breaches that have caused significant impact to the organization.

Hacker groups threatening to target an organization, causes fear and panic because history has shown us that they possess the will and ability to continuously attack an organization until they are successful. One of the goals today is to minimize the chance of being targeted. While an organization cannot live in fear, they should also be careful. It is never the victim's fault but if someone is walking in the bad part of town holding a large sum of money in their hand, the likelihood of being mugged is higher than if one keeps their money concealed and stays in the safer part of town. Many organizations, without even realizing it, are drawing unnecessary attention to themselves either by what employees say or what organization posts on their websites. Think of the impact and exposure social networking sites could cause to an organization. The good news is once an organization understands the threat and the capability of the adversaries, they can better protect themselves. It is important to note that with the APT an organization will always be targeted, but there are steps that can be taken to minimize the impact.

Since many organizations focus solely on fixing random vulnerabilities, for example patching, as their approach to security, they are not protecting against the threats that have the highest likelihood of compromise. This starts to explain why companies that spend millions of dollars each year on security still get compromised. For example, if you are the defensive coordinator for a football team, the team can be number one in the league at defending against the running game. The focus of all practices is fixing and removing the vulnerability of an opposing team running the football against the defense. While this is a noble cause and would take considerable effort, how effective would this team be against a team that primarily passes the football. The answer is not very effective. Many organizations are focusing all of their energy against a perceived threat, but if it turns out to be the wrong threat, they will still be compromised.

It is sometimes hard for people to accept this fact but in this day and age, an organization needs to recognize that they are going to be attacked with a high chance of compromise. While this might seem frustrating it is better to accept reality than live in denial. If someone claimed that they are never going to get sick for the rest of their life, you would probably shake your head and say that is a nice claim but it is not realistic. Saying that your organization will never get compromised is as naïve as saying you will never get sick. Continuing with our analogy, the goal when someone gets sick is to minimize the impact and ultimately not die. While we can eat healthy and take vitamins to reduce the number of times we get sick, when we do get sick the goal is to go to the doctor quickly and deal with the illness when it is still small. The general philosophy that we follow is prevention is ideal but detection is a must. An organization can do many things to minimize the chance of a compromise but it needs to make sure that appropriate measures are in place to detect and deal with an attack in a timely manner.

Briefly looking at APT, the advanced nature of the adversary means that they will usually find a way into an organization. What makes security so exciting is that we have a much harder job than the attacker. For the attacker to compromise an organization, they need to find one vulnerability. For the defense to stop an attack, we have to find every vulnerability. Unfortunately many companies do not understand all of their points of exposure and if the offense knows more than the defense we are going to lose. In addition, the attacker is very persistent. They will keep trying until they are successful.

The main reason the APT is successful is that it is a new threat that many organizations are not prepared to handle. The old threat was visible, went after long hanging fruit and if it failed would move on to its next target. Most of the security we have in place is prepared to handle this level of threat not the APT. While some of the APT attacks are automated, we are dealing with a sophisticated attacker who performs some of the attack with manual intervention. Since a human is involved with planning and potentially executing the attack, the adversary can adapt and utilize human intelligence to extract information from a target.

ORGANIZATIONS VIEW ON SECURITY

Over the years, the evolving and emerging threat has also changed how an organization and its executives view and assess their security posture. Over ten years ago there was a real threat but many executives were not afraid. By the mid-2000s they were afraid but did not know why. Today based on all of the breach data, they know why they are afraid but they do not know what to do about it. Many organizations are also not fully aware of the impact.

It is also common for organizations to not recognize that APT is the silent killer. It could be happening right now to an organization, but since there is nothing visible, they think everything is fine. Executives all of the time state that security has been telling us for the last three years how bad everything is and that we will be compromised, but nothing has happened which leads executives to think that cyber security is over hyped. In essence, executives say that security keeps saying the sky is falling and accuses the security group of being Chicken Little. The problem is that the sky has fallen, but organizations are not receiving the right information to realize that it is occurring.

The simple question is: if there was a system on an organization's network that was compromised and slowly extracted information out of the organization, how would you know about it? If a user received an email that looked legitimate but contained embedded malware and clicked on it, how would an organization detect it?

Organizations have heard of the phrase APT and know that it can get around most security measures; they just do not have the proper information to recognize that the problem might be occurring right now. Instead of thinking of APT as a problem that could occur in the future, we have to recognize that it is a current problem that is occurring right now. A key motto of security is to assume the worst and hope for the best. Isn't it better to act as if you are compromised and be prepared, than be ignorant and be compromised? If you assume you are compromised and you are not, you have just gained a better understanding of your organization and improved your security. If you assume you are not compromised and you are, you could go out of business.

While some organizations are recognizing the devastating impact the APT can have, some are still living in denial. What many people think is that bad things happen to other organizations not ours. The number one motivator for someone purchasing an alarm system is they or someone they know very well is robbed. Unfortunately the current motivator for organizations implementing effective security is to take action after a breach occurs. Many organizations do not think bad things can happen to them until it does. In this day and age there is enough data and confirmed attacks that organizations have to recognize it is not a matter of if an attack is going to occur but when.

YOU WILL BE COMPROMISED

We have come to a point in security where organizations have to recognize the fact that they are going to be compromised. It is also safe to conclude that any critical systems that are connected to a network and ultimately connected to the Internet have already been compromised. As a society we must make the paradigm shift that the threat has advanced to the point where no system is safe. One of the key themes that will be echoed throughout this book is Prevention is Ideal but Detection is a Must. While an organization should hope and pray that they do not get compromised, they need to recognize that it is going to happen and put measures in place to detect it in a timely manner. Having a compromise is OK if it is caught quickly and appropriate remediation is taken to prevent reinfection. Having a compromise for 6 months is not acceptable.

The ultimate goal is to make sure our organization does not go out of business. Ideally we need to detect any compromise early, react quickly, and minimize the overall damage. Looking at the amount of records compromised in recent breaches shows us that organizations are not doing an effective job at detection. If we were doing proper detection organizations would have 200 records stolen and be compromised for one week. Today it is not uncommon to see millions of records stolen over a several month period.

Saying that an organization will be compromised and most likely has been compromised is hard for some people to accept. However, it is merely the inverse of one of the fundamental truths of security—as soon as a system has any functionality or value to an organization, it is no longer 100% secure. A system that is 100% secure has 0% functionality. To put it another way a system that is 100% secure has minimal value to an organization because there is no functionality. As soon as you take a computer, plug it in to electricity, connect it to a network, and let humans touch the keyboard, the security has dropped below 100%. If the security is below 100%, then compromise could occur, it is just a matter of time.

THE CYBER SHOPLIFTER

One way to look at the APT is it is like a cyber shoplifter. The problem with shoplifting is it cannot be completely prevented. If we have a quick theoretical discussion it actually can. If you own a store you can completely stop shoplifting by locking all of the doors and windows and not allowing anyone in and not allowing anyone out. If a store is completely locked down, then shoplifting can be completely remediated. The problem with this approach is while shoplifting has been prevented, legitimate customers have also been prevented from entering and the ultimate fate of the store is it will go out of business. As soon as you allow legitimate customers into the store, shoplifters can enter and potentially cause harm.

At point of entry a legitimate customer and shoplifter look identical. One could argue that a bad shoplifter could be detected at point of entry, but in this day and age we are worried about the advanced or sophisticated attacker not the novice. A sophisticated shoplifter will enter the store and behave just like a normal shopper and therefore cannot be prevented. The only way to deal with shoplifter is early and timely detection. This analogy represents a critical piece of the puzzle which in time is not on your side. If that shoplifter is only in the store for 5 min, the store has less than 5 min to detect and deal with the problem. Otherwise once the shoplifter leaves the store there is little that can be done at that point. Therefore watching the video cameras each evening and realizing that earlier that day someone stole from the store is not very helpful in preventing the immediate loss. One could argue that there could be some long-term value in understanding how the attacker works to increase the chance of detection in the future. It is also important to point out that the quicker the shoplifter can be caught the less damage they will cause. If they are in the store for 10 min, if you catch them within 2 min they might only have stolen three items but if they are not detected until 8 min, the damage is much greater.

The way to catch and deal with shoplifters is by understanding the point of deviation or the moment in time where the person acts differently than a normal customer. If a shoplifter enters the store and acts like a legitimate customer the entire time, they are not a shoplifter, they are a normal customer. At some point a shoplifter must act differently and start to cause harm. This is known as the point of deviation and is the key to catching shoplifters and minimizing damage. The more you can understand how they work, the better the chance of catching them.

This analogy and theory applies directly to attackers and more specifically to the APT. The advanced threat will enter an organization looking like legitimate traffic. Therefore most traditional prevention devices will be ineffective against this threat. It is important to point out that we are not in any way shape or form stating that traditional prevention measures are useless. They still have value and things would be a lot worse if they were not present on a network. The trick with the APT is think augment not replace. We need to keep the solid foundation that was created over the last ten years and continue to build upon it. However, this illustrates the fundamental problem with dealing with the APT. If you look at a network diagram for your organization and you put a P on every device that is preventive and a D on every device that is detective, you should notice something concerning. About 80% of all of the security in most organizations is preventive and only a small percent is detective. This is because in an ideal world if you could both prevent and detect an attack, prevention is much better. However with the APT since prevention no longer is completely effective, detection must take a higher priority and a bigger focus in our current defensive posture. It is important to note that prevention is still important and should not be forgotten about.

Some organizations do claim that they have detective measures in place like IDS (intrusion detection systems) or similar technology. The problem is most current detection is focusing in on what is coming into the organization. If you are concerned about data theft, does the data get stolen when the attacker enters the organization or when they leave? The damage occurs when they leave. Therefore effective detection needs to focus on what is leaving the organization, not what is coming in. Only by watching what is happening on the system and what is leaving the organization can the attacks be detected and dealt with a timely manner, minimizing damage, and exposure to the organization.

THE NEW DEFENSE IN DEPTH

Defense in depth is not a new concept and is based on the idea that there is no silver bullet when it comes to security and no single technology will be able to completely protect you. Therefore multiple measures of protection must be put in place to keep an entity secure. A great example of defense in depth is a castle. Castles illustrate a key component of defense in depth because when it is done correctly, most people do not even notice it. However if we start to examine how a castle is built and structured, it illustrates the multiple security measures that were designed into the castle.

When you walk up to a castle, several defensive measures are immediate obvious. First, the castle is usually up on a hill, with a moat around it and a single entrance. This makes it very hard for an attacker to perform a sneak attack and from a defensive measure the attacker can only enter the castle at one location which allows a keen focus on that one location. In addition to only having a single point of entrance, the entrance is usually long narrow and an average person would have to bend down to enter the castle. This was all carefully thoughtout and designed. If an opposing army is going to attack the castle and the soldiers try to enter the castle with all of their armor, they will have to enter one by one, go slow, and bend over turning sideways to fit through the entrance. Assuming that the attackers were detected it would be easy to defend against this by focusing all attention at the single, narrow entrance, and picking off the opposing army as they enter.

One other important defensive measure in a castle is the stair case. When you walk up a stair case in a castle you will notice several things. First, the stair case always spirals to the right, are narrow, are uneven, and are dimly lit. As you walk up the stairs for the first time your right arm and shoulder are pressed against the wall and you walk very slowly, typically looking down since the stairs are uneven and it is easy to trip if you go to fast. When people first hear this, they wonder how this is a security measure. The first important point is that the weapons of choice when most castles were built were swords and most people are right handed. Therefore if you are attacking the castle, you are going slowly up the stairs because they are uneven, you are looking down, and your right arm is pressed against the wall giving you limited mobility with the sword. If you are defending the castle, you typically have gone up and down the stairs many times a day, are very familiar with the pattern and can move up and down them very quickly. In addition, since you are defending the castle and would be coming down the stairs, your right hand is in the open area and easier to swing. Therefore just through a careful design gives the defender a much more strategic advantage over the attacker.

The important question is whether your organization's security is as well thoughtout, built into the design, effective, and as robust as the castle. Unfortunately most organizations security makes it easier for the attacker and harder for the defender. A simple example is the lack of robust configuration control. If every system in a network is configured differently, it makes it easy for an attacker and harder for the defender. We need to start doing a better job of increasing the difficulty for the attacker. The general rule is if the offense knows more than the defense, you will lose.

While defense in depth is still a critical component of effective security, the approach and methods have changed. It is still true that no single measure can protect an organization but assuming for a second that it does exist, would we want to use it? The answer is absolutely not. If there was one single device that made you secure, how many items would an attacker have to defeat to be successful. The correct answer is one. Therefore we want multiple levels of security out of necessity, knowing that any single measure can be compromised. While we hope we never get compromised, if some of our security is compromised, it should be designed in a way that we can detect it before it gets to our critical information.

Another common misconception with defense in depth is that all security should be isolated and separated from the rest of the network. While security devices do need to be managed and controlled very closely, they also need to be integrated into all components on the network. One of the many reasons why APT is so effective is that it can easily bypass most of the existing security devices that organizations control.

Putting all of the defense in depth together requires a comprehensive approach to security. The important thing to remember is that we want to prevent on the inbound traffic and detect on the outbound traffic. By not only performing both prevention and detection but also doing it for both inbound and outbound traffic provide true defense in depth that will scale against the current and future threats.

PROACTIVE VS REACTIVE

Based on the current threat level of the APT, the porous nature of organizations and the portability of the data, organizations are going to have to spend resources to implement effective security. The question is on whether an organization is going to be proactive or reactive. At the end of the day an organization is going to have to address and spend money on security. The only difference is if you are proactive, it is a lot cheaper than being reactive. An organization is going to have to pay, you either pay now or pay later and if you pay now it is a lot cheaper and easier than paying later. It is the difference between making sure that your house is fireproof or waiting for you house to burn down and rebuilding it after the fact.

The fundamental problem today is organizations are spending money on security and do not understand that money does not equal security. Now money is definitely a good thing and is needed. However, there is a difference between effective solutions and ineffective solutions. Many organizations are spending money on good things that will help the organization overall, but they are not spending money in the right areas. An important question to ask would be based on all of the money that was spent on security for your organization, how confident are you that you could stop or detect an attack? In addition, once you understand a new threat vector, be able to adjust your security in a quick manner to address the threat?

Security threats are very dynamic and fast moving. Corporate IT environments are very focused on uptime, stability, and availability of the systems. Changes are always looked at in a skeptical way and have to be fully tested and approved. Therefore being reactive and constantly updating and changing components can be very concerning especially to CIO's. The trick is to create an environment where the analysis component is dynamic but the configurations are stable, minimizing the impact to the functioning of critical systems. Another important question to ask is when was your security devices that are being used today purchased and how often does the configuration get updated? The traditional answer is 2–3 years ago and updated 1–2 times per year. Now if you ask the attacker a similar question on when where their techniques developed and how often do they change, you would receive a completely different answer. Typically the APT reviews their methods constantly and if they are not effective adjust instantly.

LOSS OF COMMON SENSE

Security is not that difficult if organizations stick to fundamental principles and utilize the same common sense that we apply in the real world. If you were walking down the street and you saw a half-eaten candy bar on the sidewalk would you pick it up and eat it? Absolutely not. You do not know where it has been and it could potentially make you very sick. You would never do that. Why is it then if a user sees a USB stick lying on the ground, they pick it up and will plug it into their computer? It is the same threat as the candy bar but most people have been trained from an early age not to eat food off of the ground, but those same common sense principles have not been taught when it comes to cyber. Now the argument is that eating a candy bar could immediately impact our health but a USB stick could not. However, what would be the impact if your identity or credit card information was stolen. This could actually cause more long-term harm and take more time to fix than if you just got sick for a few days. The point still remains the same though that there is a difference in how people view physical harm and cyber harm. Therefore let's look at another example where the lines are much closer.

Everyone who has children knows to talk to your children about the dangers of talking to strangers. You explain that you should never ever talk to a stranger or get in a car with someone that you do not know. Even if they say they are a friend of your parents, do not believe them and run. This is taught to kids at an early age and re-emphasized throughout their lives and by teachers in schools. Most parents would agree that they have done a good job of educating their children on these physical dangers. Now, how many of those same parents would agree that they have talked to their kids about talking to strangers on the Internet. In talking with parents, one parent explained that they only allow their teenager to talk with other teenagers online so they are protected. My response was how do you know they are teenagers that they are actually communication with? Online you can be anyone that you want. Anyone reading this book could claim to be a teenager online if they wanted. In addition, most of the social media sites do not perform any validation when an account is set up. Anyone can create an account claiming to be anyone that they want.

The second argument that is often stated is that online interaction is virtual and they are not in any immediate danger like they are if they are directly talking to a physical stranger. While initially this is true, the slime balls that are targeting children will build up a relationship online and at some point convert it over to a physical relationship. They might offer to send them something and ask for their mailing address or ask to physically meet them. While your children know not to give away their address to a stranger online, if they have been chatting and talking with someone for six months online they no longer think of them as a stranger and this is where the problem starts.

The Internet has a lot of value and has enhanced our lives in many ways. It has also created many new dangers at both a personal and a business level. However many of the principles that we have learned in the real world when we were little and emphasized throughout our lives, did not happen in the cyber world. Many people who rely on computers everyday do not understand some of the basic dangers and issues. As will be emphasized throughout this book, one of the biggest dangers to an organization is lack of awareness by employees on the dangers of the Internet and how they will be targeted online.

IT IS ALL ABOUT RISK

There is an entire chapter in this book focused on risk but based on its overall importance, we wanted to briefly cover some fundamental topics in the introduction. Organizations get so tied up in trying to protect against attacks, they sometimes forget why they are doing security. They keep spending money buying more devices and they still get broken into. After a successful attack they are very frustrated and believe they are wasting money. Spending resources does not make you secure if you do not focus in on the right areas. There is a difference between doing good things and doing the right thing.

My son came home from school at the beginning of the school year and asked if I could help him study for a surprise quiz. Being a supportive parent, I of course said yes. Honestly, I was a little confused because unless they changed the definition of surprise since I have gone to school, how did he know he was having a "surprise" quiz. When I asked him he explained that the quiz is not a surprise, but the subject matter is. The teacher did not tell them what subject the quiz was going to be on. To help him properly study, I asked him what subject he thought the teacher has been emphasizing and what topic he thought the quiz was going to be on. After some thought he said mathematics, he explained that the teacher was really pushing fractions and long division. I gave him several problems and he got everyone wrong, he did not understand the concepts. We worked for three and a half hours and after that time he finally understood the concepts. He woke up the next morning and was very confident and excited to take the test. He came home from school with his head hung low, arms sagging, and as he walked in he took a long deep breathe. He looked at me and said rough day at school. I was puzzled since I knew he understand math, so I asked what happened on the quiz. He said he did not do well on the quiz. When I asked why because he knew the math, he paused and said one slight problem, the quiz was on history not mathematics. He then looked at me and said dad, I wasted three and half hours yesterday studying math when I could have been doing something much more useful like playing video games. After thinking for a moment I answered that the time he spent learning math was a good thing, was not a waste of time and will help him tremendously over the course of his life and education. In terms of passing the exam, it was not the right thing to do, but it was still a good thing to do overall.

This story is very relative because it explains the current problem we have with security and the discussion I have with many executives after a breach. When I meet with a CEO after a breach, they typically walk to the door to meet me similar to my son coming home from school, head down, frustrated, and upset. They look at me and say over the last five years we have spent over three million dollars on security and we were compromised this week. They conclude that the money that was spent on security was a complete waste and could have been used for other purposes. Similar to my son, I look at them and say the money that was spent on security was a good thing to do and things would have been a lot worse if you did not spend the money. In terms of stopping the attack it was not the right thing to do but overall it was still a good investment.

One of the fundamental problems with security today is organizations are doing good things to help protect the environment, but they are not doing the right thing which will stop advanced attackers. We need to shift our attention to the right things to successfully defend the enterprise. This book is focused on the right things that need to be done.

The right things are taking a risk-based approach to implementing effective security. Before an organization spends an hour of their time or a dollar of their budget on anything in the name of security, they should answer three questions:

1. What is the risk?
2. Is it the highest priority risk?
3. Is it the most cost effective way of reducing the risk?

While some companies think they are taking a risk-based approach, they are focusing their energy on fixing random vulnerabilities. While this is a good thing to do it is not the right thing to do. In order for an organization to make sure they are focusing in on the right areas, threat needs to drive the risk equation. Organizations should be focusing in and fixing vulnerabilities that are tied to high risk items, not just fixing any vulnerability that does not have an actual threat tied to it. Most importantly, organizations need to focus in on the high likelihood and high risk items.

WHAT WAS IN PLACE?

What continues to drive home the point that organizations are doing good things but not the right thing is by looking at what security was in place when a breach occurred. Most people think that when an organization is compromised, it is because they made a blatant error or had invested no money in security. If you look at most APT attacks, the items that all companies had in place at the time of the breach include:

- Security policies.
- Security budget.
- Security team.
- Firewalls.
- Application filtering.
- Intrusion detection.
- End-point security.
- Anti-virus protection.

What is frustrating and surprising, is if you asked most people what they need to do in order to be secure, the list would look similar to the above. Organizations are doing what seems to be common sense and still being compromised. The problem is money or common sense does not make an organization secure. An organization must be focusing in and fixing the vulnerabilities associated with high likelihood threats that have a big impact.

If you take most organizations security roadmaps and pick random items and ask them to describe the risk that item is addressing, most do not have an answer. The first fundamental problem is while organizations say security is important, they are not mapping critical decisions back to risk. Whether we like it or not, security is all about risk. Second, looking at the risk formula which at its most fundamental level is threat times vulnerability. Vulnerabilities are the items you would remediate to ultimately reduce a risk. Therefore organizations jump the gun and focus their energy on fixing vulnerabilities. The problem with randomly fixing vulnerabilities or just fixing the low-hanging fruit or the easiest vulnerabilities, is assuming all vulnerabilities are equal. Unfortunately it is not a numbers game.

Organizations need to focus in on the vulnerabilities in which there is a high likelihood of a threat that will have a big impact. Risk remediation is a quality game not a quantity game. It is better to fix 5 vulnerabilities in which there is a real threat, than 50 vulnerabilities in which no threat exists. Another common problem with vulnerabilities is that organizations hyperfocus on a vulnerability and keep working it until it is completely eliminated. It is better to reduce several vulnerabilities than eliminate a few.

By focusing in on fixing high impact vulnerabilities that are tied to high impact threats, organizations will move from doing good things to do the right things. Good things will lay a solid foundation for security but the right things will stop an attack from being successful or minimize the overall impact.

PAIN KILLER SECURITY

Everyone is always looking for a quick fix and network security is no different. One of the reasons why organizations are implementing and deploying security devices and still being compromised is because they are fixing the symptom not the problem. Fixing the symptom will give you short-term relief, similar to taking a pain killer. However pain killers do not fix the long-term problem and do not provide long-term relief. Therefore in order to provide long-term protection the actual problem must be fixed. If organizations focused on fixing the problem first and after threat the symptoms, they would then have very effective scalable solutions.

REDUCING THE SURFACE SPACE

One of the key areas of fixing the problem is reducing the attack surface or removing extraneous components that are not being used. As we will cover throughout this book, good hardening procedures and solid configuration management is the key to success. However in many cases organizations are running services that are not needed to run the business, but those services are being exploited by attackers. It is one thing if an organization is running services, have open ports or scripts that are needed to run a business and those are compromised. If that happens, it is a cost of doing business and you cannot get to upset if the decision was based off of risk. However, if an organization is running extraneous components that are not being used for any legitimate business purpose and those get compromised, you have every right to be upset. Those types of compromises should be avoided at all cost. Unfortunately, that is the common source of compromise. Many of the success APT attacks have taken advantage of functionality that is enabled but not being used for any legitimate purpose.

Organizations need to recognize that most software, applications and systems have more functionality that what is needed to run the business. If organizations spent the time to remove those components, not only would security be simpler, but it would make the attacker's job much more difficult.

To give an example, the following are common points of compromise for APT and other attacks. What is frustrating and ironic is that these components are enabled/running on most networks/systems, yet very few organizations require the functionality to run the business. The following should be looked at very closely and if not used should be removed:

HTML EMBEDDED EMAIL

Some people utilize the HTML features of email to change the color of their background or have embedded content. In many cases they use it because the feature is available to them. The real question is do organizations really need HTML embedded content in order to run their business? In most cases the answer is no. The reason why HTML embedded content is a big problem is this is a common source of spear phishing attacks use by the APT. The adversary would send an email with a link. Most users see the link in their email and believe that is where they are actually going. However they do not realize that there is a separate HTML field that lists the real link the user will be connected to. In addition, embedded code that runs in the background can also be hidden within the html. Therefore if organizations turned off HTML embedded email, the vector of many of the spear phishing attacks would be greatly minimized.

BUFFER OVERFLOWS

The cause of a buffer overflow is based on the ability of a program to write more information to memory than what was originally allocated in the program. As a simple example, a program would allocate 20 characters but allow the user to write

30 characters and in essence overflow the buffer. This would allow an attacker to overwrite the written pointer and have malicious code executed on the system, potentially giving the attacker access to the system. The reason this is allowed is because of a data structure called a dynamic link list which bypasses the ability of the program to perform proper bounds checking. The problem is very few programs actually utilize dynamic link lists today. Most applications that have been compromised via buffer overflows were not utilizing dynamic links lists. This means the feature could have been removed with no negative impact to the application. Think about how concerning this is. One of the top methods of breaking into servers is buffer overflows and it is using a feature that has no legitimate purpose; which meant the feature could have very easily been removed and the problem remediated through proper hardening.

MACROS IN OFFICE DOCUMENTS

One of the other common methods of spear phishing is to send an office document that has embedded macros than run malicious code on the victim's system. While Office 2010 has macros turned off by default, the problem is previous versions of Office had macros turned on by default. In addition, users can still turn macros on in Office 2010. In working with clients, less than 5% of most employees need macros turned on to do their job. Once again this means if macros were turned off it would have had minimal impact to the organization but would have taken away a main vector from the attacker. Now some people reading this will state that some people in our organization use macros as part of their job. That is fine but we need to change our approach to security. The traditional approach to security is if only a small number of people need a feature or functionality, turn it on for everyone. The new approach is if only a few people require some functionality, turn it off for everyone and only turn it on for the people who need it.

THE TRADITIONAL THREAT

One of the many challenges that we are dealing with today is the threat has changed but the defenses organizations have used are still the same. The threat of five years ago is quite different than it is today. Five plus years ago organizations were dealing with distributive, visible, low-hanging fruit attacks. Most of the security was built on looking, blocking, and stopping evil from coming into a network. This worked well when attacks were static, did not change and were often targeting known vulnerabilities on a network.

In most organizations, if you ask when most of the security devices they are using where purchased the answer is typically 3–5 years ago. This means the solutions we have in place were built to deal with the traditional threat, not the advanced persistent threat.

COMMON COLD

The traditional threat that organizations have dealt with is comparable to the common cold. The way most people deal with the common cold is they wait to have a symptom, a fever, a running nose, or a sore throat. They go to the doctor, the doctor determines what is wrong, provides medicine and in a few days the patient feels better. Traditional security is very similar. An organization would look for a visible symptom or sign of an attack, take action and recover the organization in a timely manner.

While common colds are a concern, if treated correctly, have minimal impact to an individual. The traditional attack that many organizations face, if identified and remediated quickly usually have minimal overall impact to an organization. The reason some organizations thought the traditional type of attack was so bad is because they did not identify it in a timely manner. A common cold, if left untreated could turn into pneumonia and be very serious. While some traditional attacks had serious impact to an organization, it was only because it went untreated, not because it was very damaging.

REACTIVE SECURITY

The method that organizations used to dealt with the traditional attack is reactive security. We wait for a visible sign and we take action. If we are dealing with an attack that is more of a nuisance and goes after the low-hanging fruit, than reacting to the attack makes sense. The general premise of reactive security is that the time it takes an attacker to perform damage is greater than the amount of time it takes to detect and react to a problem. For example, if it is going to take an attacker 3 h to cause damage and we can detect/react in 1 h, than reactive security is effective. The problem today is that attackers are utilization automation and targeted attack methods; therefore reactive security is no longer effective. As we will see throughout this book, to deal with the APT we have to move from reactive to proactive and predictive security.

Reactive security also has another fundamental flaw. An organization must actually know about or have already been impacted by an attack in order to be able to detect and react to it. Therefore as attackers move from standard exploits taking advantage of known vulnerabilities to zero day or custom exploits, that we have not seen before, reactive security continues to decline in value.

AUTOMATION

While not all APTs are completely automated, one of the many reasons why attacks in general and APT specifically are successful is that they utilize automation and many organizations are still relying heavily on manual methods of detection and analysis. It does not matter how smart or sophisticated you are, manual methods will not scale against automation.

Several months ago a friend of mine asked if I wanted to go play paint ball this coming weekend. Since I have had a stressful week it seemed like a fun idea. Now I have not played paint ball before so I signed up for the standard package which included a manual paint ball gun. Essentially you would pump it three times, pump, pump, pump in order to shoot a ball. Hopefully no one reading this will take offense, but some of the people who play paint ball are a little crazy ☺ Some of these folks arrived with very expensive guns with backpacks and auto reload, automatic weapons. When we started the first game, I thought I had pretty good skills. I snuck through the woods, bypassed many potential attackers and the only thing standing between myself and the enemy flag was one person who did not move the entire game and was guarding the flag. As I stood up to take him out, I started to load my gun, pump, pump and before I could perform the final pump he turned around. At that point I realized this was a mistake since he had two guns, one he each hand. He started firing his automatic weapons in a cross fire fashion. We were playing with blue paint balls so in less than 10 s I looked like a smurf. After wiping off some of the paint, regained my composure, I upgraded to an automatic weapon for the next game. The person guarding the flag did not move the entire game but at the end of the day no matter how good you are, manual methods cannot win against automated methods.

Many organizations have a similar situation. They have really smart people who are working around the clock performing very advanced analysis of attacks. They are given six packs of energy drinks every day and can keep going non-stop. However if you are dealing with over 5000 variants of malware a day there is no way that manual methods will scale. One of the many keys to success is to deploy automation in order to keep pace with the attacker.

THE EMERGING THREAT

Many organizations continue to spend time, money and resources on cyber security but at this point, hopefully you realize that one of the fundamental problems is organizations are spending money in the wrong area. Spending money on security does not help if we are not focused on the right areas. The problem is that the threat has changed but our approach to security has not changed. Offense must guide the defense.

There is no such thing as 100% security, which means we cannot fix every vulnerability associated with every risk. We must focus in on the risks in which there is a high likelihood of a given threat and a high impact if a compromise occurs. The only way to be effective is to constantly understand what the threat vectors are and keep pace with the attackers. The advice from Sun Tzu in The Art of War still holds true today. In order to be victorious, you must understand both your enemy (threats) and your own weaknesses (vulnerabilities). Every organization should have a list of their critical assets, the business processes that support those assets, the most likely vulnerabilities and the common points of compromise.

APT—CYBER CANCER

Earlier in the chapter, we talked about the traditional threat being compared to the common cold. However over the last five years the threat has changed and now what we are dealing with is cyber cancer. The problem with cancer in the human body is our traditional measure of detection does not work. Detection is based on the premise of looking for a visible sign and taking action. The problem with cancer is if you wait for there to be a visible sign it is too late. Once there is a visible symptom the cancer has grown to the point where it is usually inoperable and therefore terminal. Any doctor will tell you the way to deal with cancer is prevention is ideal but if it cannot be prevented early detection is critical.

In its simplest sense, the advanced persistent threat is cyber cancer which means traditional detective and reactive measures will not work. At point of compromise there is nothing visible and by the time there are visible signs of attack, the damage has already occurred. We have to assume that even though everything looks fine on the surface, underneath the surface the network might be compromised. Organizations need to look for problems even though there is no visible sign of an attacker on the network. One of the key rules of cyber security is plan for the worst and hope for the best. It is better to assume an organization is compromised and have it clean, that assume an organization is attack free and be compromised. In addition, today the chance of a network not having at least some malware or attackers on the network is very slim.

Two interesting facts about APT continue to highlight this fact. First, most organizations determine that they are compromised because someone else notifies them. While there are some organizations that detect the APT themselves, in many cases a third party such as law enforcement or an ISP notify them they have information leaking out of the organization or that they have been compromised. Second, many organizations are compromised for 6–9 months before they determine that they are compromised.

Based on the stealthy nature of the APT a critical rule is prevention is ideal but detection is a must. In a perfect world it would be great if we could prevent all attacks. However that is not realistic. In this day and age you must accept that you are going to be compromised. In cases where attacks cannot be stopped, the earlier we can catch an attack, the less overall damage. Imagine for a second if an organization that was compromised for 6 months, could have detected the attack even 3 months earlier. They would have saved tremendous money and reduced the overall damage. Our goal is even if an organization cannot stop an attack, the early they can catch it the better. This is also an area where automation can continue to help speed up the time of detection.

ADVANCED PERSISTENT THREAT (APT)

The advanced persistent threat is used to describe an adversary, typically a foreign government, that will target an organization, not-stop until they successfully compromise the entity, with the goal of data extraction and long-term access. The key words with the APT are stealthy, targeted, adaptive, and data focused. While the APT is not new, the large scale nature in which it is attacking systems and the fact that more organizations are realizing that their current way of defending against traditional attackers has to change is new. The important shift with APT is that we are now dealing with well-funded, organized professionals, not hackers from the 1990s. Many people when they think of cyber security and attackers think of images of the movies "War Games" and "Hackers" and envision teenagers trying to break into systems with no real target or goal other than to wreak havoc. Now that sensitive critical information is stored on computers, organizations use networks to run an entire business and e-commerce is over a billion dollar industry, attackers have gone professional. Essentially any information that someone wants is available on a computer somewhere in the world. If you can find that information, the Internet becomes your oyster where any pearl is only a keystroke away. APT is cyber cancer and is the organized sophisticated method of compromising systems.

The term APT—advanced persistent threat sounds so simple but the terms are often misunderstood. When people hear advanced they think of state-of-the-art advanced, sophisticated ways of breaking into the system. As you will learn throughout this book, the common point of compromise for APT is targeting a user and convincing them something is legitimate so they open an attachment or click on a link. Not very sophisticated, but very effective. Advanced does not stand for the sophistication of the attack, it stands for the sophistication of the attacker. The adversary, originally used to refer to attacks from China, is very advanced in what they are capable of doing. However they are going to launch targeted attacks and focus on what works. While the adversary is very advanced the methods they use are very standard, common and most importantly they work.

The next word in APT is persistent. The attacker is not going away. They are going to keep trying until they are successful. Standard hackers utilized worms that would try a few ways into a system. If they worked the system was compromised. If they did not work, the worm would move on to the next target. This meant you were hit for a short period of time and if you defended against it, you lived to fight another day. Today, the attack is non-stop, it will not go away which means are defensive measures have to be 24/7, 365, and just because we defended against an attack today means they will keep trying. The persistent nature is the reason why APT causes so much damage. Many organizations will prevent the first several attempts and properly defend their organization for several weeks. However, as soon as an organization lets down their guard, the attacker will take advantage of it and break it. What makes this game so frustrating and exciting at the same time is the attackers only have to find a handful of vulnerabilities in order to win. On the other hand we have to find and fix everyone vulnerability to win. Today because networks are so complex, porous and data is so portable are chances of winning against persistent threats are slim. We need to de-scope and use good configuration management to properly minimize the size of the attack surface.

APT—STEALTHY, TARGETED, AND DATA FOCUSED

Another way to describe the APT is stealthy, targeted, and data focused. This really differentiates it from the traditional threat and shows the areas that an organization needs to focus on to properly defend and protect against this threat. The main goal of APT is not to get caught. Sneak in, acquire what you need and sneak out, leaving no visible trace and make it hard for anyone to know what really happened. This means if an organization is looking at their traditional detective measures looking for signs of an attack, nothing is going to show up. On the surface everything looks fine when in reality bad things are happening below the surface. This way cyber cancer is a great way to describe the threat. Someone could be in the early stages of cancer but they feel fine, they are exercising and they look very healthy. Little do they know there is a deadly disease growing inside of them. Unless they actively get examined and look for an illness when they feel healthy, by the time they realize they have cancer it would be terminal. This describes the current challenges with organizations today. The executives say everything is working fine and there are no visible problems, therefore we must be in great shape and secure. Little do they know that several systems on their network have been compromised and by the time they realize it, the damage has been done. Therefore a paradigm shift has to occur where executives understand that we are no longer dealing with a visible attack like the common cold, we are now dealing with a stealthy attack, cyber cancer.

In addition to the APT being stealthy, it is also very targeted. Traditional attacks went after the low hanging fruit. A worm would walk an entire IP address space looking for vulnerable systems. It was merely a numbers game. Today the professional attacker or the APT is more interested in quality than quantity. They are going to identify information they want, determine who has it and target that organization and/or individual. It does not matter the size of your organization or the business that you are in, you need to recognize that you are a target. Not only does a target mean that they are going to focus all of their energy on your organization, more importantly it means they are going to study your organization. The APT is going to gather as much information about your organization so they can customize the attack to be successful. They are going to determine the weak points within your organization and target those individuals as the point of entry for the compromise.

Finally, the APT is focused on organizations information, its high worth assets. The attacker does not care about defacing a website, they want an organizations most critical intellectual property. What is the most critical information to your organization? What differentiates you from everyone else in the market and gives you a competitive advantage? That is the information that is going to be targeted. This means that if the APT is successful, the amount of damage to your organization is significant.

CHARACTERISTICS OF THE APT

While the APT is stealthy, targeted, and data focused, the following are the important things to remember:

1. APT focuses on any organization, both government and non-government entities. Some people make the mistake of thinking that the APT is only focused on Department of Defense (DoD). When it comes to the Internet the lines between government and commercial are blurring and anything that could cause harm to a country or give an adversary an advantage will be targeted.

2. While the threat is advanced once it gets into a network, the entry point with many attacks is focusing on convincing a user to open an attachment or click on a link. However, once the APT breaks into a system, it is very sophisticated in what it does and how it works. Signature analysis will be ineffective in protecting against it. Advanced attacks are always changing, recompiling on the fly, and utilizing encryption to avoid detection.

3. Many organizations make the mistake of thinking of attacks like the weather. There will be some stormy days and there will be some sunny days. However, on the Internet you are always in stormy weather. In the past, attackers would periodically attack an organization. Today attacks are nonstop. The attackers are persistent, and if an organization lets their guard down for any period of time, the chance of a compromise is very high.

4. Attackers want to take advantage of economy of scales and break into as many sites as possible, as quickly as possible. Therefore the tool of choice of an attacker is automation. Automation is not only what causes the persistent nature of the threat, but it is also what allows attackers to break into sites very quickly.

5. Old school attacks were about giving the victim some visible indication of a compromise. Today it is all about not getting caught. Stealth and being covert are the main goals of today's attacks. APTs goal is to look as close (if not identical) to legitimate traffic. The difference is so minor that many security devices cannot differentiate between them.

6. The driver of APT is to provide some significant benefit to the attacker, the benefit being either economic or financial gain. Therefore the focus will be all about the data. Anything that has value to an organization means it will have value to an attacker. Since data has become so portable, and with cloud computing increasing in popularity, data is now available from the Internet, via many sources.

7. Attackers do not just want to get in and leave, they want long-term access. If someone is going to spend effort breaking into a site, they will make sure they can keep that access for a long period of time. Stealing data once has value, but stealing data for 9 months gives the attacker even more value.

Putting all of this together means that you will be constantly attacked and compromised, making it necessary for an organization to always be in battle mode. This is a never ending battle. Since the APT is meant to be extremely stealthy, there is a good chance that an organization might be compromised and not know about it for several months. Before you discount this, if you were compromised and the attacker was not doing any visible damage, how would you know?

DEFENDING AGAINST THE APT

While there are entire chapters in this book focused on defending against the APT, as means of introduction there are some high-level strategies organizations should use. Always remember that prevention is ideal, but detection is a must. Most organizations focus solely on preventive measures but the problem with the APT is that it enters a network and looks just like legitimate traffic and users. Therefore, there is little to prevent. Only after the packets are in the network do they start doing harm and breaking in. Based on the new threat vectors of the APT, the following are key things organizations can do to prevent against the threat:

1. *Control the user and raise awareness*—the general rule is you cannot stop stupid, but you can control stupid. Many threats enter a network by tricking the user into opening an attachment or clicking a link that they shouldn't. Limiting the actions a user is allowed to do with proper awareness, sessions can go a long way to reduce the overall exposure.
2. *Perform reputation ranking on behavior*—traditional security tries to go in and classify something either as good or bad, allow or block. However with advanced attacks, this classification does not scale. Many attackers start off looking like legitimate traffic, which means they would be allowed into the network, and then once they are in they turn bad. Therefore, since the goal of attackers is to blend in, you need to track what the behavior is and rank the confidence level of whether it is looking more like a legitimate user or more like evil.
3. *Focus on outbound traffic*—inbound traffic is often what is used to prevent and stop attackers from entering a network. While it will catch some attacks and is still important to do, with the APT it is the outbound traffic that is more damaging. If the intent is to stop exfiltration of data and information, looking at the outbound traffic is how you detect anomalous behavior, which is tied to damage to an organization.
4. *Understand the changing threat*—it is hard to defend against something you do not know about. Therefore, the only way to be good at the defense is to understand and know how the offense operates. If organizations do not continue to understand the new techniques and tactics of the attackers, they will not be able to effectively tune their defensive measures to work correctly.
5. *Manage the endpoint*—while attackers might break into a network as the entry point, they ultimately want to steal information that exists on endpoints. If you want to limit the damage, controlling and locking down the endpoint will go a long way to protect an organization.

While the current threat is advanced, persistent, stealthy, and data focused, organizations can implement measures to effectively deal with the threat.

APT VS TRADITIONAL THREAT

As organizations adjust their security posture and defensive measures to protect against the APT, it is important to focus on the key differentiators of how the APT works. The approach of the APT is different from the traditional threat in three areas: the goal, the structure of the attacker, and the methods. The ultimate goal of APT is to maintain a long-term beachhead on your network. The attacker wants long-term access to all of your resources so that they can constantly at will extract and capture any information that they want. The traditional threat was about the immediate need. A worm would target an organization, extract that they wanted, and leave. Typically with APT there is both an immediate need and a long-term focus. Not only does the attacker want to be able to compromise information today, but it is also about future attacks. In essence, the attacker wants to have strategic targets compromised so as new information is needed in the future, the access exists; they just need to extract the data.

The APT is not an individual or a small hacker cell that was used with traditional threats. Today they are very well organized, well-structured organizations. The steps of the attack are broken down into clear division of labor and each person on the team is well trained in their respective skill. Think of a fortune 500 company focused on offensive operations and you are starting to understand the structure of these organizations. Many of the attack methods are under strict change management and are constantly updated to increase the success rate and decrease the chance of being caught. One of the reasons on why defensive measures have to move from reactive to proactive is because that is what happened with the APT. The traditional threat was reactive. A patch was released and a worm was written to take advantage of the vulnerability that was not present on a system. The adversary was reactive and would wait for the vendors to release information on vulnerabilities and react to those announcements. The APT is constantly tracking how organizations implement security, determining what their next move is going to be, and create offensive measures that will defeat an organization's security, giving the adversary access to the information they want. In some cases, by the time an organization deploys a new measure of protection, the advanced adversary has already figured out a way around it.

The methods used by APT also take advantage of advanced technology. Most malware that is used is customized for maximum success against a specific client. In cases where malware might be re-used, the code would be changed and recompiled so that traditional security measures like signature detection are no longer effective. Essentially many of the attacks are built for one-time use. Therefore any analysis that the defender performs has minimal impact because the next attack is going to be different and unique. One of the scariest features of the APT is they turn our biggest strengths into our biggest weakness. What is the one technology that the APT is using to slip under the radar and bypass most of the security devices that are deployed on networks today? Encryption.

Encryption was created to stop attackers from accessing critical information. It was built to help defend our networks. However encryption does not just stop the attacker from reading our information, it stops anyone from accessing the contents of the encrypted payload. Most security devices are not capable of reading encrypted packets and the ones that can, cannot do it very efficiently. The number one trick of attackers is after they break into a system, they set up an encrypted out-bound tunnel to an attackers system. Since the data is encrypted it goes virtually undetected on the network. This is a prime example of using great technology for evil.

SAMPLE APT ATTACKS

To highlight the damage and devastation that the APT can cause, we will look at a few sample APT attacks to highlight the principles we have been covering and to show that traditional security measures do not always properly scale.

Company: Large Oil Company.
Motivation: Attackers sought valuable data about new discoveries of oil deposits (this data can cost hundreds of millions of dollars to produce).
Result: Companies unaware of extent of attack until alerted by law enforcement; APTs had been persistent for 14 months and actively exfiltrating emails and passwords of senior executives.
Company: Technology Company.
Motivation: Attackers sought persistent access to cutting-edge intellectual capital.
Result: Chinese attackers successfully exfiltrated sensitive data from large Fortune 100 organizations.
Company: Nuclear Facility.
Motivation: Attackers sought to disrupt critical industrial infrastructure, specifically targeting nuclear facilities.
Result: Attackers successfully infiltrated several nuclear sites and damaged uranium enrichment facilities.

APT MULTI-PHASED APPROACH

The APT adversary achieves their goal of stealthy, persistence, and data focused through a multi-phased approach. In order for APT to be successful the attacker has to perform careful planning and analysis.

The following are the general phases of an APT attack:

Phase 1: Reconnaissance—gathering of information about the target, looking for specific areas that can be focused on to achieve long-term compromise with the minimal amount of energy or effort. This usually involves finding an individual that can be targeted to be used in phase 2.

Phase 2: Initial Intrusion—determining and finding some way into the organization to establish a foothold. This usually does not require exploitation and is most commonly achieved by convincing a user to open an attachment or click on a link they are not supposed to open.

Phase 3: Establish Backdoor—ultimately the APT wants to be able to communicate with the network they are targeted. After initial intrusion has been accomplished a remote way in is established so the attacker can continue to move around the compromised network.

Phase 4: Obtain Credentials—an attacker wants to own the entire network and maintain long-term access for both current and future use. This usually requires obtaining, cracking or hijacking admin, and privileged credentials.

Phase 5: Install Utilities—at this point the attacker wants to establish persistence and total control of the network. This is usually done by installing customized tools to create a complete command and control communication with the compromised network.

Phase 6: Data Exfiltration—the final step is to steal and extract the critical information off of the network in a stealthy way. This is usually done with encryption and masking the data to look like legitimate traffic.

Since every APT attack is unique and different there are many variations, but these are the general steps that are often followed.

SUMMARY

APT is only going to increase in intensity over the next year, not go away. Ignoring this problem just means there will be harm caused to your organization. The key theme of dealing with APT is "Know thy system/network." The more an organization can understand about network traffic and services, the better they can spot/identify anomalies, which is the better way to defend against the APT. Remember that the APT is quite different than traditional attacks. First, the APT is very target aware. They are going to spend time to understand the target organization and built custom malware to increase the chance of a successful attack. Second, they are highly organized and structured like a corporation. The malware they use is highly customized to achieve maximum impact and be very stealthy. Third, APT is very competent and motivated and in many cases backed by nation states. This means they have the resources that are need to be successful. The good news is, by focusing in on understanding the threats and an organization's vulnerabilities; you can properly defend against the APT.

Why are Organizations Being Compromised?

2

INTRODUCTION

It would be nice if we lived in a world where bad things only happened to bad people. Unfortunately we live in a world where bad things happen to good people. People who drive the speed limit, always stopat stop signs, and wear seat belts still get into accidents or hit by drunk drivers in which they had no control over the situation. Similar things happen in the cyber world. Organizations that try to do the right thing and follow all of the rules still get compromised and broken into. Many executives of organizations, after they are notified that are compromised, are surprised. A common theme is we have spent millions of dollars on security, how could this have happened. The underlying reason is no matter how hard we try you cannot control the threats. The only things that you control are the vulnerabilities that are present on your systems.

Now this can be a slippery slope. It is impossible to remove all vulnerabilities from a system, just like it is impossible to remove all vulnerabilities from our lives. Even though some people reading this book might believe so, there are no super humans or people that are perfect. We all have weaknesses. Those who are successful in life focus in fixing the weaknesses that we can, accepting the ones that we cannot and create situations that maximize our strengths and minimize our short comings. Security needs to take the same approach. On the one hand an organization cannot remove all vulnerabilities, which mean there is always a chance of compromise. This chapter is about playing to our strengths and avoiding the slippery slope of spending a lot of effort on security and still being compromised. By better understanding the threats and why organizations are compromised will allow us to build better more effective defensive measures.

In the real world and in cyber there is no "E" for effort. In elementary school, I use to receive an "E" for effort as my grade for PE (physical education). Essentially this was a nice way of saying that while I tried harder than anyone else in class, I really sucked at this particular activity. School is about learning and instead of giving me an F which is what I deserved, since I was not very good at the activity, it would have really discouraged me, and they wanted to show my parents that I was trying very hard and putting in a lot of effort, even though the results did not show it.

Unfortunately once you leave school, regardless of whether you try hard or not does not matter, you are judged solely on the results. This causes frustration for many people because they are trying hard to secure their organization but are still compromised.

Back in the 1990s, understanding and assessing why organizations were compromised was straightforward. Organizations that were compromised back then were making obvious mistakes. They had no firewalls, no detection, all systems had public IP addresses, and no patches were applied. After an incident it was pretty obvious that organizations needed to put resources against security to minimize this from happening again. Just like in the medical world, we understand the common cold very well and there are many solutions for dealing with it. While cyber security is never simple, it was straightforward because we were dealing with a visible threat and organizations knew what had to be done to secure the enterprise.

Today the threat is much harder because we are dealing with cyber cancer which we are still trying to understand and determine exactly how it works. Today cyber security can be downright frustrating because organizations can do what they believe to be the right things but still get compromised. Just like people can exercise, eat healthy, have low blood pressure, and still get cancer. Organizations can still get cyber cancer even though they believe to be following good sound cyber security principles. The problem that will be discussed in this chapter is there is a difference between doing good things and doing the right things. Good things will help you in the long run, but the right things will stop and defend against the current threats.

DOING GOOD THINGS AND DOING THE RIGHT THINGS

One of the first rules that many people have learned throughout their lives is that money does not solve all problems. In the cyber world, many organizations are learning the same principle. Money does not equal security. Just because an organization buys a lot of products does not mean they will be secure. First, there is no such thing as a silver bullet or 100% security. No matter what you do, an organization will have vulnerabilities. There is no single product that an organization can implement that will make them secure. Therefore products will help manage an organization's risk but regardless of what products are purchased; continuous monitoring must be performed to detect attacks that traditional security measures might have missed.

Second, security products must be implemented correctly in order for them to be effective. Many organizations will purchase a security product, plug it into their network or install it on a server, and assume they are secure. Most security products have to be configured and properly managed in order for them to work. Many organizations have a false sense of security because they have a firewall, IDS, IPS, and DLP installed and therefore feel they are secure. When in reality those products are not stopping the advanced attacks because they are not configured correctly.

Third, security products must map against critical risks to an organization. Are the security products that are being implemented actually solving the problem that is needed for an organization to be secure? There are all of these fad diets available that will help people lose weight. The problem with many of these diets is they are not very healthy for your body. Most people will agree that being healthy is what is most important. However people get so focused on losing weight, they will do anything, regardless of whether it is healthy or not. Many organizations do the same thing with security. They get so caught up in implementing products, they forget to ask the most fundamental question of whether it made them more secure or not.

While we know that buying security products might seem like a good idea, it might not always be the best option. Ultimately the question of doing good things and doing the right things comes down to the fundamental and core principles of security. Whether we like it or not, security has and will always be about understanding, managing, and mitigating risk to an organization. Buying products that does not reduce or map against a high priority risk is a good thing to do. Mapping any purchase or activity against proper risk reduction is the right thing to do to protect against an advanced threat. Remember the key questions. Before you spend a dollar of your budget or an hour of your time on security, you should always be able to answer three questions:

1. What is the risk?
2. Is it the highest priority risk?
3. Is it the most cost effective way of reducing the risk?

Organizations that focus on these questions are doing the right thing and winning the cyber battle and organizations that are not focusing in on risk are typically compromised with a high degree of frequency. If you want to take a quick test and see how well aligned your security budget is with doing the right thing, perform the following steps. Take your current yearly security plan or roadmap and for each item on your plan ask the above three questions. If you can answer them for most of the items on your roadmap, your security is properly aligned. If you cannot answer those questions for most items on your security roadmap then you are doing things that are very similar to organizations that are being compromised. If an organization's security decisions are not mapped back to risk, they are not focusing in on the areas that matter in defending against the APT.

SECURITY IS NOT HELPLESS

With all of the attacks that are occurring and the perception that any network could be compromised, it is important not to get frustrated, unplug your systems, and go Amish. While it is a reality that systems will be compromised, it is not hopeless. By focusing in on the right areas, cyber security can make a positive difference and help improve the functionality of an organization. We have to recognize the bad things that are going to happen and properly prioritize and focus in on preventing, minimizing, and detecting the threats that can cause the most harm.

Always remember that there is no such thing as a risk-free life. People get into car accidents and still drive. People get injured on a daily basis but people still exercise and play sports. Relatively speaking, cyber security is relatively new so the media focuses energy and effort when compromises occur. If one large Fortune 500 company is compromised it will make headline news but what about the other 499 that did not get compromised? We are making a positive difference in increasing overall security, but we have to remember that it is never going to be perfect.

In order to be effective within an organization, we have to make sure the executives understand that while attacks are going to occur there are actionable things that can be performed that will make a positive difference. I have heard executives say if attacks are always going to be successful then why bother wasting money on cyber security. Just let the attacks occur. That statement is as foolish as saying well there is a chance I could get into a car accident so I should just drive drunk. Yes, car accidents could occur but by being a safe driver you can greatly reduce the chances of it occurring. Cyber security is the same way. While attacks are going to be successful, things would be a lot worse if all of the energy and effort was not put into securing an organization. Make sure your executives and company understand how many attacks are being stopped and all of the positive impacts security is having instead of focusing in on the negative.

While one could argue that ultimately the number of goals determines who wins and who loses, it is also important to look at the shots on goal. If there were 50 shots on goal with one score that is a lot different than 1 shot with 1 goal. Today the number of shots on goal or attempted attacks are increasing at an alarming rate which means the number of successful attempts are also going to increase.

Cyber security, especially with the APT is going through an interesting transformation. Several years ago, many security people would say that the best thing that could happen to us is that we have a compromise. The logic was that executives were not giving the security team the resources they needed because they did not think there was a problem. They thought security was just being Chicken Little saying the sky is falling when everything was fine. When a breach occurred it showed the executive team that there really was a problem and they started giving them the resources they needed. This was very concerning to me because it meant we had a suicidal mindset when it came to security. What would you do if a friend of yours said the best thing that could happen to me is if I can shot or get into an accident? You would be very concerned. There was the same concern for many clients when they would say the best thing that could happen was something bad occurring.

Today that has changed. Now security folks are taking back their words that they wish their organization would have a compromise and today they are saying, we are going to die at some point so why bother living. That is also a defeatist attitude. Yes, bad things might happen but the goal is to continue to move from reactive to proactive and predictive security postures. The more you can understand what might occur and take defensive measures, the less impact it will have to your organization.

BEYOND GOOD OR BAD

The new approach to security to deal with APT focuses in on constantly analyzing behavior and as someone exhibits good behavior we increase their access and as they exhibit bad behavior we reduce their access. This is in contrast to traditional security where activity is either blocked or allowed. Firewalls have and will continue to be an effective means of protecting an enterprise. However they are essentially a binary device. The firewall ruleset will examine traffic and determine whether it is good (allowed) or bad (blocked).

This approach has a fundamental flaw. It assumes that something is always good or always bad. If a firewall blocks activity it assumes that it is 100% bad. What if something is bad 80%? In this case the firewall must allow it into the network. The reason is simple. If the firewall blocks this activity, it will be blocking 20% legitimate sales, customers, or business emails. Today, APT is constantly changing its behavior and therefore the behavior that it uses to compromise a site is not always 100% bad. Therefore one of the reasons organizations are compromised is because they are relying on technology that can only block 100% and most of the advanced attack methods do not fall into this category.

Effective security today needs to be adaptive. Instead of allowing or blocking activity, we need to use degrees of access. As an entity exhibits good behavior they are given more access to resources and as they exhibit bad behavior, their access is reduced. What is interesting about this approach to security is that it changes the paradigm. Traditional security often hurts the user and impacts the ability for them to perform their job. This new approach hurts the attacker. If a system is compromised with malware and the user does not know the system is compromised, they are still going to use the system for legitimate purposes. With this approach, as the malware tries to do malicious things on the same system as the legitimate user, our new approach to security will reduce the amount of access the system has. In most cases the access that is taken away is associated with the malicious behavior not the user. Therefore the malware is prevented from doing harm but the user can still perform the work they are doing. Application aware, next-generation firewalls, and DLP (data loss prevention) products are focusing in on making a more granular distinction, allowing better protection against APT.

ATTACKERS ARE IN YOUR NETWORK

In cyber security, things are not hopeless and through careful focus and attention you can make a positive difference and protect the critical information. While it is important to be positive, it is also important to be realistic. Unfortunately today you have to recognize the fact that if you have a large network with critical information, most likely there is an attacker in your network. One of the key attributes of security is plan for the worst and hope for the best. It is better to assume that you are compromised and if you are not, no harm and no foul. However if you assume that you are not compromised and you are, significant damage could be happening right now and your organization could continue to lose money. This approach is why we all get a physical each year. Even though you feel healthy and fine you still go to the doctor and get blood work and other tests done so if there is something wrong in which there is no visible symptom, you can detect it and deal with it early.

One of the sayings in cyber security is paranoia is your friend. It is always good to be paranoid and try to stay one step ahead of the attacker. More importantly, APT is so persistent that we are at a point in time where we have to recognize that attackers are like spiders. No matter what you do there will always be spiders in your house. Even very large mansions could have spiders. The reason is simply, there is no way to stop them 100% of the time. Based on the advanced and persistent nature of current attacks, they are going to be in your network. The trick is to minimize and control them. Building on our spider analogy, it is OK to have a few spiders but you want to catch them before they make a nest and have baby spiders running around.

The real question is if there was a system on your network that was compromised how would you know? This is the bigger problem that we have to deal with. The concern is not whether there is an attacker on your network, the question is how can we detect them early and minimize the overall damage. Organizations need to enhance their existing security measures to deal with the new advanced persistent threat that will continue to grow in severity and impact.

This brings up a critical point which is many companies that are compromised with APT do not detect it themselves. The way that many organizations know they are compromised is because another organization, such as law enforcement, calls them. This tied with the fact that many companies are compromised for 6–9 months before detecting it shows the severity of the problem. We have to continue to do what we can on prevention but put more and more energy on detection. What if an organization that was compromised for 7 months and notified by an outside entity that they were compromised, detected it within two weeks? In a perfect world, we would say taking 2 weeks to detect a threat is way too long. However, if normally it would take you 7 months and you are catching it within two weeks, think of how much damage was controlled and how much information was saved from being stolen.

Remember that APT is cyber cancer. There is not going to be any visible sign of a problem until the impact is so great to your organization. You need to recognize that your organization is compromised and start looking for it before it is too late. Based on the current state we are in, an organization has to accept the fact that they are compromised or will be compromised in the near future. By accepting this fact changes the approach we take with security. Traditional security is focused on proactive prevention and reactive detection.

If an organization understands this new approach, it not only explains why organizations are compromised but also changes everything in terms of how we approach security. One of the reasons why organizations are compromised is they focused all of their effort on prevention but they do not know what exactly they are trying to prevent. If you do not know what something looks like or if it looks identical to something that is allowed, prevention is going to have minimal impact.

Now we must be careful of how we approach this. In no way shape or form are we saying that prevention has no value and should not be done. Prevention is critical for laying out a foundation and stopping a critical set of attacks. However prevention alone is not going to get the job done on the new breed of attacks we are dealing with.

Since the attack has changed, we must make sure that our defensive measures scale against this threat. From a quick checklist perspective let's examine what is required for a solution to scale and detect the APT:

- *Automated*—the current threat is persistent and nonstop. As depressing as it sounds, we have to accept the fact that for the foreseeable future, your organization is going to be attacked and compromised. Not only do attackers want information today, they also want to gain a foothold so they can have access in the future. Therefore more and more of our security needs to be automated to keep up with the changing threat. While some manual method is required from an analytical perspective, more and more decisions need to be automated.

- *Adaptive*—since the attacker is persistent and continuously trying to get in, if something fails they are going to try something new. If the attacker is always performing different attacks to get in, our security also needs to be adaptive. What will work today will not work in the future. This is what we often refer to as attacker leap frog. The attackers will figure out a way into the system. The defenders will deploy a defense mechanism to prevent it. The attackers will re-evaluate the situation and find a new way in. The defenders will identify the vulnerable and fix it. This sequence of events will continue. If we only focus on stopping an attack once we will have short-term victory but long-term defeat.

- *Proactive*—the philosophy of traditional security was to only spend money if you are absolutely sure there is a problem. This lead to reactive security. Wait for the attacker to perform some damage, detect it and fix it before there is significant damage. This approach makes two assumptions that are not true today. First, there will be something visible early on to detect. Second, the damage will be minimal and slowly increase so if it is detected early it can be stopped. Today, neither of those statements is true. Therefore security must be proactive and fix a problem as soon as it is discovered, not after it is compromised.

- *Predictive*—in order for proactive security to be effective, we must also anticipate what the attacker is going to do. While the threat is very advanced and persistent, there is also some predictive nature to how they behave. By studying and understanding many types of attacks, we can begin to understand what vectors the threat is going to target and focus most of our defensive measures in those areas.

- *Data Focused*—many traditional approaches to security focused in on signatures and ways an attacker might break into a system. Today since we have to recognize that systems are going to be compromised and attacks are stealthy, the traditional approach is futile at best. Once again if we do not know what to look for, how can we stop it? Upon further analysis we do not want to look at just the signatures of attack, we want to look at what the attacker is ultimately after. New approaches to security have to focus on the data and ways it might be compromised.

Now, look at all of the security that you have deployed on your network and see how many of those requirements the current security solutions meet? This is not criticizing the approach that was taken but pointing out why organizations have been compromised.

PROACTIVE, PREDICTIVE, AND ADAPTIVE

If you want to properly protect your organization and keep it secure, there are three critical words that we need to always follow: proactive, predictive, and adaptive. This is the defensive posture that will allow organizations to properly protect against the APT. Many organizations are still focused on traditional reactive security. While some have put energy and effort into security and think they are being proactive, in reality they are just detecting attacks early. If you ask organizations to rate how well they are doing in these three areas, you will notice an interesting trend. Organizations that are not performing proactive, predictive, and adaptive security are being compromised and those that are performing these measures are not being compromised and if they are, the damage is contained.

Proactive emphasizes the stance that we cannot let the attackers make the first move. When we are dealing with a visible attack, early reaction to a threat works. However now that we are dealing with a stealthy threat, there is nothing to react to and by the time there is a visible threat for an organization to react to, the damage is already done and the data has been stolen. Alarm systems are effective against a thief that is trying to actively break into a house and performing actions that they should not be performing (the traditional threat). However, an alarm system is not effective against a cleaning person who has access to the house, the alarm code and is allowed access but using that access to steal items instead of cleaning the house (the advanced threat). The only way to handle this threat is to recognize that it is a threat and proactively perform background checks on the individual and monitor what they are doing. With the APT, we have enough data and information to understand how they work and what they are targeting. Therefore we can start to minimize and reduce the vulnerabilities that those threat vectors are going to use.

Predictive is closely tied with proactive in that we need to anticipate what the attacker is going to do. If you play chess and you understand the sophistication of the person you are playing you can start to predict how they are going to behave and anticipate their next move by planning ahead. While this is not always a 100% perfect, is does provide an effective way for winning a game. By understanding that the APT is going to target users, especially users that have been out in the public domain and are visible to attackers, we can begin to provide additional security for those users, warn them and even block any attachments that are coming from external addresses. In emphasizing the point that predictive security does not always work it is important to always balance the choices that are made. A key aspect of security is to always ask, what do you gain and what do you lose? If the losses are less than the gains, then it should be done; if the benefit does not outweigh the losses, then other alternative countermeasures should be considered. For example, one of the main ways the APT compromises a system is by sending an email to a user that looks legitimate, with an infected attachment or a rogue link.

What is interesting about targeted spear phishing is that it is fairly low on the sophistication list but very effective. I knew over 10 years ago that we were in a lot of trouble in terms of targeting people with email. I was traveling on the west coast and was woken up at 4am because the "I love you" virus was causing havoc across the industry. What was interesting about the virus was that it was obvious it was not legitimate communication. It is not normal that co-workers would send each other I love you messages. Even though people knew that this type of activity was not normal, they still clicked on the links. At that point I realized that if people would click on email attachments that were clearly not legitimate, what would happen when the attacker made these emails look legitimate. The concern now is the attackers carefully use social media and public information to target an individual with a legitimate email so that they will open the attachment and/or click on a link. Think of a simple example. What if an attacker researched your company and realized that you fiscal year ended in April. Early March you received an email that was spoofed to contain your boss's return email address. It stated that your boss just got out of a budget meeting finalizing next year's budget and adjustments are being made based on difficult economic conditions. Several of your projects have to be reduced and attached is a spreadsheet with the new financial information. Your boss asks you to review and provide back any comments by COB. Most people would click on the attachment. Now if the attacker did additional research and saw that you gave a presentation at a recent conference on how to deploy wireless within an organization and in the presentation you stated that you are working on integrating wireless into your control systems. What if the attacker put that specific project in the email? There would now be even a great chance that the recipient would trust that the email came from their boss and open the attachment. Essentially what attackers do is target an individual and determine what level of confidence needs to be presented to the user for them to fall victim to an attack. They gather as much information as possible to make the email look legitimate, increasing the confidence to the point where there is a high guarantee that the attachment will be opened. This is where effective proactive, predictive security comes into play. If you know people in your organization are going to be targeted and you know the attacker is going to gather open source information to find their target, you can stay one step ahead. On a regular basis you should create a list of people who are publicly associated with your organization. What information is available and how would they be targeted? Provide this information to the individual and raise their awareness. Also, additional countermeasures can be put in place to minimize the damage. For example, with one client the main avenue of attack was spoofed email addresses, making an external email look like it came from an internal address. One initial solution was to have the email system mark an email that came from the outside as external. All emails received from an external mail server had {EXTERNAL} pre-pended to the beginning of the subject line so it was obvious where this email originated. Employees where trained that if the email address was internal but {EXTERNAL} appeared on the subject line they should not trust the email.

For some clients they also decided to just block any email addresses in which external emails contained internal addresses. Now whenever you start blocking emails this could impact the business and many organizations are very hesitant to do this. However, to watch out for the best interests of the organization, security needs to change their position from picking a dog in the fight to being the honest broker. The traditional way of performing security is for the security team to decide that all dangerous emails need to be blocked. They would go to the executives and make their case to try and block all emails. Some executives would bring up the point that this would disrupt the business and have negative impact. The more the security team pushes the more they keep spinning their wheels in the mud. The problem is that the executives assume there is no pain with the way things are currently being done. Therefore when security suggests a change, they are immediately hesitant because they are basing their decision on false expectations. The problem in this case is security picked a side in the fight and tried to argue their position.

The better solution is for security to step back and present both sides of the equation. Option one, keep doing what we are doing today allowing the organization to be targeted and continue to lose $2 million per year. Option two, block all potential dangerous emails and based on research this would cause some productivity issues and frustrations and would cost the company $150k. Now that you are presenting both sides of the equation you can tell the executives which option would you like. Since security is all about presenting risk and options while the executives' job is to determine the appropriate level of risk to the organization, this solution scales well. Whatever option the executives decide on security has now done their job by effectively presenting the appropriate risk options.

Another option that works is when an email is detected as harmful or dangerous, the attachment opens in a non-executable virtual machine. Now the content can still be viewed to determine if it is legitimate but because it is in a virtual machine and nothing is allowed to execute, any malware is contained and there is minimal to no damage to the client. While there is an entire chapter covering solutions to the APT, these paragraphs where meant to show that once you understand the problem, there are reasonable workable solutions that can be deployed.

This also shows that the approach to good security is always centered around a simple principle: offense must guide and inform the defense. The more you understand how the offense works, the more you can predict what they are going to do and build defensive measures to protect against it. Not to depress anyone but in talking about predictive and proactive solutions it is important to remember that the threat we are dealing with is persistent. This means we can never rest. With traditional attacks, if we successfully defended against the threat, the attack would stop. So we had times in which we were defending and times that we were preparing for the next attack. Today the threat is persistent and never stops. Defending against one avenue of attack just means they will try something different until they are successful. Now defending and preparing both have to occur simultaneously. This also explains why organizations get compromised. Many clients successfully defend against one attack, take a rest and while they are resting the attacker sneaks in. In addition, many companies think once they reach a certain level of protection they can stop. Today defensive measures may be better than the attackers but if you stop and the attacker continues, it is only a matter of time until they surpass your defensive measures and break in. Always remember when implementing security to never ever underestimate your adversary. Once you do, you will lose. This means that your security must also be adaptive and change in response to the new threats. What works today will not work tomorrow. The attacker is very advanced. Remember that the A in APT does not refer to the advanced nature of the attacks, it refers to the advanced nature of the attacker. The traditional attacker used low sophistication worms and would try the same attack over and over again until it worked, going after the low hanging fruit and trying to break into as many organizations as possible. Today the threat is targeted. This means they are determined and focused to break into your organization and will not stop until they are successful. If they try something and it does not work, they will not try it again. Not only do you have to understand what they are going to initially try and stop those threat vectors, you have to predict what they are going to try next and adapt your security to defend against what is going to happen and most importantly proactively deploy those defensive measures before the attacker targets your organization. While proactive, predictive, and adaptive can have value by themselves, using them all together is where you get super-charged APT grade security.

EXAMPLE OF HOW TO WIN

While the focus of this chapter is on why organizations get compromised and highlighting the problems that organizations have, we want to take a short commercial break and talk about a solution of how to switch your organization from a position of weakness to a position of strength. While there are entire chapters on the solution, the focus of this book is on solutions and methods to defend against the APT. Therefore even in the early chapters we want to provide some solutions that you can immediately apply to secure your organization. Another point we are going to emphasize is in many cases to provide appropriate security to deal with the APT, you do not need to purchase additional products, you can often use what you have. On average when we survey an organization and look at what they have purchased, they are using less than half of the functionality that they paid for. Therefore very often by surveying what an organization has already purchased and configuring features that are not currently being utilized, organizations can create a solution by using what they already have, in a more effective manner.

One of the technologies that is often underutilized in many organizations is NAC (network access control). NAC is solution that will query a system and based on policies determine which VLAN (virtual local area network) a system is placed on. For example, when a system is plugged into a network, NAC would scan the device and determine if is patched, running the latest version of endpoint security and whether it has indicators of compromise present on the computer. If the system is fully patched and compliant it is placed on the private, trusted VLAN. If it is missing a patch it is placed on a limited VLAN in which it can download and install the patch. If the system is infected it is placed on an isolated VLAN and quarantined. While NAC is very effective and works very well, NAC is often only used when systems are initially connected. After the system is connected and NAC determines what VLAN it should be placed on, NAC does not provide any additional services.

Determining the correct VLAN at the time of connection is important, but why not utilize NAC for continuous monitoring. One of the techniques that attackers use to bypass current network security devices is to set up an outbound encrypted channel on an infected system. Since the attacker has compromised a system that they will use as a pivot point, they need to make an outbound command control channel to interface with the compromised system and potentially exfiltrate data out of the organization. The attacker does not want to get caught so they will utilize their own encryption keys to create an outbound tunnel. This one trick makes the entire connection stealthy and slips right by most currently deployed network security devices. Application level firewalls, IDS, IPS, and DLP all need to read portions of the packet to make a determination of the security level. If the packet is encrypted, the devices are essentially ineffective at catching or stopping the attack. An effective measure for dealing with the APT is to move from signature analysis and packet detection to behavioral analysis. The following are four things that can be used to differentiate between normal and attack traffic, even if the traffic is encrypted:

1. *Length of the connection*—normal users typically make short outbound connections, while attackers usually make long connections.
2. *Number of packets*—normal connections typically send small number of packets out of the organization while attackers typically send a higher volume of packets.
3. *Amount of data*—normal connections typically are sending requests to servers, (i.e. web servers) to request information and therefore is a small amount of information. Attackers since they are extracting information normally send large amounts of information.
4. *Destination IP*—the outbound connections for normal users typically go to a set amount of legitimate IPs, usually within a certain list of trusted countries. Attackers typically make outbound connections to anomalous IPs or IPs in foreign countries that are not normal sites the company connects to.

It is important to note that every organization is different and these four points have to be sometimes adjusted and adapted based on the specific details and applications an organization is running. The bottom line is even if the above points have to be slightly adjusted for an organization, there is almost always a difference between normal connections and attacker connections.

Therefore NAC can be used to do continuous monitoring of each switch port building a baseline of what is normal activity for each user, profiling the average number of connections, packets and data leaving the organization. In addition, a list of common destination IPs can also be tracked. When the average number of packets, connections, or data is exceeded by 30%, NAC will move the user to a less trusted VLAN. If the average number is exceeded by 50%, they are moved to an even less trusted VLAN. When their activity returns to normal, they are moved back to their original VLAN. Essentially as a system shows bad behavior or indicators of a compromise, NAC will move the user to a less trusted VLAN and contain the damage. As the user exhibits good behavior, they are moved to a more trusted VLAN. Now real-time monitoring of the APT can be achieved. For this solution to work it is important it is adjusted to the unique needs of an organization. For example, if at the end of the quarter finance performs different transactions than they normally do, all of this has to be taken into account. Security is not always easy but with proper configuration can scale very effectively to deal with the advanced threats.

DATA CENTRIC SECURITY

Cyber security is an interesting problem. On the one hand, the fundamental methods to secure an enterprise against a specific threat have not changed that much over the years. For example, let's go back to 1988 and briefly look at the Morris worm. The main reason on why that worm was successful was organizations were all running default installs that contained extraneous services and many patches were not applied in a timely manner. In addition, there was minimal configuration management so organizations did not fully understand their exposure. If we fast-forward to today and look at any modern worm and ask the same question on why are those worms successful, you will get a similar answer. Many systems still contain extraneous services and ports and a vulnerability that one system has, many systems have. Essentially organizations do not know what vulnerabilities exist on their systems because configuration management is still lacking. The fundamental method for protecting against a worm has not changed that much over the years. If organizations focused on minimizing the attack surface or exposure of an attack and managed it holistically across the organization, they can effectively protect against a various types of malware like worms.

The problem is the specific threats that we are focused on have changed. Traditional security focused on the system and tried to prevent someone from breaking in. Weaknesses in systems typically included open ports and extraneous services. Today's APT focuses on the human. Weaknesses in humans include trusting items that look legitimate, being naïve and the ability to easily be tricked. However many organizations are still focused on protecting the server. First, many organizations do not realize that the threat has changed. Second, securing a server is easier than securing a human.

Even though we have talked about it for years, many organizations still have traditional security which focuses on a strong outer perimeter to try and stop the attack from coming in. Once you are in the network there is minimal security and the network is fairly flat. This is what is offered referred to as the M&M model of security which is hard on the outside and gooey on the inside. Organizations have focused their energy on creating a strong robust perimeter, between the Internet and the private network. This means it is easy to move between systems and access the data than an attacker wants once they gain access to the private network. When the attacks against a network were mainly server based and visible, this approach was effective. Organizations knew what the attacks looked like and they could be prevented and minimized. However today by targeting the user, most attacks can easily sneak past the perimeter and by targeting a user, compromise an internal system. Now that the attacker has a foothold or beachhead on the internal network bypassing the strong perimeter, there is minimal protection and one of the many reasons why attackers can easily cause damage and compromise so many organizations.

Dealing with the human threat is a much harder problem because it is not static. Blocking port 25 on a firewall or looking for a specific behavior of an attack is static and can be effective against certain types of attacks. Humans utilize judgment and the attacks can always change but be crafted in a way to trick someone to fall victim with a high degree of success. Therefore while awareness and isolation of systems are critical, the most important component is to take a data centric view of security. Where is your data, who has access to your data, and how is it protected? We no longer have the luxury of stopping all attacks. As we have talked about, you need to accept the fact that you are going to be compromised and most likely already have been compromised. The goal of an organization now becomes minimizing the damage and impact to an organization. By focusing in on the data will allow organizations to get ahead of the curve. If someone breaks into a test system, but there is no information on the system, the impact is minimal. If someone breaks into a system and can directly or indirectly steal critical information and extract it from the organization, this now has a big impact. One of the main concerns for most organizations is reputational damage. No one wants to be on the front page of the newspaper or headline news. By focusing and controlling the data, this threat can be minimized.

MONEY DOES NOT EQUAL SECURITY

We often talk to organizations and they are confused after they are compromised since they have spent over $3 million dollars on security. We also hear organizations state that they have increased security by 5% while all other budgets have been cut. They then ask us, isn't that good enough. Unfortunately money does not equal security. Having a security budget is important, but if an organization is not spending money in the right areas, the organization will still be exposed and compromised.

Remember that today's threat is like a cyber-shoplifter which means preventive measures will do minimal to protect an organization. How much of your security is focused on detection? Also, not only is detection important but it must be focused on outbound traffic. While inbound detection has some value, ideally an organization should have inbound prevention and outbound detection.

We often ask the question that if a system on your network was compromised, would you be able to detect it? While asking this question is important, we often urge you to take it a level deeper. Set up a system on your network and slowly send out sanitized information and see if anyone notices. It is easy to claim that an organization is secure but the best way to validate it is to actually test your security.

THE NEW APPROACH TO APT

APT is a completely different problem that what most organizations are used to dealing with. When you switch from detecting visible attacks to looking for stealthy and data focused attacks, we need a new way of approaching the problem. We now have to look for signs of a compromise when everything on the surface looks fine. Remember when dealing with the common cold looking for visible signs to know that you needed to see a doctor worked. With cyber cancer it did not work because by the time you saw a symptom, the problem was so bad it could not be treated. To deal with cancer you have to get examined when you feel healthy and fine. The important question is if a system on your network was compromised and extracting information, how would you know? In many cases looking at a single system would not give you enough details. In addition, since many attackers hide on a system using a variety of techniques to include kernel level rootkits, you could be given false information if you only examine the system. Rootkits are installed by attackers to hide and cover their tracks by manipulating the system to give back false information. Knowing that the information the system provides might be false information, it is important to use data from other sources. If you correlate all of the logs from all devices, systems, and applications, you can now get a clearer picture of what is happening.

The first approach to do this is reducing the attack surface. The more systems, applications, and services you are running, the bigger the problem and the more information you need to look at. Many organizations are still not adhering to the principle of least privilege. The principle of least privilege states that you must give an entity the least amount of access it needs to perform a job function. With a server or a client system, any extra services should be removed off of the system. The first question to answer is do you even know what software is installed on your system. Pick your home or work laptop. If you took out a piece of paper, would you be able to write down all of the services and open ports that exist on the system? If you do not know what is running, how can you secure and protect your information?

Least privilege also needs to be followed for every user on the system. The APT targets an individual user and compromises their system. What is interesting is the individual user is not necessarily targeted because they have the key information on their system. They are targeted because they are an easy target and have a high chance of being compromised. In addition, while the critical information is not on their system, they might have access to that information or at least have visibility to a server that contains the information. Therefore if an attacker can gain a pivot point on the system, they can use that as an entry point into the system to ultimately gain access to the information they want. One of the main reasons why this attack works is the principle of least privilege is not being followed for users. Many users have more access than what they need to do their job. If this access was minimized, the attacker's job would be more difficult.

Performing a better job at reducing the attack surface through least privilege is important, keeping a pulse check on everything that is happening on a network is also critical. There is no single solution to protecting against the APT, however the more organizations can correlate what is happening across their entire network, the more visibility they can get into the problem and the better chance they will detect anomalies. SIEM (security incident and event management) products can be used to correlate and analyze logs to help find useful information that could be indicative of an attack.

SELLING SECURITY TO YOUR EXECUTIVES

A key reason why organizations are not doing the right thing with regard to security is executives do not understand security and the security team does not know how to communicate with executives. In many organizations, executives and security have tried to communicate but since they do not speak each other's language they easily get frustrated and most communication has completely broken down. It is analogous to someone who only speaks English and someone who only speaks German trying to communicate. They will often try and become very frustrated since neither side understands what the other side is saying. After they become very frustrated they will give up and stop communicating. To emphasize the problem, when was the last time you talked with your executives about security and had a useful conversation?

In the 1960s a group of anthropologists were exploring the Amazon and found an Indian tribe and made initial contact with the tribe. After interacting and examining the tribe, they realized that there were very few older people in the tribe. By performing testing of the local water supply they realized that it contained bacteria that after many years of drinking was lethal and the reason why there were not many older tribe members. The anthropologist explained to the people that if they would just boil the water before drinking it, it would kill the bacteria and the tribe would be much healthier. Several years later the anthropologists visited the tribe again and realized that they were still drinking the water directly and still dying. The anthropologists were very frustrated because they gave the tribe an easy solution but they refused to listen. It turns out the reason the tribe did not listen is that they did not understand what was being told to them. The tribe did not have a unit of measurement and did not know what the word boil meant. The anthropologists thought they were giving very clear advice but it turned out the people they were talking to did not understand what they were saying, failed to implement their recommendation and still suffered the negative consequences. In order to communicate with someone and have them listen, you must speak their language and make sure they understand what you are saying.

The reason we covered the story of the anthropologists is it mirrors the current problem we have in security today and the reason why so many organizations get compromised. To help align the story, replace the word anthropologist with the security team and the word tribe with executives. How often do security people get extremely frustrated because they told executives about the problem, gave them a solution, they refused to listen and the organization was compromised. All of the time security people so frustrated because they told the company what was going to happen, gave them a reasonable solution, and no one listened. While the language that security folks speak is very clear to them, it often does not make a lot of sense to the executives and therefore they do not listen. In some cases, the reasons why organizations get compromised is not because of resources or technology, but because the security team is not able to communicate the correct information to the executives and/or the executives are not able to ask the right questions. The net result is there is a misunderstanding of what needs to be done to protect the organization and bad decisions are made. Compounding the problem, executives also do not understand the value of security and think that the energy put forth on security was wasted.

Based on all of the attacks that have been occurring, there are some people who have claimed that security is a zero sum game. No matter what you do you will not come out ahead. Essentially that security is hopeless and you will lose. If you do not focus in on the correct areas that might be true; however, many organizations have shown that by focusing in on the right areas security can be a business enabler, not only protecting the organization but allowing the organization to operate more efficiently. One of the reasons people think security is a zero sum game is because there is minimal useful communication between the security team and the executives. If the two groups are not clearly communicating on a regular basis so both sides understand each other, you cannot win at security. One of the best ways to increase communication and show value is by showing the return on investment (ROI) or in our case, the return on security investment (ROSI).

In order for security to be successful, we have to show that we are focusing in on the correct areas and that the organization is getting a valuable return for their investment. The main value of ROSI is (1) show executives that they are getting value and benefit from security; (2) explain to executives that their money is best spent in security because it will provide the best benefit to the organization; and (3) have security speak a language that executives understand. For ROSI to work, you have to keep it simple. I had someone tell me that they tried this and it did not work. They explained that they created a 75 page report, spent 3 days working on it and no one read it. I looked at him and said I would not read it. In order to effectively show the ROSI, you need to produce short and simple graphs that executives can easily understand that highlights the value add of security and shows that things would be a lot worse if the security measures were not put in place. One of the mistakes often made with calculating ROSI is people often say security is very difficult to measure because if security is done correctly nothing happens. Therefore at the end of the year, the executives see nothing has happened and concluded that security has no value because they did not see anything tangible. They assume that nothing would have happened even if money was not spent on security and budgets are cut. Unfortunately that logic is not correct. If security is done correctly there are lots of bad things that are being prevented, but there is nothing visible happening so executives jump to the wrong conclusion. Therefore security needs to do a better job of showing the value that security is providing and emphasizing that things would be worse if security was not properly implemented. In addition, we need to train executives on how to ask the correct questions to gain better insight into what is happening.

In order to show how you can present ROSI to executives, let's look at two examples. First, many executives do not understand how bad things are with security and how often an organization is under attack. As the media continues to push these topics, executives slowly understand but they still do not have a clear picture that this is a constant battle and attackers are constantly trying to break in. If you want to understand the extent of the problem, the next time you see your executives, ask them a simple question: "How many attempted attacks do you think our organization has every week?" When I ask this question I often receive responses like 20–30 attacks per week. One executive said to play it safe I will bet on the high side and say 70. Those of us that work in security know that many of these organizations have 70 attempted attacks every hour and some every minute. There is clearly not an understanding of the problem space and how much organizations are being attacked. The good news is this information is readily at your fingerprints and can easily be provided to executives. What is another word for attempted attacks?—dropped packets from your firewall. Every time a firewall drops a packet it is an attempted attack. If it wasn't an attack or undesirable traffic, it would have been allowed through by the firewall. Tracking dropped packets is something most firewalls automatically perform and organizations should be tracking it on a regular basis. If for some reason you do not have this information it is as easy as putting a single line at the end of your firewalls ruleset:

ANY ANY ANY ANY – DENY - LOG

Your firewall should be implementing a default deny strategy and anything that is not explicitly allowed should be dropped. This is automatically done by most firewalls, however if you allow the default implicit deny, usually the packets are not logged. By adding in an explicit deny all, you can have all dropped packets logged. Now that you have the number of dropped packets or attempted attacks against your organization, create a simple chart. Ideally produce this for a year but 6 months will work if you do not have a full year's worth of information. Create a graph that shows the number of dropped packets for each month or week. Use a simple line chart so it is easy to read and not confusing. At the top of the chart list the average number of dropped packets per month. At the bottom of the chart list the average cost of an attack against your organization and/or DMZ servers. What is interesting is most organizations have over 100,000 dropped packets per month and the average cost of an incident is $1.2 million. By providing this information to the executives on a monthly basis shows the huge return on investment. Now spending several million on security makes sense because you are preventing billions of dollars of potential damage to your organization. A simple chart like this provided to your executives on a periodic basis will move security from being something organizations do not understand to an area that is providing one of the best returns on the organizations investment.

A second example of showing the return on investment is anti-virus and/or endpoint security products. As the economy continues to be tight, more and more organizations are cutting budgets. Even security is suffering cuts in the investments that are normally made. The main reason is organizations do not understand how big a problem it is and what needs to be done to protect the organization. As you learn to show the ROSI on security, do not be surprised if your budget increases! One area that is often scrutinized today is AV (anti-virus) software. Many executives say that viruses are no longer a problem because you do not hear about major viruses like you did many years ago when several times a year you would hear about Melissa, I love you, or other large- scale viruses. In the last few years there has not been a major virus outbreak. However, stating that viruses are no longer a threat is jumping to the wrong conclusion. Viruses are as much a threat if not more of a threat than they were in the past. The difference is the means and methods of how viruses target and compromise systems have changed. Viruses use to be visible and large scale, so everyone knew that they were occurring and organizations acted in a reactive manner. Today viruses are causing more damage because they are now focused, stealthy, and going after an organization's critical information. Since they are more focused and typically going after a smaller number of organizations, they are not noticed and therefore it is easy for executives to jump to the wrong conclusion. If security does it job correctly, once again we can show the huge benefit and value add an organization is getting from implementing an AV solution.

Once again the trick to showing the ROSI is a simple, concise, and effective message. A simple graph with some short labels is the best way to show executives all of the great work that security is performing. Remember, if it is complicated or hard to read, they will not understand it. To show the ROSI on AV, create a graph showing the number of quarantined viruses your AV software stops every week. Plot it on a simple graph showing this for the last 6 months. At the top list the average number of viruses prevented per week. At the bottom list the cost a virus outbreak has on your organization. Your incident response team should easily be able to provide this information. I have had executives that wanted to cut the yearly license for AV software. After they see that they have hundreds of quarantined viruses every week and each one could cost the organization half a million dollars, the investment becomes a no brainer.

One of the main reasons why organizations get compromised is the executives and security team do not know how to communicate. Based on the increased exposure of attack and the significant monetary loss, executives and the security team should be communicating on a regular basis. The best way to do this is for security folks to understand what is important to executives and learn to speak their language. The language you need to learn to speak is easy: money. By showing how bad the problem is with simple graphs and emphasizing the value add that organizations are gaining by implementing security, organizations can better align security with their business need and protect their critical information.

TOP SECURITY TRENDS

As we finish up this chapter in answering the question on why do organizations get compromised, it is important to remember that security is always changing. By understanding the top trends that are occurring in cyber security, will allow your organization to better align your resources for the future.

My son played basketball and while his team tried very hard, they lost every single game. The kids and coach where getting very frustrated. In talking with the coach he could not understand what was happened. He said that he played and coached basketball 15 years ago and these plays always worked and his team went to the state championship. The first mistake that was made is while the general rules of the game are the same, the approaches and strategies have changed. Also, every team is different and has unique players so things that worked in the past will not work in the future. To help the coach, we started watching other teams who were similar in makeup to his team who were winning and watched what they did. If team x played team y and won and this week we are playing team y, guess what. We started to copy and adapt the plays of team x and we started winning games. Now at some point if we wanted to beat team x we would have to develop our own unique plays, however the moral of the story is while ultimately you must take a customized approach to be state champions, if you are losing every game, by copying what the winning teams are doing, you can start to increase your chances of winning.

Cooker cutter security does not work. If you want to have an advanced security program, it must be customized. However, regardless of what position you are in with security you should understand what organizations that are winning and those that are losing are doing and minimize doing anything like the losers and maximize patterns of the winners. While this chapter was focused on why companies are compromised and things to make sure you avoid doing, we want to finish with key trends that organizations that are winning are doing so you can start to align your activity with the correct areas. While it is important to know what you should not do, it is also important to know what you should be doing.

The following are some key trends that organizations need to make sure they are focused on:

- *The exponential growth of mobile devices and the commercialization of IT drives an exponential growth in security risks.* Every new smartphone, tablet, or other mobile device, opens another window for a cyber-attack, as each creates another vulnerable access point to networks. Mobile computing continues to increase in popularity because it offers flexibility and the ability to access information from anywhere and any location. Often new technologies and especially mobility is driven by functionality. Very often minimal if any security exists in these devices. Reactive security still plays a key role where organizations will wait for these devices to be compromised and figure out how to secure them after the fact. What we often forget is that security should be based on the data, not the form factor of the device. If a laptop, tablet, and mobile phone all contain the same data, why does one have 15 characters passwords and another only have a 4 digit pin. Why does one device have endpoint security and patching and the other device has nothing. The policy should be written for the sensitivity of the data and any device that contains that information should have the same level of protection. What also makes mobile devices more of a problem than laptops is laptops are often owned by the company and mobile devices and tablets are owned by the individual. Since the individual owns the mobile device very often by default, any data on their device they also own. Therefore organizations must make sure that in their policy that every employee must sign before connecting a device to the network, they take away the expectation of ownership. Any corporate information residing on a personal device still belongs to the company and the company can remotely protect this information including deleting and securely wiping the device if they feel it represents a threat. It is also a good idea to take away the expectation of privacy so the company can fully monitor any activity.

- *Increased C-suite targeting.* Senior executives are no longer invisible online. Firms should assume that hackers already have a complete profile of their executive suite and the junior staff members who have access to them. While executives often have the highest level of protection, they are also targeted more and more based on the information they have access to. Attackers are looking to profile potential targets by correlating and analyzing online information. Since more and more executives have a public facing component, there are more details to gather about them and they can be an increased target. While this is important to keep in mind, we must always remember that anyone who has a public profile can be targeted. We have found that by analyzing online information about employees, there is a direct correlation between the amount of information someone has publicly available and the increased likelihood they will be a target.

- *Growing use of social media will contribute to personal cyber threats.* A profile or comment on a social media platform—even by an employee's relative—can help hackers build an information portfolio that could be used for a future attack. It is important to remember that online there is no such thing as private information. Any information in electronic form can be found and used against an individual or a company. There is also no such thing as temporary information online. Once you hit send or save, you have to assume that the information will exist forever. Electronic information is backed up and with people forwarding and re-posting information, you have to assume that someone will always be able to find a copy of the information. While information is always available, with the rising popularity of social media it has just compounded the problem. Previously there were clear boundaries between work you performed as an employee and work you performed as an individual. Most people had two separate computers and while there was some overlap, there was a separation. Today with social media there are no lines. Since your online identity can often very easily be associated with your employer, it is easy for anyone to cross reference the information. Information that is meant for a small private group of people, could easily be accessed and used to harm an organization. This raises an interesting question on whether an employer can tell an employee what they can do on their personal time.

- *Your company is infected, and you'll have to learn to live with it.* Security should remain a priority, but today's risks and threats are so widespread that it will become impossible to have complete protection—the focus of cyber security tactics increasingly must be to isolate, limit and control intruders inside your system. Resilience is a key word that comes to mind today with cyber security. Organizations must learn to fight through an attack and make sure that the critical business units can continue to function and the impact an attack has to an organization is minimized. It is no longer a question of if or even when an attack is going to take place. Organizations need to accept that attacks are ongoing and that their organization is compromised. The trick is early identification and containment of the problem to minimize exposure to the organization.

- *Everything physical can be digital.* The written notes on a piece of paper, the report binder, and even the pictures on the wall can be copied in digital format and gleaned from tools to allow a Wikileak-type of security violation to continue to occur. The word data theft is very misleading. If someone steals your car, you notice it is stolen because it is no longer available to you and you suffer direct harm by having to replace the physical asset. When someone steals your data, they are not physically stealing it, they are just making a copy. Your data is still available to you and therefore is much harder to notice and detect. With physical assets you can control and manage distribution and copying. With digital assets they can be copied at the speed of light and very hard to control. Based on how portable information is, it can now exist in so many places and locations. By giving a user access to a file, that file can now exist on a large number of different devices which makes it much harder to control.

- *More firms will use cloud computing.* In some cases, today's clouds are more secure, controlled, and protected than traditional networks. They also offer the means to offer data analytics on a larger scale, a more effective use of servers, and the savings of power and cooling costs. Bottom line is you cannot argue with financial savings. The financial benefits of moving to the cloud are so large that organizations are going to move to the cloud, you cannot stop it. What you can do is make sure organizations do it in an efficient and secure way. Instead of saying no cloud. Analyze your applications based on risk and create three categories: (1) cloud ready; (2) potentially cloud ready if certain changes are made; and (3) not cloud ready. Now by having a risk-based approach, organizations can make more logical decisions. The other key point of the cloud is in some cases it can definitely create security risks. However in some cases cloud providers are more secure than the organization.

- *Global systemic risk will include cyber risk.* As banks and investment firms continue on the path to globalization, they will become increasingly interconnected. A security breach at one firm can create negative ripple effects that greatly impact systemic risk in financial markets. On the Internet, there are no country boundaries. In the real world, if you move between countries it is obvious and there are clear control points to enter and leave a country. On the Internet you can seamlessly move between countries without any indicators because it is completely transparent. More importantly is the infrastructure that controls the Internet: core routers and DNS are now controlled by international entities and governments. How do you know that domain name resolution is accurate if you are going through a country that you do not trust?

SUMMARY

Those that do not learn from the past are forced to repeat it. It is critical to understand why organizations are compromised and try to avoid these behaviors as much as possible. While the adversary is very advanced and capable of doing whatever it takes to break into your organization they are also opportunistic and efficient. Why would they use an advanced attack if a simple one will work and is easier to perform? Attackers prefer to use automation and repeat methods that have successfully worked in other organizations. It is quicker and easier for them. Only in cases where it is very difficult will they perform more advanced, adaptive manual attack methods.

While the attacker is very persistent, you want to force them to work very hard to compromise your organization. Automated methods are very hard to defend against and happen very quickly. Advanced manual methods take longer and are easier (relatively speaking) to detect. Therefore the more you can understand how attackers have broken into systems in the best, the more effective your defensive measures can be.

How are Organizations Being Compromised?

3

INTRODUCTION

Regardless of the profession you are in, you cannot be very good at the defense if you do not understand the offense. Organizations are being compromised because they do not understand how the offense operates and in many cases are not fixing the right problems. If you look at a football team, the best defensive linemen are the ones who study and know how the offense calls plays. Sometimes when you are watching a football game and the defense makes a really good play, the announcer will say that the defense knew exactly what the play was that the offense was going to make. The analogy of how many organizations approach defensive security is they decide what vulnerabilities to fix independent of how the offense is actually breaking into systems. The defense cannot create their game plan in a vacuum, they must use the details from the offense to make sure they are building an effective plan that works. If you want to be effective at the defense you need to understand how the offense operates and protect against those threats. Defending against a threat that is not used by the attacker, means that your organization still gets compromised. Doing good things is fixing random vulnerabilities, doing the right thing that actually stops attacks is understanding how the attacker comprises an organization and focusing in on those areas.

The spirit of this chapter is you cannot defend against a threat if you do not fully understand how the attacker breaks in. By understanding how organizations are compromised, you can identify what are the most likely threats that would cause the most impact to your organization and focus your energy against those areas.

While this approach seems sound and straightforward, the problem is the threat is always changing and the point of compromise is different based on the threat that an organizations is facing. The original way attackers broke into systems was targeting known vulnerabilities on a server. Since the attackers knew that organizations were not applying patches in a timely and effective manner, they knew that if they wrote a worm that compromised a vulnerability in a newly released patch, there would be a certain subset of systems that would not be protected and they would be able to get in. This threat was treating all targets equally. It did not matter which organizations they broke into, as long as they compromised one or more systems. These attacks were typically focused on resources since most large organizations have similar resources. The goal was to compromise as many servers as possible, but the specific organizations were less important than the number of systems ultimately compromised. These resources such as servers and Internet connectivity were typically used to launch attacks against other organizations. Even with Website defacements, breaking into a large number of organizations sent a message, regardless of which ones were compromised. With Website defacement, the attacker was trying to make a statement against an organization they did not believe in (hacktivism) or show how smart they were. With this style of attack an organization was playing the odds and typically needed to have slightly better security so an attacker would break into someone else and leave their organization alone. It was almost as if attackers had a certain quota they needed to make each month and once the quota was met, they would stop. Therefore the approach was to make sure you were above the line.

This is often called the faster than the bear syndrome. There are two friends who are hiking through the woods and they notice a bear following them. The bear looks very hungry so they keep walking faster and faster and the bear keeps following them. After a few minutes, one of the friends stops, takes off his boots and starts to put on his sneakers. The other friend looks at him and says why are you putting on your sneakers you are not going to be able to outrun the bear. His friend looks at him and says I do not have to outrun the bear, I just have to outrun you! The bear is going to get one of us and I do not want it to be me. With the traditional threat, the attacker was going to get some organization, your organization just had to be better than the rest. In many cases by having a robust and timely patch management system tied with solid configuration management would allow an organization to be faster than the bear and protected. Today the threat has changed.

Many attacks today are targeted. Based on a variety of reasons an attacker will determine that a specific organization is their target. This is usually done for monetary reasons or critical intellectual property but could also be political or based on affiliations the particular organization has. Either way, the quota model no longer works. Even if your organization has better security than others, the attacker is focused solely on breaking into your organization. It might take them longer but they no longer will be happy if they compromise 10 organizations, they will only be satisfied if they compromise your organization. The trick today is to minimize the chance of an organization being targeted. In some cases it is inevitable. For example if you are a government contractor with the plans for a new fighter jet, other than not winning the contract, you will be targeted and there is not much you can do. In other cases by limiting public information of executives and employees, can minimize and limit the exposure. For example, speaking out about certain issues or against certain hacking groups can cause your organization to be targeted and compromised. This would not only cause damage but could also impact the reputation of the organization. Sometimes the name of your organization can also cause you to be targeted. Organizations with the word United States or America could cause additional focus drawn to the organization from groups who do not like the USA. Some of the groups who are not very familiar with the country might even think these organizations are associated with the government.

The other big difference with APT attacks is the persistent nature of the adversary. With typical worms, there would be a surge of activity targeting the specific vulnerability or vulnerabilities that the worm was after and if you properly defended against it, once the worm stopped, the organization would have a chance to rest. Today, the threat is non-stop 24 h a day, 365 days a year. There is no time to rest and the second you let your guard down the attacker will sneak in. In the past there were some sunny days and some stormy days. Today it is non-stop storms. Some people ask, how does the future look and my response is we have a lot of work ahead of us, but it is a good time to be in security.

WHAT ARE ATTACKERS AFTER?

In order to understand how an organization is compromised, it is important to understand what the attackers are after and trying to compromise. The traditional threat was mainly about bragging rights. In the later 1990s and early 2000, many attackers focus was on being able to show that they could break into an organization but not do deliberate damage to an organization. During this time period Web site defacements were very popular. This was an easy and visible way to show an organization had been compromised. Other than embarrassment there was no deliberate harm to the organization. Today the APT is mainly focused on disclosure and extraction of critical information or intellectual property. While the goal of APT is to maintain long term access to a site, the main reason for this is the ability to extract information that can be used for the advantage of an adversary.

What has muddied the waters today is we have seen an increase in hactivism where hacking groups are targeting an organization or country try to make a point or stop them from doing something. In these cases public embarrassment and reputation damage are the goals. This means there has to be a public or visible component to the attack. These attacks are not typically classified as APT because they often involve the standard customary way of breaking into an organization. Since one of the goals of APT is not to get caught, being stealthy is the name of the game and they do not want an organization to find out or know what they are doing. Therefore the APT normally does not have an obvious visible component to the attack. The goal of the APT is to blend in and look like normal traffic.

ATTACKER PROCESS

How organizations are compromised is often different depending on whether a client or server is being compromised, however, the general attack process is similar.

Attackers usually follow a five step process for breaking into an organization:

1. Reconnaissance.
2. Scanning.
3. Exploitation.

4. Create backdoors.

5. Cover their tracks.

One of the key themes of dealing with the APT is knowledge is power. If the offense knows more than the defense you are going to lose. Therefore organizations need to constantly perform penetration testing and try to break into their organization to find weaknesses and exposures. While the defense would perform similar actions as the offense, they often take a modified approach:

1. Determine the scope.

2. Information gathering.

3. Scanning.

4. Enumeration.

5. Exploitation.

To be effective at the defense, you must understand and know how the offense works and operates. It is critical that an organization understand the tactics, techniques, and procedures (TTPs) that the attacker is going to use. Therefore let's look at each of the five steps an adversary would take and how a focused effort can allow the defense to stay one step ahead.

RECONNAISSANCE

Reconnaissance involves finding out information, normally public information, about an organization to better understand how they operate and is used to identify people or potential points of compromise that can be used to successful exploit an organization. What is interesting is many traditional attacks, for example worms, actually perform little reconnaissance and play the numbers games. They know that there are enough systems that will be vulnerable and unpatched and they do not care which organizations they get into as long as they break into some. Essentially if an attacker is going after quantity not quality, moving directly to step three, exploitation is fine. However, if you want to target a specific organization, identify vulnerabilities and have a high chance of compromise, performing reconnaissance is critical.

One of the questions that often gets asked is why does the APT have such a high-success rate and almost always able to get into an organization they target. The reason is reconnaissance. The more information that is collected through reconnaissance, the easier it is to break into an organization. The amount of information on the Internet is tremendous and with the introduction of social media, information is growing at an exponential rate. If you gather enough information and perform enough reconnaissance, the chances of an attack being successful increase dramatically.

The idea of reconnaissance is not new and has always been performed by attackers. Even in the 1960s and 1970s if someone was going to rob a house, they would drive through a neighborhood and see which houses did not have any lights turned on to indicate that someone might be on vacation. They would also look and see if there were newspapers piled outside the door which indicated that someone was not home for a few days. All of the subtle information can be quite valuable if it is correlated and gathered in a proper manner. Today cyber reconnaissance via the Internet, allows anyway (including an adversary) to gather and correlate a large amount of information with relative ease.

Let's look at a brief example to show the value of reconnaissance. A publicly traded company is performing state-of-the-art research on a new project and there is information on their Website about how the company is going to change the way business is performed. For various reasons a foreign government wants to find out what they have discovered and obtain the research. Since it is a publicly traded company, they can go to the SEC public Website and pull down the financial reports that the company is required to file by law. In the findings they realize that the company has had a pretty flat year and business has been tough. The company is doing fine but they are going to have to look at ways to cut expenses and be more lean. The attacker also finds out that the organizations fiscal year ends in June. The attacker now begins to search the Web on the company name and finds out that one of the senior engineers on the project is giving a presentation on another topic at an upcoming conference. The presentation is on how to roll out technology X across the enterprise. After the presentation, the slides are available and by going through the slides the attacker can see that the company is planning on rolling out Phase II of this project next fiscal year. By going through social media sites, they are able to locate other people who work at the company, including the name and email address of the CIO, who this person reports to. The attacker now crafts an email in April to the senior engineer and spoofs the from field to be the CIO's email address. The subject line is budgetary constraints for Project X Phase II. The email states that the company is finalizing their budget for next year. While the CIO did everything possible to protect the project, because of tough economic times, budgets are being cut and reallocated. The CIO asks the engineer to please review the attached spreadsheet and confirm that the updated numbers will still allow Phase II of the project to be rolled out. Is there anyone who would not open the attachment? Because the attacker did such a good job on reconnaissance, the likelihood of compromise is almost guaranteed. When it comes to compromising an organization everyone wants to jump the gun and go right to exploitation. However by doing your homework and gathering information about the adversary, it can make the attack easier and the chance of success much higher. The APT knows and understands this and is one of the reasons why, they might take 4 months to perform reconnaissance to increase their chances of success but at the end, it is well worth the effort.

An interesting exercise is to perform analysis and determine what information and threat intelligence is publicly available on the Internet. Many times announcements, news articles, and press releases can inadvertently mention an organization or a person in an organization and put the organiztion at risk. However, many organizations do not even realize the information is out there. While you cannot stop the information from being published, if you know it is out there you can build a better defense and recognize you are going to be targeting. With many clients, once you know how the adversary targets an organization using public information, you can start to predict with a high level of accuracy who is going to be targeted. Knowledge is power and the more you know the more effective defenses you can build. Threat intelligence is a critical component of understanding an organization's exposure and building a proper defense against the APT.

SCANNING

Once reconnaissance is performed and an attacker has general information about the target, they now start probing the organization to find out more information and potential weaknesses that can be exploited. Reconnaissance involves gathering (usually) open source information and typically does not touch any of the victim's system. This is one of the reasons it is very difficult to detect reconnaissance. However, scanning is where the attacker takes the open source information and uses it to start to gather specific information about the target. Reconnaissance usually involves identifying a specific target and scanning is finding out additional details about the specific target.

To illustrate scanning, let's continue with our traditional example of a robber driving through a neighborhood to perform reconnaissance of who might be on vacation. Once a house has been identified as a target, scanning would involve finding out specific weaknesses about the house that could ultimately be used to rob it. One method might be for a robber to dress up as a repair person and show up at the front door. By knocking on the front door, they can check and see if any doors or windows are open or unlocked. They can look inside the house to get a better idea of what is inside. If scanning is done correctly, exploitation should be relatively straightforward.

The traditional method of scanning typically involves using domain names to identify IP addresses and scanning a range of IPs to find active visible systems. Once these systems are identified the attacker would look for open ports and try to identify the services that are causing the ports to be open. Once the services are identified, specific vulnerabilities in the services would be probed to find weaknesses that can be exploited.

This method of scanning is still seen in some cases but is often not the method of operation of the APT. The reason is twofold. First, Internet facing systems are traditional locked down and even if they are compromised are usually on a segmented firewalled network. Therefore breaking into a DMZ still requires work to extract information. Targeting internal systems with private addresses through services that are allowed like email is often a better method. Second, if an organization is performing logging and event correlation, traditional scanning would show up in the logs. If you are looking in the right areas, you can tell when someone is scanning your systems. From a logging perspective it is pretty noisy. If one of the goals of the APT is stealthy, this method does not work very well. Therefore while some scanning is done, it is usually more covert and people based. This would include calling the help desk to try and gather information or targeting someone on a social media site.

One example of APT scanning would be to perform reconnaissance and identify an individual in the company that is going to be targeted. By performing research, you identify a previous worker or colleague who currently does not have a social media account. The attacker would create an account of this friend and convince the target that this is really the person they think it is. They will use this account to scan, find out additional details and probe the individual to provide information they normally would not provide if they knew that person was actually an adversary.

While reconnaissance and scanning are both performed, the APT relies more heavily on the recon piece and less on the scanning. The main reason is recon is much easier to hide and be stealthy and the scanning is more visible and likely to tip off an adversary that they are being targeted. A good way to deal with the APT is to understand what the attacker knows. In building an effective defense, knowledge is power. It is important to perform your own recon, identify people who are more likely to be targeted and put them on high alert. Make sure they understand that they are going to be targeted more than others and should be on the lookout for any suspicious behavior. While anyone in your organization can be targeted by the APT, it is important to find the people that have a high percent chance of being targeted. For many of our clients, performing threat intelligence allows a list of individuals to be created and a percent chance of being targeted to be calculated. Anyone who goes above 60% is given a special briefing and more closely monitored.

EXPLOITATION

Once an attacker gathers information about the target using external information (reconnaissance) and starts to probe the organization directly (scanning), they are now ready to exploit or compromise the organization. With traditional attacks against DMZ servers this usually involved exploiting a known weakness (i.e. buffer overflow or SQL injection) or utilizing a zero day exploit that they either developed or was available in the underground. While the attackers had a high success rate, it was still some work and access was not guaranteed.

Today, the APT is all about the quickest, easiest most effective way into an organization. It turns out that targeting a user with a well-crafted email that contains a malicious attachment, is the easiest way to exploit an organization. What is interesting is with the amount of information and details about an organization publicly available, if an attacker performs steps 1 and 2 correctly, step 3 exploitation is almost guaranteed. The threat of the APT was foreshadowed over 10 years ago with viruses like Melissa and I love you. These viruses send non-work related emails to people that obviously were a virus and people opened the attachments. It was obvious that something was wrong and that it was an attacker; however people still opened the attachments. If people are going to open attachments for emails that obvious are not legitimate, what do you think is going to happen when the emails look and sound legitimate because proper reconnaissance was performed—access is almost guaranteed. By understanding how the attacker compromises an organization will allow the organization to better defend against the attack. However, never forget that the attack is always evolving. Attackers used to break into DMZ servers using the traditional threat. Since organizations protected against it, the APT now targets users via email. What we have to remember is that the threat will always evolve. Once we protect against the current vectors that are being using by the APT, APTv2 will use a new vector. We always have to try and keep pace or get ahead of the attacker. Proactive and predictive is better than reactive and compromised.

CREATE BACKDOORS

Typically the way an attacker gets into a system is not the easiest or most direct way into the system. Therefore after initial compromise, they want to create a backdoor to make it easier to get in and out of the system. For example, if after reconnaissance and scanning, the robber finds that the window on the second floor above the garage is open, they would get a ladder, climb on the garage and use that to break in. While that will allow them access to the house, they are not going to use that method to steal your TV and electronics. It would make no sense for them to carry everything to the second floor, out the window, across the garage and down the ladder. Instead they would realize it would be easier to back their van to the back of the house, open the door and use that to rob your house. They would create an additional backdoor to make it easier.

Cyber attackers take the same tactic. After compromise they typically would create an encrypted outbound session, that looks like legitimate traffic, slipping under the radar and making it easier to steal information.

COVER THEIR TRACKS

Attackers do not want to get caught. While the APT will target an organization with the goal of extracting certain information, their ultimate goal is long term access. Any organization that they are going to target because they have valuable information today, will continue to generate valuable information and will have critical information that the APT will want in the future. Therefore it is most economical to create a foothold or beachhead within the target organization and covertly maintain that access over a long period of time so they can continuously extract information out of the organization. This is another area in which APT is different than traditional attacks. Traditional attackers focused mainly on scanning, a lot on exploitation and a little on creating backdoors. They skipped steps 1 and 5, which are critical for success. The APT on the other hand focuses most of its energy on steps 1 and 5 because gathering data and creating long term access is key to a successful attack.

When evaluating the state of an organizations overall security, it is important to remember that the APT spends effort on covering its tracks to be stealthy. Therefore, even though everything might look fine with no visible signs of an attack, that does not mean that your organization is not compromised. Remember we are dealing with cyber cancer which means detailed analysis is required to find the problem.

COMPROMISING A SERVER

Attackers ultimately want information and data. Since this information traditionally resides on a server, compromising a server will give them the information they need. This is analogous to asking bank robbers, why do they rob banks? The traditional answer is because that is where the money is. In asking why do attackers break into organizations and compromise servers, you receive a similar response, because that is where the data is.

While there are a lot of books and information on hacking and breaking into servers, hacking a server really comes down to three conditions:

1. *Visible IPs*—You cannot break into what you cannot see. Therefore, an attacker must be able to see and connect to an IP address in order to compromise it.
2. *Open port*—Ports are the entry point into a system, the more ports that are open, potentially the easier it is to break in.
3. *Vulnerabilities in the services*—Ultimately for an attacker to compromise a system there must be a vulnerability present on the system. While the vulnerability could be misconfiguration, or stolen credentials, a common point of exploitation is a weakness in the service that is causing a specific port to be open.

If we look at this in more detail, typically an attacker starts with a domain name such as syngress.com. From the domain name the attacker needs to be able to find an IP address. A simple way of performing this is by pinging the domain name. Even if ICMP traffic is being blocked, the program needs to convert the domain name to an IP address before the packets can be sent out. This can be seen in Figure 3.1.

From this analysis we can see that the IP address of the Web server is 69.163.177.2. The more detailed way to find out an IP address is to perform a whois lookup to determine the authoritative name servers and use nslookup to identify the IPs. There are many whois services like network solutions but the following information can be obtained by searching the public records:

Domain Name: SYNGRESS.COM.
Registrar: SAFENAMES LTD.
Whois Server: whois.safenames.net.
Referral URL: http://www.safenames.net.
Name Server: NS.ELSEVIER.CO.UK.
Name Server: NS0-S.DNS.PIPEX.NET.
Name Server: NS1-S.DNS.PIPEX.NET.
Status: clientDeleteProhibited.
Status: clientTransferProhibited.
Status: clientUpdateProhibited.
Updated Date: 15-dec-2010.
Creation Date: 10-sep-1997.
Expiration Date: 09-sep-2015.

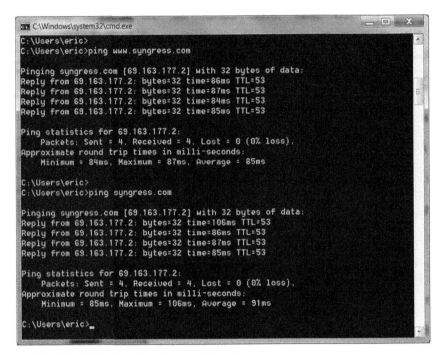

FIGURE 3.1 Basic Way to Determine an IP Address

There is a lot more information that is available within a whois search but what we are interested in is the name servers for the domain. With the name servers we can now perform an nslookup, as seen in Figure 3.2.

The first thing we need to do is connect to one of the authoritative servers by issuing the command:

- Server ns.elsevier.co.uk

where ns.elsevier.co.uk is one of the authoritative name serves that was acquired by performing a whois lookup.

As you can see, we tried to perform a zone transfer which would give us a listing of all of the domain name to IP address mapping, but that is typically blocked. At a minimum we were still able to probe the single domain name and arrive at the same IP address by issuing the command:

- ls syngress.com

By performing this command we received the IP address which is 69.163.177.2. As you can see this is the same IP address that we acquired by performing a ping.

Now that we have a single IP address we need to determine which portion of the IP address belongs to the organization. Since 69 is between 1and 127, it is a class A

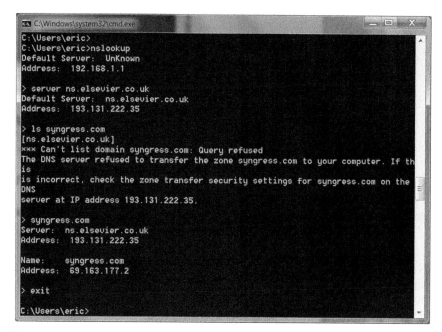

FIGURE 3.2 Performing an Nslookup to Identify an Organizations IP Address

address. It is very unlikely that an organization has a full class A address, so we now have to determine what portion belongs to the organization. If it is an US address, you can use ARIN to identify the range of the address to target, see Figure 3.3.

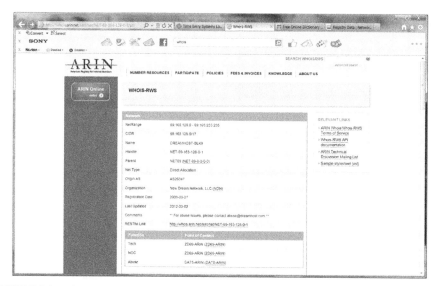

FIGURE 3.3 Using ARIN to Determine the IP Address Range

FIGURE 3.4 Tools Like Nmap and ZenMap Can be Used to Find Visible IPs and Open Ports

Now that we know the IP address range we would scan the range to find visible IP addresses and open ports. This can be done with tools like nmap, see Figure 3.4.

While port scanner tools are of value, an attacker ultimately wants to be able to find vulnerabilities in a service. In these cases, vulnerability scanners can be used to not only find visible IPs and open ports, but it can provide the services to look for vulnerabilities. Tools like OpenVAS can be used to identify vulnerabilities or exposures, Figure 3.5.

While vulnerability scanners are of value, ultimately an attacker wants to break into the system. The next evolution of tools are exploitation tools. These tools, like

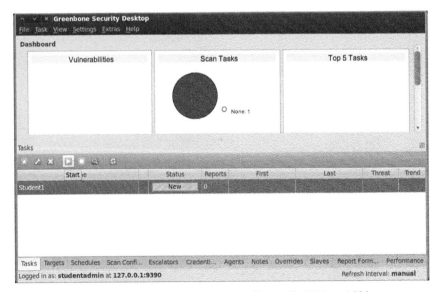

FIGURE 3.5 Tools Like OpenVAS Can be Used to Identify and Find Vulnerabilities

Core Impact, will actually find vulnerabilities in a system and if vulnerable exploit the service and give the person access to the system, see Figure 3.6.

By understanding how an attacker breaks into a system, can help an organization better improve its defenses. Remember one of our core rules, if the offense knows more than the defense we will lose. Therefore an organization needs to perform all of these steps so they can identify their exposure and increase their security. This is often done by creating a network visibility map, see Figure 3.7.

While we covered the specific details of how servers are compromised, one of the fundamental reasons why attacks are successful is because the adversary does their homework and organizations do not. What is scary is if you look at what an APT adversary did in order to perform an attack and compromise an organization, in many cases they have a lot more details than the organizations that is compromised has. If there is any single lesson that can be taken out of this chapter, it is to do your homework. At a minimum if

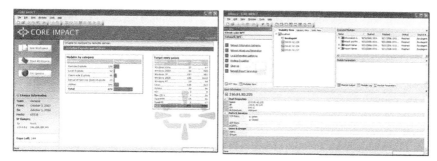

FIGURE 3.6 Exploitation Tools Like Core Impact Can Find and Compromise Vulnerable Services

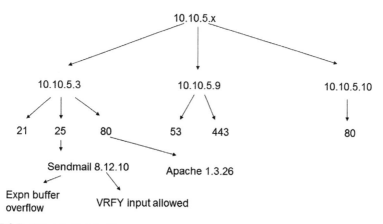

FIGURE 3.7 Network Visible Map

you pay anyone to do a penetration test, or if you perform the work yourselves, you need to have a network visible map created. An organization cannot protect what it does not know about it. Therefore, understanding visibility and exposure is critical.

Remember, what makes an attack very successful is when the attacker focuses in on step 1, 2, and 5. They perform detailed reconnaissance, in-depth scanning and work hard to be stealthy and cover their tracks. Most organizations when they defend against the attacker, focus their energy on mainly step 3, exploitation and looking for the attacker by finding backdoors that were created with step 4. When you look at it in this manner it is obvious where the disconnect is. The attacker is all about steps 1, 2, and 5 and the defender is all about steps 3 and 4. Can you figure out what you need to do in order to do a better job? Focus more energy on steps 1 and 2 to better understand where the vulnerabilities and exposures are in your organization. Now you will know what the attacker knows and have a better chance of winning. After you have better knowledge and you switch from having the offense know more than the defense to the defense knowing more than the offense, you now have to remember step 5. The APT is all about being stealthy, they do not want to get caught. Therefore an organization's security must be focused on looking for things that are not visible on the surface, trying to detect and find the unknown. One of the classic quotes to illustrate the current concern level is from Donald Rumsfeld where he states "There are known knowns…there are known unknowns…but there are also unknown unknowns…" What he is referring to is we know for a fact we are not catching all of the APTs that are out there. The scary question is what percent are we actually catching? The unknown unknowns is what concerns everyone because these are truly the stealthy attacks that no one even knows exist. The problem we are addressing is known as the iceberg problem, see Figure 3.8.

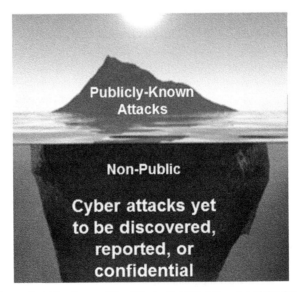

FIGURE 3.8 We are Catching Some of the Attacks But What Percent of the Attacks are Being Missed

The unknown is why proactive security will work and reactive security will fail when it comes to a stealthy attack. If there is a stealthy attack that we do not know about but there is nothing visible on the surface (the portion of the iceberg below the surface) unless we specifically hunt for the APT, an organization will be compromised for a long period of time.

COMPROMISING A CLIENT

Even with proper reconnaissance and scanning, compromising a server still requires skills. However, when a client is being targeted if you do proper reconnaissance and scanning, success is almost guaranteed. This is why targeting a client is becoming the method of choice for the APT. The reason is simple—no matter how hard you try or no matter what you do, you cannot stop stupid. People will click on links or open an attachment that they shouldn't. A great example is during tax season in the United States many people get stressed out. A common attack technique is to send an email similar to Figure 3.9.

While this approach is very simple, many people have fallen victim to it. The problem is the IRS will never communicate with a tax payer via email. They understand the risks and in order to play it safe, they utilize other forms of communication. Many tax payers do not realize that and therefore a simple email will easily trick a user into getting their system compromised. Once an attacker can compromise a trusted system on the network, it makes it easy and simple for them to navigate internally, compromising information and extracting it out of the organization.

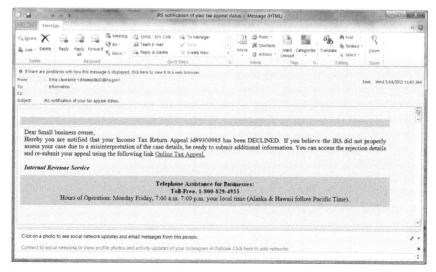

FIGURE 3.9 Spoofed e-mail Looking Like a Legitimate Tax Return Issue From the IRS

Compromising the client, while very low tech, is very effective in the results because you are playing the odds and with proper research, the odds are very high in favor of the attacker.

INSIDER THREAT

"I trust everyone, it is the devil inside that I do not trust," is a great line from the movie the Italian Job. Everyone has the potential do to harm, including your employees. If you look at the minimal background checks that most companies perform off their employees, why should you trust them? Why is it that once a total stranger is hired at your company, you now have complete trust in that person. Just because they are now called an employee does not mean they now have loyalty to your organization and would do nothing to hurt the company. We do not want to be so paranoid that your company cannot function, but a healthy dose of paranoia is good. Always remember that paranoia is your friend!

When most people think of the insider threat, they think of deliberate evil insiders like Aldrich Ames, Robert Hanssen. What is interesting and scary is that most spies have one thing in common, they passed the polygraph (lie detector test) with almost a perfect score. How could a machine that tests whether people are lying not catch the biggest liars that cost so many people their lives. The reason is a polygraph does not detect lies, it detects guilt. In these cases, either the people felt justified with their actions and did not feel guilty about them or they were trained to be able to bypass and deceive people. Therefore, only by closely watching people over time will you start to understand that there are certain people who cannot be trusted.

Insider threat and corporate espionage rely on the fact that it is sometimes better to live in denial and be happy than to know the truth and have to deal with it. Most organizations of any significant size have either been or will be compromised by the APT in the near future, yet many organizations prefer to ignore the threat. As one executive pointed out to the author, if I know about a problem I need to deal with it. In some situations in life, what you do not know cannot hurt you. With the APT, what you do not know can put you out of business. While most executives might not be as bold to admit it, it is easier to ignore a problem that you cannot see. It is easier to trust your employees and keep life simple, than have to suspect everyone and deal with the complexities it creates. However if it will put your company out of business, cost hundreds of million dollars worth of loss or cause people to die, you might think differently about the answer.

Nobody wants to believe the truth but corporate espionage via the insider threat is causing huge problems, but many organizations either do not have the proper monitoring to detect that it is happening or do not want to admit that it is happening to them.

Organizations tend to think once they hire an employee or a contractor that they are now part of a trusted group of people. While an organization might give an employee additional access that an ordinary person would not have, why should they trust that person? Some organizations perform no background checks and no reference checks and as long as the hiring manager likes the individual, they will hire them. Many people might not be who you think they are and not properly validating them can be a fatal mistake. Since many organizations, in essence hire complete strangers who are really unknown entities and give them access to sensitive data, raises the profile of why the insider is of such importance.

If a competitor or similar entity wanted to cause damage to your organization, steal critical secrets or put you out of business, they just have to find a job opening, prepare someone to ace the interview, have that person get hired and they are in. That fact that it is that easy should scare you if not terrify you. Many organizations have jobs open for several weeks and it could take a couple of weeks to setup an interview. You mean to tell me that if I was focused on your company that I could not within a 4-week period, prepare someone I know to ace an interview. This is what foreign governments do when they plant a spy against another government. They know that a key criterion for that person is passing the polygraph. Therefore they will put that person through intensive training so that they can pass the polygraph with no problem.

In terms of the importance, I often hear people say that it is only hype and that it cannot happen to us. This is synonymous with people thinking that bad things only happen to others, they never happen to you; until they happen to you and then you have a different view of the world. I remember several years ago when my father got diagnosed with having a cancerous brain tumor. It shocked, devastated me, and changed my views forever. Prior to that I knew that people had brain cancer but it was something that I could not relate to or understand because I never thought it could really happen to myself or someone I love. Bad things happened to others not to myself. This is the denial that many of us live in, but the unfortunate part is bad things do happen and they could be occurring right now and you just do not know about it.

Insider threat is occurring all of the time, but since it is happening within a company it is a private attack. Public attacks like defacing a Web site are hard for a company to deny. Private attacks are much easier to conceal.

Since these attacks are being caused by trusted insiders, we need to understand the damage they can cause so we can build proper measures to prevent the attack, minimize the damage and at a minimum, detect the attacks in a timely manner. Many of the measures organizations deploy today are ineffective against the insider. When companies talk about security and securing their enterprise they are so concerned with the external attack, forgetting about the damage that an insider can perform. Many people debate about what percent of attacks come from insiders and what percent of attacks come from outsiders. The short answer is who cares. The real answer is this:

- Can attacks come from external sources?
- Can an external attack cause damage to your company?
- Can an external attack put you out of business?

- Can attacks come from internal sources?
- Can an internal attack cause damage to your company?
- Can an internal attack put you out of business?

Since the answer to all of these question is YES, the exact percent is less important. Both have to be addressed and both have to be dealt with. I would argue that since the insider has access already, the amount of damage they can cause is much greater than an external attacker and the chances of getting caught are much less. If an attacker comes in from the outside they only have access to systems that are publicly accessible and they have to break through security devices. If an attacker comes from the inside, they have more access and less security devices to deal with. As our digital economy continues to grow and the stakes increase, anyone who wants serious access to an organization is not even going to waste their time with an external attack, they are going to go right for the trusted insider.

An organization will never ever be able to completely remove the insider threat because companies need to be able to function. If you fire all of your employees, you might have prevented the insider attack but you will also go out of business. The key is to strike a balance between what access people need and what access people have.

While insider threat has been and will always be a concern it is important to understand it in the context of the APT. The deliberate malicious insider has always been a common method of espionage both in government and corporate organizations. While it is still a viable method, it is not necessary in most cases today. Finding someone within the organization, convincing them to deliberately steal information and cause harm to the organization takes time, energy, and effort. An individual needs to be targeted, convinced, and usually paid, so it is also more expensive. Plus, there is only a small subset of people who would be willing to do this and if you approach the wrong person, they might notify the organization of who is targeting them and will allow the organization to build better defensive measures. The deliberate insider works but it requires significant amount of resources and is a higher risk.

Remember one of the goals of an advanced adversary is to utilize the minimal amount of energy and effort for an effective attack to work. For the current APT, the easier and preferred method is to target and utilize an insider in such a way that they do not even realize they are being targeted. This is what we call the accidental insider. This is someone who honestly believes they are acting in the best interest of the organization and has no idea that their actions are causing harm and allowing an adversary to compromise and steal significant information. In many cases this is good old fashion social engineering, think of it as I love you or Melissa on steroids. In addition, today's attacks have plenty of resources to make the chance of compromise, almost guaranteed. What is scary about the accidental insider is not only is it easier but from an attacker's perspective the insider that is helping them does not even realize it, plus it is free because you do not have to pay them like you would with the deliberate insider.

While today's APT utilizes the accidental insider, hopefully with enough aware-ness and controls put in place this will be harder and harder for the attacker to use for a successful attack. In the future when this approach works with a lower frequency, it is predicted that we will see the deliberate insider become a common avenue with APTv2. Remember, the attacker will never waiver or stop trying to break in so once today's methods stop working, they will have to adapt and the deliberate insider is on possible natural evolution.

TRADITIONAL SECURITY

As we finish up the chapter on how organizations are compromised by the APT, we often hear organizations say that they are protected because they have invested mil-lions of dollars in security. While traditional security devices are useful and things would be a lot worse if they were not in place, they are not enough to stop the APT. We did a study to investigate what organizations that were compromised with the APT had in common. When asked this question many people think of unpatched sys-tems, but that is only a percent. What all organizations that have been compromised with the APT have in common are:

- Security policies.
- Security personnel.
- Security budgets.
- Firewalls.
- Intrusion detection systems.
- Encryption.
- End point protection.

Organizations have all of these key elements in place and they are still compro-mised. What is scary is if we asked you to create a list of what an organization needs to do to be secure, the list would be fairly close to what is listed above. While we have to remember that traditional security is not enough, we also have to remember that we still need this foundation. If these core items were not in place, things would be a lot worse. In addition, in many cases the products/solutions were not configured and installed correctly. The best technology in the world will not do its job correctly if it is not installed, configured, and maintained correctly. To ensure that security is properly implemented, we will examine prevention and detection technologies and how to configure them for success against the APT.

FIREWALLS

Firewalls play a critical role in an organizations security and are often one of the first devices that an organization purchases. The problem with firewalls is even today organizations make two fundamental mistakes. First, executives believe they are the silver bullet and having a firewall will prevent and stop all attacks. While executives do not need an in-depth understanding of firewall technology, they need to have a high level understanding of what works and what does not. Having your executives believe that your organization is at a different level of security then where you are really at is very dangerous. This is why creating metrics that can be used to make sure everyone is on the same page is critical.

The second mistake that is made is technology personnel believe that if you have a firewall in place you do not need to fix the root cause problems. In performing a recent assessment, the organization had systems on their DMZ that were not patched with extraneous services open. When we talked with the IT team their response was that it was OK because the firewall is blocking those ports so there is not a need to fix the problem. This is very dangerous because while a firewall can block traffic, it is treating the symptom which is pain killer security. Blocking traffic with a firewall is important, but just as important is to make sure that any system is properly hardened and configured to minimize the chance of an attack.

From a technology standpoint a firewall is a router with a filtering ruleset. It is an inline device that connects multiple networks together with the ability to block and stop traffic. The blocking and allowing of traffic is dictated by a ruleset that tells the firewall what to do. It is important to remember that a firewall is a binary device. It either allows or denies traffic. This is very powerful because it has the ability to prevent and stop attacks from occurring but this also means that there are limitations. Since a firewall is a preventive device it can only block attacks that are 100% bad. If something is always bad the firewall can block and prevent the attack. The problem is today more and more traffic, especially with the APT is meant to blend in and look like legitimate traffic and is only bad 60% or 70% of the time. The problem with this traffic is the firewall has to allow it through. Traffic that is bad 60% of the time means it is good 40% of the time. If a firewall blocks traffic that is not 100% bad and it is only attack traffic 60% of the time, it would be blocking 40% of an organization's business and customers which would be unacceptable. Therefore this traffic has to be allowed through. By nature of how a firewall works, it will not be able to block all attack traffic, some will be allowed in.

Just having a device called a firewall will not make an organization secure. There are two critical rules that must always be followed:

1. *It must be designed correctly*—the golden rule of firewalls is all connections must go through the firewall. Not some connections, not most connections but all connections must go through the firewall. A firewall cannot protect what it does not see. While many organizations claim they are following this rule, when we analyze their networks we find that they have wireless connections, modems, and extranet connections that bypass the firewall. With mobilization, consumerization of IT continuing and cloud services, networks are becoming more porous and data is more portable which make this rule more difficult to enforce. However with proper planning an organization can utilize technology

and still be secure. An organization might have to install multiple firewalls, but as long as all of the traffic goes through some firewalls, they can achieve a high level of security.

2. *It must be configured correctly*—The best firewall design is not going to help if the firewall is not configured correctly with a properly designed ruleset. The ruleset is ultimately what tells the firewall what should be allowed and what should be dropped. Since we are not able to identify all of the evil that is occurring on the Internet and drop all of those packets, it is recommended to use a default deny approach to building a robust ruleset. The premise is based on specifying what traffic is allowed and dropping all other packets. The other problem with how organizations configure a firewall is they usually do not develop a firewall policy ahead of time. The way the firewall is configured is a smart person sits in front of the firewall and creates a ruleset on what they believe to be allowed and if everything works, they declare victory. If you do not create a security policy/requirements document that specifies what exactly is allowed in and out of an organization, how do you know if the firewall is configured correctly. The problem with most firewall testing is they only test the positive—are the things that are supposed to work working. After a firewall is configured an organization would test email, Web, and other services and if everything works they assume it is configured correctly. The problem is additional traffic could also be allowed that represents a risk or compromise. Therefore in addition to testing the positive, it is also critical to test the negative—are the things that are not supposed to work, not working. The million dollar question is how confident are you that all attack traffic or anything that is not legitimate and part of your business is being blocked. You need to be able to answer that question to confirm that the firewall is working correctly.

DROPPED PACKETS

The last key piece of validating the effectiveness of a firewall is to look at the number of dropped packets. Ultimately the point and reason for having a firewall is for it to block and stop traffic that should not be allowed. Based on that assessment, can you answer a simple question: "How many dropped packets does your firewall have every day and if there is an anomaly, would you be able to detect it?" One of the most effective ways of tracking and validating the effectiveness of a firewall is by looking at the number of dropped packets. We had one client that was so proud of their firewall because they had 237 rules in their firewall. The problem was when we examined the number of dropped packets, they had 0. This meant that their 237 rules where equivalent to ANY ANY ANY ANY—ALLOW. Their firewall was a very expensive pass through device. Only by checking the number of dropped packets, can an organization better understand how effective their firewall is. Ultimately the success of the firewall is based on how many packets it drops. Therefore by tracking the number to make sure it is aligned with the type of business you are in and look for changes is a key piece in measuring the effectiveness. Every organization is differ-ent but on average you should have several thousand dropped packets a day or more. Some organizations might have several thousand every hour, but if your organization only has a hundred dropped packets a day either you are plugged into a safe part on the Internet (not likely) or your firewall ruleset is not configured correctly. It is also critical to check the number of dropped packets after a change is made to the ruleset to make sure you understand the impact that rule had on your security.

For example, we were performing an assessment for a client and part of the evalu-ation was examining their firewall ruleset and a key component is looking at the number of dropped packets. The assessment was being performing in November and by looking at the dropped packets we noticed that there was a significant change back in July, see Figure 3.10.

We went to the firewall administrator and asked what changes they made to the firewall in July since some change to the ruleset had to account for 30% less packets being dropped. The admin said he would research it and get back to us. He came back a day later and said how did you know that I changed the firewall ruleset back in July. I said if you tell me what you did I will tell you how we knew. He said that a new business application was being deployed and he had to make a minor change to the firewall to allow that traffic through. I said I do not think the change did what you thought it did. I told him the reason we knew he had made a change is because whatever he did allowed a significant amount of more traffic through the firewall. When we showed him the change in dropped packets that was associated with his change, his eyes got really big and he said I think I made a mistake. After carefully examination of the change, the rules were incorrect. After fixing the change and con-firming that the ruleset was correct, the number of dropped packets increased back to

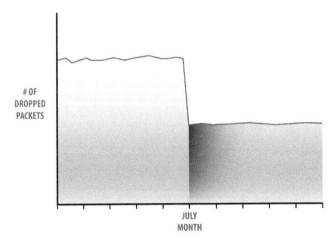

FIGURE 3.10 Number of Dropped Packets From a Client Assessment

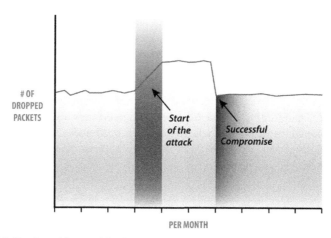

OF
DROPPED
PACKETS

Start of the attack

Successful Compromise

PER MONTH

FIGURE 3.11 **Number of Dropped Packets Showing Indicators of a Potential Compromise**

where they were prior to the July change. By showing him the chart made a believer out of him to always check the number of dropped packets and hopefully it will make a believer out of you.

In addition, most attacks are not successful on the first try. The P in APT comes from the fact that the attacker will keep trying until they get in. This means that normally at the beginning of an attack, the number of dropped packets increase and once an attacker compromises the organization they drop back down, see Figure 3.11.

By carefully tracking and watching the number of dropped packets you can identify not only when an attack starts but also when the attacker is successful.

While firewalls do play a key role in protecting an organization, an adversary can figure out what traffic is allowed into an organization. By crafting their attacks to look like legitimate traffic, they can slip through a firewall. This is one of the problems with the APT. One of the common methods of attacks is sending a well-crafted email, targeting at a specific individual. Since email is allowed into an organization and the email is crafted to look legitimate, in many cases it can slip through even a well-configured firewall.

INBOUND PREVENTION AND OUTBOUND DETECTION

To illustrate one of our key rules of defending against the APT, prevention is ideal but detection is a must, let's look at how this can be done with a firewall. Most people when they build and configure a firewall they focus on inbound prevention. The reason is that is where most attacks originate and can be effective at blocking malicious traffic. Building off of our discussion on dropped packets, let's look at a simple question: Is the Internet filled with evilness? The answer is simple, absolutely.

There is a lot of attack traffic on the Internet and therefore we should have a large number of dropped packets coming into our organization.

Now let's look at outbound traffic or packets leaving your trusted network going to an untrusted network. Asking a similar question: Should your internal network be filled with evilness? The answer is no, remember we asked the question with the word should. While your internal network might be compromised, it should not be compromised. Therefore, if you have a well configured firewall that is tracking and blocking outbound traffic, should you have any dropped packets—the answer is no. If you have a dropped packet and there has been no authorized change and nothing stopped working, you just detected an anomaly which could be indicative of an attacker.

If you have a very tight outbound filtering ruleset, there should be no dropped packets. If there are dropped packets it either means that legitimate traffic is being blocked or a system just got compromised and trying to make an unauthorized connection. Now by performing outbound filtering with a strict change control process organizations can more quickly and easily detect the APT.

We had one client that was getting compromised with the APT and in some cases it took several months for them to detect the compromised systems. After careful examination of their network, we determined that there were only a limited number of sites in which users could send encrypted traffic to. We created a very tight outbound filtering ruleset, filtered out the noise and once it was tuned there were no outbound packets being dropped (which is what you want). Now when a user opened an attachment and gets infected with the APT and it tries to make an encrypted outbound connection, they were able to catch the system and the attacker within minutes. Just by understanding the technology and configuring it correctly, they were able to move from a position of weakness (being compromised for 6 months) to a position of strength (being compromised for minutes).

Now there are other technologies that you can use like DLP (data loss prevention) to perform similar analysis but we wanted to show you that by understanding the attacker and understanding the technology, you can deploy creative solutions that are not expensive.

INTRUSION DETECTION

One of the key rules of security is prevention is ideal but detection is a must. While firewalls are very effective at preventing attacks, they can only block things that are 100% bad. An IDS (intrusion detection system) is a passive device or in the case of a NIDS (network IDS), it is a sniffer with an alerting component. When a NIDS sees unusual or strange traffic it can set off an alert. Since it is not inline it can be more aggressive and have a higher rate of false positives. To make sure we are all on the same page, let's briefly review the four types of alerts that security devices can generate:

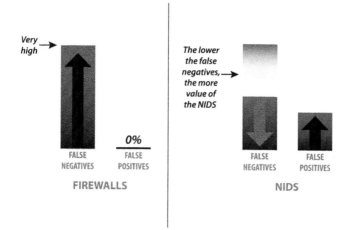

FIGURE 3.12 The Lower the False Negatives the More Value a NIDS Provides

- *True positives*—The NIDS generates an alert for attack traffic.
- *True negatives*—The NIDS does not generate an alert for normal traffic.
- *False positives*—The NIDS generates an alert for normal traffic.
- *False negatives*—The NIDS does not generate an alert for attack traffic.

What is important to remember is that false positives and false negatives are an inverse of each other. If you increase one you decrease the other.

A firewall cannot block legitimate traffic. It would be disruptive and not scale. Therefore a firewall has zero tolerance for false positives. If we make the false positives in a firewall zero, this means the false negatives are very high. The value of an NIDS is it has some tolerance for false positives because it is not an inline preventive device, it is detective. Therefore we can now push down the false negatives, increasing the false positives. The lower the false negatives can be pushed the more value the NIDS is adding over the firewall, see Figure 3.12.

Since a NIDS can detect and find items a firewall misses, together they provide a complimentary level of protection.

SUMMARY

Security is not easy. In this day and age organizations are going to be compromised and broken into. While we always prefer to prevent an attack before it occurs, we need to be able to detect attacks in a timely manner. Just like we are going to get sick, we have to accept that our organization will be compromised and the more proactive and detective we can be, the less impact it will have to our organization.

By understanding how attackers break into systems, an organization can build more effective and robust solutions that properly scale. While the main source of compromise today is the accidental insider, targeting someone within the organization to open an attachment or click on a link to infect a system. We have to remember that the attack vectors will always change. Educating your employees and contractors on the danger of social engineering and the fact that they are the target, will help protect against the accidental insider. Awareness is critical. While the dangers of social engineering are evident to people who work in the field many users do not recognize that they will be targeted and do not understand how to surf the Web in a safe manner. The more education and awareness that can be provided to your employees, the more effective they will be at dealing with the APT. While user awareness will never be 100% effective, because some users do not care, you can increase the effectiveness by making it personal. Instead of talking about what an employee needs to do to keep the organization safe, talk about what they need to do to be protected at home and at work. Show them the dangers of identity theft and how their children could be targeted. By making it personal people will listen and therefore you have a better chance of changing behavior.

However, we always have to look towards the future and be prepared for the next iteration of the APT or what we call APTv2. Our prediction is the attacks of the future will switch back to the deliberate insider. Therefore putting energy and effort against all insiders will go a long way in protecting the enterprise.

Risk-Based Approach to Security

4

INTRODUCTION

Security is a topic that organizations are concerned about. Most people do not even get surprised anymore when they hear about information being compromised and organizations being attacked. Security is a top priority for some individuals, many organizations, and most nations. However, while everyone likes to talk about security, very few organizations really know what it means to "be secure." It is easy to say you are secure but it is hard for people to quantify and validate that they are implementing the proper level of security. Most people focus on the devastating impact that the APT can have on an organization but do not spend enough time on how to defend against it.

Organizations not properly understanding or approaching security correctly have always been a problem, we just never noticed it based on the type of threats that we were dealing with. When organizations were dealing with typical script kiddies who were performing known attacks and using common tools, buying products helped and organizations could get away with not approaching security correctly because the threat vector was easier to deal with. Today, the approach of faking it until you can make it when it comes to security no longer works, because the threat has changed. When it comes to APT if you are faking it when it comes to security you will not make it, and you will get compromised by the adversary.

What is important is to understand that the fundamental principles of taking a risk-based approach to security is not new and has always been the recommended way to secure an enterprise; some organizations have done it, others have not. The critical shift is in the past it was recommended and today based on the APT it is required. We hear security evangelists state all of the time that if you do not focus on risks you will lose. Organizations ignored the advice for ten years but since there was minimal damage, they concluded that the advice was flawed. The advice was 100% correct, it was just a little ahead of its time. The good news is if you do security correctly today, it will last tomorrow. If you did not perform security correctly in the past, it does not matter how many band aids you put on the problem, it is not going to work in the future. While it may take work, if you determine that your security program is not aligned with risk, fix it now because it will not be easier in the future. Products do not make an organization secure, only solutions that are mapped to risk will protect against the advanced threat. Dealing with the APT mandates a risk-based focus with regard to security.

PRODUCTS VS. SOLUTIONS

After a breach in which an organization is compromised with the APT, the Number 1 response we receive back is tell me the amount of money we need to spend to fix the problem. Essentially what do we need to buy in order to be secure? While you absolutely need money in order to secure an organization, money alone will not make an organization secure. Organizations have gotten into bad habits because if you have no security products and you have a low-grade threat, products can help. For example, if you get hit with a virus and install anti-virus software on your system it will help protect your organization. Since that was many organizations, entry point into security, they are still comfortable with that approach today. While that was never a viable approach, organizations had the perception that it worked.

Today we have to switch from looking at buying products to implementing solutions. A product solves a problem but a solution implemented correctly reduces risk. Now products are absolutely a key part of implementing an effective solution but it needs to be wrapped with configuration, monitoring, and validation to make sure that the risk that it was meant to address is being lowered to the appropriate level. For example, installing AV software on everyone's system is a product. Configuring it to look for the correct malware, updating it, and performing event correlation to understand the threats and react to any attempted attacks in a timely manner is a solution. Buying less products and spending more time on implementing better solutions that map against risk is a better approach to security.

LEARNING FROM THE PAST

Those that do not learn from the past are forced to repeat it. That phrase is true in the real world and it is true in cyber. A perfect example is looking back at worms in the 1980s and 1990s. First, it is important to remember that the world was a different time and a different place 20 years ago. The World Wide Web was not invented, e-commerce was not a viable business, most people did not have computers in their home and if they did it was a slow dial-up modem, and very few people had laptops. The general acceptance of technology was much less and therefore security was not a priority.

In examining any worm, the important question is what was the reason the malware was able to spread so quickly and cause so much damage? The answer is because everyone was running default installations with extraneous scripts, systems were not patched, robust configuration management was not in place, and people did not know what was on their network. Many organizations that were compromised were surprised because they did not realize the services that were exploited were running and that they were vulnerable.

Now fast forward until today and pick any of your favorite worms or attacks that caused devastating impact. What was the reason so many sites were compromised with the worms? The answer is the same. Organizations are running default installations with extraneous scripts, systems are not patched, robust configuration management is not in place, and people do not know what is on their network. In addition, many organizations do not realize they are exposed. The fundamental problem is if the offense knows more than the defense, you will lose. Even more fundamental, if the defense does not know what is on their network, they will lose because they will not know what to protect. The solution for fixing the problem 20 years back is the same solution for fixing the problem today, organizations must harden their systems, remove extraneous scripts, and perform better asset management.

Many organizations do not understand what is connected to the network, what is running on the systems and how they are configured. Very often when we perform incident response and we de-brief the client, they are surprised with the list of vulnerabilities that are presented. For example with one client when we notified them that they had a prototype server that contained sensitive data with minimal authentication plugged into the network, their reaction was you must have made a mistake, that was removed 4 months ago. One of the sayings we always jokingly use is tools do not lie, people do. They are not intentionally lying but they actually thought the server was removed, but they never validated and checked it. Unfortunately if you do not check and understand your network, there are many adversaries including the Chinese that would be happy to check for you.

The short answer is organizations are not properly assessing, understanding, and prioritizing their risk. Not to jump too far ahead but if we look at the APT closely, one of the biggest risks is targeted emails sent to a user in the organization and compromising the system so that it can be used as a pivot point for other attacks. What are the risks? (1) macros; (2) HTML embedded content; and (3) email clients with direct access to the host operating system. If organizations just disabled macros, turned off HTML embedded email, and ran their email client in a virtual machine, there will be minimal impact to the user and it would be much harder for the attacker. This will not solve all problems, but this is a simple example that if organizations focused more on risk, security would be more scalable and achievable. All three of the examples reduce the risk to a lower level, increasing the overall security posture of the organization.

WHAT IS RISK?

We have been talking about risk in the context of security, but what exactly does it mean? Risk is the probability for loss. Risk is essentially asking questions like:

- *What could happen?*—The question is focusing in on the threats or things that could cause harm to an organization. What is important to remember is to focus on realistic things that could occur to an organization. It is also important to focus on the damage component or impact of the attack. When answering the question, stating APT as what could happen is not a good answer. Stating that a competitor in a foreign country could steal all of your critical information is a better answer.

- *How bad would it be if it happened?*—The question is focusing in on the damage that could occur. This is tying in what the impact of an attack would be to an organization. For example, what would be the reputation or monetary loss to an organization if a given threat occurred? Many organizations are using this as the primary driver of which threats to focus in on. They recognize that attacks are going to occur but will focus in on the ones that could cause the most damage to the organization.
- *How often could it happen?*—Frequency is also an important question to ask because this adds a multiplier effect to the threat. If the damage a threat would cause is $20k, that might not seem like a big problem. If it occurs 1000 times that is a much bigger concern. When we talk about calculating risk for an organization one of the key components is the ARO or annualized rate of occurrence, which ties directly to the frequency of the attack.

Risk is all about determining what are the potential dangers that could successfully cause harm to an organization. For risks that are really bad, we would want to predict when they are going to occur and proactively fix them before they happen. Ideally we would want to proactively fix all risks but organizations do not have unlimited budgets or the ability to predict the future with perfect accuracy. Therefore in cases where we cannot mediate the risk, we need to put together a plan for detecting and reacting to the risk in a timely manner. Prevention is ideal but detection is a must.

The last question we need to ask with regard to risk is how much confidence do we have in our answers. We always have to remember that uncertainty is a critical component of risk. Once something becomes a guarantee it is no longer a risk decision.

FOCUSED SECURITY

Security has and will always be about understanding, managing, and mitigating the risk to organization's most critical assets. The problem is many organizations say this but very few people really do this. With your current organization see if you can answer the following questions:

1. *What is your organization's most critical information?*—We have to recognize that attacks are going to occur and prioritize our efforts against the information that would cause the greatest impact to an organization. The impact of the attack is tied directly to criticality of the information and how valuable it is to our organization. If you do not know what your critical information is, how can you protect it?
2. *What business processes support that critical information?*—Knowing what your critical information is, is a good start; however, you need to trace it across your organization to determine what business processes use and store that information. The ultimate question you are trying to answer is where does your critical information reside and map it down to a server level. Ultimately attackers break

into systems or computers, so if you do not know which specific systems contain the critical information you cannot protect it.

3. *What are the areas that you are most concerned about?*—As we will see throughout this chapter to effectively deal with the APT, you must map everything you do against risk and threat drives the risk equation. While understanding what threats an organization is most concerned about is important, the threats need to be grounded in truth. For example, there are some people that will not fly because they are concerned with safety but will get in a car multiple times a day. While they might have personal reasons for that decision, if it is truly based on data, flying is much safer than driving in a car. The point we are making is make sure that when you map out your threats that the data that is driving the decision is accurate. Often we hear executives say they are concerned about *x* and want to spend money on reducing the risk, but it is not a real risk, founded on factual data.

4. *What are the vectors that could cause the most harm?*—Once you understand the threats, what are the ways that an attack can manifest themselves against your organization? What are the vectors that an attacker would use to cause harm and/or compromise an organization?

5. *Do you have exposures that would allow these threats to happen?*—Ultimately in security, you control your own destiny. While attackers will try to break in, they will not be able to compromise an organization, if you created a vulnerability that allows them to be successful. Vulnerabilities or weaknesses in your organization are what allow an attack to work. Knowledge is critical in dealing with the APT. You need to understand your exposure in order to be able to defend against it. It is also important to remember that when you focus on vectors to make sure that you identify and fix the right vulnerabilities, not just the ones that are easy to remediate.

6. Is *your organization's security sufficient to deal with these threats?*—This question forces an organization to do their homework. If you do not understand your critical data and key business processes, you cannot make an accurate assessment of how well you are dealing with the threats. A key component is determining what an organization's risk posture or risk appetite is. What is an acceptable risk for one organization might not be acceptable for another organization. Unless you have criteria and metrics it is hard to make a determination of the effectiveness of an organizations security.

If you are able to answer these questions go and ask five different people in your organization including the stakeholders the same questions. Are all of the answers the same? In most cases not only will it be hard to answer all of these questions but if you received answers from different people none of them are the same.

What is scary is if you ask the adversary who is targeting your organization these questions, you will probably get more complete and accurate answers. One of the many dangers and differentiators of the APT is that they do their homework and in many cases understand a target's environment better than the victim. One of our golden rules continues to be true, if the offense knows more than the defense you will lose.

A key part of risk is making sure that everyone is on the same page and there are unified marching orders across your organization. You cannot protect against the APT if you do not understand what you are up against. There are five critical pieces of information that are needed to ensure that everyone is on the same page:

- *Critical assets/key business processes*—Every organization, whether you are in government, business, not profit, or educational, there is some information that gives an entity a unique differentiator and if it was compromised would impact the ability of the organization to meet their operational goals. What is interesting is regardless of the business an organization is in, a major concern for most organizations is reputational damage. It is important to identify the information that if it was compromised or exposed would cause significant reputational damage to the organization. Critical assets can also be an abstract term, so it is important to identify the specific information, what server or servers does it actually reside on, what applications utilize it, and what are the critical business processes that are needed in order for the organization to properly function.
- *Threats based on likelihood*—it is hard to fight an enemy that you do not know. Therefore, it is critical to determine what are the specific threats that could impact an organization. The key focus is to make sure that they are prioritized based on likelihood. While there are numerous threats, it is important to focus on the ones that really matter and that could cause real harm to your organization.
- *Vulnerabilities based on impact*—it is critical to understand the potential for harm and what an enemy can do; however that is only of value if we understand which of those attacks will be successful based on weaknesses in an organization's infrastructure. It is important to always understand where your exposures are and which weaknesses are going to lead to a successful compromise.
- *Overall risks*—performing analysis is important but risk is where we put it all together to focus on which APT vectors will have the greatest chance of success based on an organization's overall exposure. When we define the actual formula, risk $=$ threat $\times$ vulnerability.
- *Focused Countermeasures*—understanding risk is important but the main reason for calculating risk is so a decision can be made about it. A list of methods for reducing the risk need's to be determined. The important piece in selecting a countermeasure is to figure out what is the acceptable level of risk. Normally we are not going to eliminate a risk because that is too expensive but ultimately it depends on the value of what is being protected. Instead we are going to reduce the risk to an acceptable level based on the critical information we are protecting. With APT it becomes an interesting decision because for many organizations you have to accept the fact that you will be compromised. The question is not how we stop from being compromised, but what is the acceptable level of damage? Finally, we have to remember that organizations do not have unlimited budgets and therefore it is important to always make

sure the countermeasures that are selected provide an appropriate return on investment.

One thing we recommend for all of our clients is to produce, get buy-in, and finalize a single focus sheet for your organization, similar to Figure 4.1.

Assets	Threats	Vulnerabilities
Countermeasures		

FIGURE 4.1 Sample Security Focus Sheet

By putting down on paper and putting it up in everyone's office not only drives awareness but also keeps everyone focused on the prize. An organization cannot win if everyone is using a different play book. An organization must also have a way to measure the effectiveness of their plan through common metrics. This is the only way to protect and keep pace with the APT.

FORMAL RISK MODEL

Every decision, every purchase, and everything performed in security should be mapped back to risk and be justified by risk. Actually the correct way of generating a yearly roadmap and budget should be based on performing proper risk calculations and mapping those back to solutions. Unfortunately many organizations ignore risk when determining budgets and purchase random products. They try to map it back to risk after the fact, but that does not work.

A simple, easy test to see how aligned your security program is with risk is to perform the following test of your current security roadmap. For each item on the security roadmap, ask the following questions:

1. What is the risk?
2. Is it the highest priority risk?
3. Is it the most cost-effective way of reducing the risk?

If your roadmap was created based off of risk, this exercise will be easy and you will pass with flying colors. If you cannot answer these questions or if you are struggling, you should regroup and build your security roadmap from a risk perspective, using Figure 4.1 as a guide.

We keep talking about risk but let's break it down into its fundamental areas. At its most basic level risk is defined as:

$$risk = threat \times vulnerabilities.$$

Risk is looking at what could potentially happen and how bad could it be if it happened. With security on the front of everyone's mind and attacks increasing and occurring on a regular basis, the common question is what do we need to do to protect our organization? This is often translated into what needs to be purchased and how much money needs to be spent. Firewalls, IDS, IPS, DLP, and other security devices can absolutely help protect your organization but they will only provide long-term protection if they are actually fixing a risk. The reason comes down to how the devices are configured and deployed. Security devices only work if they are designed and configured correctly. Design focuses in on where the device is deployed and configuration focuses in on what the device is looking for and how it works. Since every organization is different, you must always step back, identify risk, figure out the most cost-effective way of reducing the risk, and focus in on deploying the device in a risk reduction manner.

We often hear organizations talk about how they must defend against the APT, but do not know where to start. Some organizations focus in on buying products to defend against the APT and because writing a check seems like an easy solution, this is the approach that is taken. For a short period of time, the executives sleep well at night because they feel that they are properly defending and protecting their organization. It could be a week, a month, or a few months but if an organization's approach to the APT was solely to purchase a product and not implement a solution, they eventually will be broken into and compromised. The problem is that while purchasing a product probably increased an organization's overall security, the real question is whether it defended against the risk that you are most concerned about.

The reason we emphasize and spend an entire chapter on risk is having risk determine what needs to be done in security always works. More importantly it is one of the few things that *does* work against the APT. We have some clients that happen to get lucky and just by spending money on security, they happened to address the right risk and defend their enterprise. The problem is it does not always work. The method that will always work is focusing in on fixing high likelihood and high impact risks as the focus of a security program. We have studied many organizations who have been compromised and many organizations that were successfully winning and the main difference is organizations that loose do not focus in on risk and those that win map everything they do back to risk. Actually let's take it a step further. Organizations that are winning do not map everything they do back to risk. They actually start with risk, which drives all of their security decisions, which guarantees they have a recipe for success.

The main reason a risk-based approach works is it forces you to understand your environment so that there are no surprises. By simply buying a product, you still do not really know what is in your environment and where an organization's biggest exposures are. In order to calculate risk you need to understand asset management, configuration management, and control change which are the recipes for success when it comes to APT.

In continuing our discussion of risk, everything begins with threat.

Threat

Everything you do with security is driven based on what we are concerned about in terms of what could cause significant harm with a high likelihood of occurrence. Many people reading this book will obviously say the APT, the advanced persistent threat, is a major concern for organizations today. While that is a good starting point, in order to take action we need to drill down further in determining the specifics threats that will be used by the APT to compromise an organization. Most traditional attacks focus in on compromising a system that is visible from an external network (i.e. the Internet) and using that as an entry point into the organization. This means the systems on the DMZ are a common starting point, focusing in on the Web server, DNS, and mail server. Through the years we have seen a large number of buffer overflows, SQL injection, and other attacks successfully break in via this attack vector.

While it has been very effective there are two reasons on why this threat is not the common method of attack for the APT. First, many organizations have been focusing a lot of energy and effort on defending against this threat. While it is not perfect there are not as many entry points as there have been in the past. Second, attacking servers is not only becoming more difficult but it is not the easiest way of breaking in. The reason is DMZ servers typically do not have significant amounts of sensitive information on them and they are isolated from the private networks via firewalls. If there is an easier method why no one uses that instead. Third, attacking servers is not a guarantee of access because more and more networks are being segmented, where DMZ systems are segmented and isolated from the critical data which is what attackers are after. This means that even after a system is compromised and owned on a DMZ, there is still a lot of work to do and other systems to break into in order to get access to the information the attacker is after.

Today the threat that has the highest chance of success is going after the end user. Not only is the end user an easier target but there are a lot more of them for an adversary to go after. Strictly from an odds perspective there are more potential targets to go after and they give direct access to the corporate network, where the critical information is. Unfortunately many organizations today have flat private networks, which means once an attacker gets access to an internal system it is relatively straightforward for them to find and access the information they are after.

The question that often gets asked is how to measure the sophistication of the threat. The reason this question is asked is because with the increased numbers of compromises and the relative ease in which attackers can break into systems, the logical conclusion is that threat has increased in sophistication. The problem is you cannot examine sophistication of the threat in a vacuum. The sophistication only matters when you tie in the sophistication of the vulnerabilities. If the defensive measures of an organization increased, then the sophistication of the offense would also have to increase to keep pace. The problem is the threat has changed and is now targeting a vulnerability that has decreased in sophistication, the end user. The reason this is the case is based on the increased functionality demands of the user. Data is much more portable, exists in many locations and personal devices being connected to corporate networks are much more common. While sophistication is a good starting point, a better measure of the current threat is to look at effectiveness. The APT has one primary goal, access to critical information that is being targeted and the adversary wants to accomplish this goal with the least amount of energy and effort required. The threat has absolutely changed in the last few years. It has gone from being visible and mass targeted to stealthy, targeted, and data focused. One could argue that the sophistication of the threat has actually decreased. Crafting an attachment to an email that looks legitimate, compromising a system, and creating a foothold on a network is less technical in some aspects than utilizing a buffer overflow to compromise a system. Bottom line is regardless of sophistication, the threat is completely different with the APT than with traditional attacks. However, you have to look beyond the specific threat. While one could argue that the specific way initially into a system has decreased in sophistication, once they get into a network the sophistication has increased. Traditional worms might have used a sophisticated payload to launch an overflow or injection attack, but the general sophistication of the attacker was low. They were just trying a large range of IP addresses to see which systems were vulnerable. The goal of these attackers was all about quantity. Breaking into as many systems as possible, hoping there was some valuable information.

Today the attacker not the attack is much more sophisticated, and is where the advance in the APT actually comes from. This is the part of the threat that is very scary. I would prefer a low sophisticated attacker with a highly sophisticated attack because the chance of success is still not guaranteed. However, when you take a very sophisticated attacker, that has sophisticated attacks, but they do not need to use them because the low sophisticated attacks work extremely well and are very easy, that is why we should be worried about the threat today. The real concern today from an APT perspective is we have not reached maximum velocity. The low end methods are still working as initial entry point into a network. What is scary is what happens when we defend against the current attacks and they start using the nuclear grade weapons. Bottom line is we need to get in front of the curve before it is too late. The bottom line is having a highly sophisticated attacker with a range of attacks they can use means the effectiveness of the attack is almost guaranteed. The other piece of the APT that is interesting is the sophistication of the threat used to gain control of the network and the sophisticated of the attack once they get in the network. While the initial entry point into an organization is fairly low sophisticated but highly effective, once they get in the sophistication increases tremendously. Once a system is compromised and a beachhead is established, the attacker normally automates their exploit and it can attack very fast with high accuracy, target the information they are after, exfiltrate the information, and slip under the radar so it is not detected by traditional cyber security products. Once again this illustrates that the adversary has the capability for going as advanced as needed but will use the simplest and easiest way to get into the system and accomplish their goal.

If that is not bad enough, if we take the advanced nature of the attacker and add in another fatal ingredient, persistence, life becomes very different for the defender. In the past if a new worm was released and you defended against it or patched your system, you were protected for a while. Today the attacker will not stop. Some argue that blocking an attack is merely just a diversion, since the attacker will keeping trying until they break in. That is why one of the techniques we talk about later in the book is honeypot jails instead of traditional blocking and tackling. The problem with a traditional firewall is an attacker knows when they are successful or not. Therefore if an attacker tries to get in and is blocked, they will keep trying for hours, days, or weeks until they are successful. A firewall still has its place in our security arsenal but if it is not properly managed and watched, it is just postponing an attack, not actually stopping it. Therefore one of many techniques we can use to deal with the APT, is instead of blocking an attacker when we detect malicious activity, we allow them into a jailed honeypot environment. It looks and acts like the real system so the attacker thinks they were successful, but it contains and controls the attacker and limits the amount of damage they can do. Now the attacker thinks they got into the system and could move on to another target as opposed to being blocked and keep trying until they are successful.

External vs. Internal Threat

If we look at threats from a most basic level, threats can really be broken down into two general categories external and internal. External threats come from outside of the organization, usually via the Internet and are typical worms and viruses. Internal threats come from within the walls of your organization and are often an employee stealing information. One of the debates that people often have when it comes to threats is what percent comes from external and what percent comes from internal. Many people state that the external threat is higher than the internal threat. The problem today is differentiating between the source and the target of the threat. For example, if an employee at a company is careless and posts information to social media sites and gives out information they should not be giving away and a foreign entity targets that person. They use open source information provided by the employee to build a profile and target the user. The user is sent a well-crafted email that looks legitimate so they open the attachment; it infects their system, compromises their network, and steals sensitive information. Was that an external or an internal threat? From an initial source perspective it was absolutely an external threat since it was an entity outside of the organization that compromised and stole information. That is the reason why many people think the percent for external threats is often higher. However, if we dig deeper it is important to point out that the external theft would not have been success-ful if it was not for the help of the insider threat. The insider clearly contributed to the external attack being successful. Many people when they hear insider threat, they think malicious insiders that deliberately will harm and steal from an organization. Incidents like wiki leaks come to mind. While that is and will always be a concern, the bigger concern today is the accidental insider. The person who is not deliberately trying to cause harm and in many cases does not even realize they are, but through their actions or carelessness, they represent a threat to the organization. The acciden-tal insider is a user who really things they are helping out a customer when they give away corporate secrets to an attacker. Or someone who holds the door open for who they believe to be a fellow employee, but it really is a competitor in disguise. The most common cases today are of course a legitimate employee who believes they received an email from a customer or their boss, they open the attachment or click on a link and compromise a system. With the accidental insider they do not even realize the harm they caused to their organization. Regardless of the percent whether it is 50/50 or 60/40 is both types of attacks can cause damage to an organization.

Bottom line is we need to be concerned about both threats and properly protect against them. In the past focusing in on one threat vector could provide benefit, today's APT usually utilizes both together. Therefore if you focus only on one you will lose.

Vulnerability

Vulnerabilities are weaknesses that allow an attacker to be successful. As we stated earlier, you control your own destiny. Vulnerability is the one part of the risk equation that you control. If there is no vulnerability, there is no compromise. Clearly that is overstating it because there will always be vulnerabilities. There is no such thing as a perfect, vulnerability free human and there is no such thing as a vulnerability free system or vulnerability free organization. What is scary is that every single system in your organization, no matter how secure you think it is, has vulnerabilities today that you do not know about. The reason we know that is the case is because there has never been a single operating system in production that has never had a patch. At a basic level a patch is the vendor telling everyone that there is a vulnerability in their system and the patch is the way to fix it. Even systems that have been out for years still have patches that are released on a regular basis. Therefore while it is easy to say that combatting the APT is as simple as removing all vulnerabilities, it is not practical because if you remove all vulnerabilities you also remove all functionality. We have to accept that our systems will always have vulnerabilities, the goal is knowledge is power, making sure you prioritize and remediate the exposures that have the highest impactful.

In talking about vulnerabilities it can sometimes get depressing because the job of the offense is easier than that of the defense. The offense only has to find out about one vulnerability to compromise your organization and the defense has to protect against all of them. Tying that to the fact that you will never ever fix every vulnerability means that you always have the chance of compromise. Unfortunately with APT you have to accept the fact that you will be attacked, you will be compromised, and most likely you might have compromised systems that you do not know about today. This continues to drive the point of prevention is ideal but detection is a must. It is OK if you get sick and miss a day of work. It is not OK to get sick, ignore it, and be put in ICU (intensive care unit) for 8 months. Early detection is critical to minimizing the impact of an attack. If a test server gets compromised that contains minimal information and it is completely isolated on a separate network, that is probable acceptable. If a critical database gets compromised and all of your data is stolen, it is absolutely not acceptable. All decisions made with regard to defending your network need to be based on prioritized focus mapped back to critical assets, high likelihood threat, and high impact vulnerabilities.

After reading the previous paragraph, many people might be depressed because it seems hopeless. Attackers only need to find one vulnerability and the defense needs to fix everyone; it almost seems like this is a losing battle. It is and it is not. Saying that the attacker only has to find one vulnerable is not completely correct. Very often for most attacks to be successful there have to be several vulnerabilities all present together for the attack to work. Even if one vulnerability is missing the attack will not work. To emphasize this, let's look at a recent attack in which an adversary was able to compromise an organization's Web server through a SQL injection attack and steal sensitive information that was stored on the server. In performing post-mortem analysis, what were the vulnerabilities that allowed this specific attack to work?:

1. Sensitive information was stored on a DMZ system, not the private network.
2. Extraneous services were running on the server.
3. Stored procedures were not being used to reduce the impact of an injection attack.

4. Proper filtering was not set up at the firewall to limit certain connections.

5. Proper patching was not performed on all services.

If you pick any number from 1 to 5 you will see something interesting. If anyone of those vulnerabilities was removed, the attack would not have been successful. Therefore an organization does not have to fix all of the vulnerabilities, they just have to fix the most critical ones. If the kingpin vulnerabilities are removed, regardless of whether other exposures are present the attack will still not work. In performing incident response, in most cases attacks are successful today because all of the following vulnerabilities are present:

1. Extraneous software/services are running on a system.

2. The software is not running at the proper permission level.

3. The software/service is not properly isolated.

4. Patches are not applied in a timely manner.

5. Sensitive data is not properly protected and controlled.

6. Proper isolation is not performed on the network.

7. High risk applications are not running in isolated environments.

While it would be ideal if an organization fixed all of these items, they should determine which one is most critical and focus on fixing the few high priority items. If they do that, even though the other vulnerabilities are still present, the attacker will have limited success.

Known and Unknown Vulnerabilities

Fixing known vulnerabilities is often the focus of most organizations. This involves applying all relevant patches to the systems across the network. We sometimes forget but a patch is the vendor's way of telling everyone that there is a vulnerability in the system and the patch is the way to fix it. While patching is a critical foundational component to security and must be done, it is moving from a primary form of security to a secondary measure. The reason is that the attack methods and vectors have changed. When worms were the primary method of compromise, they would go after known vulnerabilities. Traditional worms are often built after a patch was released and was betting on the fact that many organizations did not patch or took too long to patch. The APT often is more targeted and will identify a specific vulnerability or exploit in which a patch is not available. It is important to note that an advanced adversary will utilize the easiest and most effective way into an organization. Therefore, client side patching is very important and if the client is missing a patch, it will potentially be exploited by the adversary. In addition, with a worm it would try to get in via a few known methods and if they did not work, move on to the next system. Today's threat is persistent which means if the known methods do not work, the attacker will quickly turn to advanced methods and zero days to break in. Patching is a must but it cannot be viewed as a primary means of protection, other measures must be put in place.

The debate that people often have is that you can only protect what you know about and therefore can only protect against known threats. While on the surface there is some general logic to this thinking, with proper host hardening we believe that you can also protect against the unknown threats. Let's imagine that there is a system that is a Web server and also happens to have an email server running on TCP port 25. There is no reason that the Web server should be running email, so after careful analysis the service is removed and the port is closed. Five days later a zero day exploit for email is released. Based on the actions that were performed was the host properly protected against the zero day attack—absolutely. Now in hardening the box, we did not know the specific threat we were defending against but we were still able to defend and stop a zero day attack from being successful. While patching is important, the best way to secure a service is not to patch, it is to remove a service from a system.

The traditional bottom-up approach is to apply all patches to any software running on the system. We propose a top down approach asking the following questions:

1. *Is the system absolutely required to be on a given network?* This is especially important when talking about DMZ systems. Does the system have to be on the DMZ? If not, move it to the private network. An attacker cannot break into something it cannot see. Remember the first thing an attacker needs to break into a server is a visible IP. If the system is moved to a private address it cannot be attacked directly. However, we have to be careful because if a client system on the private network is compromised by the APT than internal systems are now visible. Therefore, even internal systems need to be segmented the same way DMZ systems are to protect against the APT. The real question is from an internal perspective, does every server have to be visible to every user. If not, put them on isolated network segments with proper filtering. The APT is counting on the fact that this is not done and if it is, we have just made it harder for the attacker.

2. *Is every port required to be open on the system?* The ports are the entry points into a system. The less ports, the less points of entry and the harder for an attacker to break in. A very secure system is one with no ports because there are no direct access points into the system. The problem is the usefulness of a server with no open ports is minimal, so while ports are required to be open you want to limit and control the number.

3. *Can any services or software be removed?* A service might be needed to be running but often services have extraneous components that are also running that are not needed for the system to function. For example are their extraneous libraries, sample scripts, or other software that can be removed.

After these steps are performed, whatever is left on the system is patched and updated. The important thing to notice is that one of our main goals of dealing with the APT is to reduce the surface space or attack surface that can be used as a point of exploitation. Typically a system has a large amount of software installed with many services running. Since an organization has to find every vulnerability to be secure and attacker only has to find one, the more complexity the harder it is for the defender and the easier it is for the attacker. What we are trying to do is reduce the size of the problem. If there is less software and less complexity, it is easier to understand what is going on and easier to secure. What we are now doing by making systems simpler is making the defender's job easier and the attacker's job harder. There is less software, less chance for vulnerability, and less chance of compromise.

Disabling service and reducing the surface space sounds easy but the first question is how do we decide which services to turn off. A good starting point is to run a sniffer in front of the system and if there is not any traffic or communication with the port, you would check with the data/business owner and if the service is not needed it can be put on the list of services to remove. The common mistake that is made is to stop there and assume that just because traffic is going to the port that it is legitimate. The traffic going to the port could be legitimate or it could be attacker traffic. Therefore, ports that have traffic or communication still need to be examined with protocol analysis tools, determining whether the traffic is authorized and coordinate with the administrator of the system. If the traffic is legitimate and the port is needed, leave it on, otherwise put in on the list.

Once you have the list of services that are no longer needed, the question is whether the services should be disabled or removed. The initial response is to disable the service because that is easier for the defender because now if a mistake is made it can easily be enabled. The problem is if it is easier for the defender to enable a service, it is also easier for an attacker. Therefore to make it harder for the attacker we want to remove the service. The problem is if we made a mistake it also makes it harder to easily fix the problem. The solution is a middle ground. All services that are determined not to be needed should be disabled for 30 days. After the 30-day window if the service is still not needed it should then be uninstalled and removed from the system. We now have the best of both worlds. The last question to answer is whether we still need to patch. The solution is easy, any software on your system always needs to be patched even if it is disabled. Any software that is removed from your system does not need to be patched. Put all of the pieces together, our final rule becomes any software that is not needed is disabled for 30 days and during the 30-day period the software is still patched. After 30 days the software is removed and it no longer needs to be patched because it is no longer on the system. If the software ever needs to be installed at a later point in time, the latest version is installed, all extraneous components removed, and the latest patches are applied.

Putting the Pieces Back Together

Organizations that are properly defending against the APT are taking a risk-based approach and those who are losing are not because other factors are driving their decisions. While we have talked about and covered risk in detail, lets exam what it actually means. Risk is the probability for loss which means there is uncertainty when calculating risk. If something was guaranteed it would not be a risk decision. In calculating risk, two pieces are involved threats and vulnerabilities. Previously in this chapter we have covered these topics in detail but looking at Figure 4.2, let's take a different perspective. While threat is the potential for harm, it is really what the

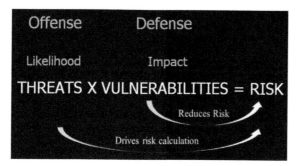

FIGURE 4.2 Formal Model of Risk

offense is capable of doing. It is what the attacker or enemy is capable of performing. Another way to look at vulnerabilities are what is the defensive position. Vulnerabilities are the defensive posture of an organization and ultimately what would have to be available for a threat to be successful. A threat without a vulnerability and a vulnerability without a threat is not a concern. Only when both are present do we have a high risk item.

If we have a high risk item that means that there is a real threat and an actual vulnerability. Now looking at the equation closely if the two factors are multiplied together to get risk, you only have to lower one of the two items in order to reduce your risk, you do not need to eliminate both. The question is choosing between threats and vulnerabilities, which one do we control? The answer is vulnerabilities. We have no control over a threat. You cannot control hurricanes, earthquakes, attackers, or foreign governments. A threat is what it is, but you have no control over it. The only piece you control is the vulnerabilities or the weakness in your environment. Based on this logic, the focus of risk reduction should be on fixing vulnerabilities. The common mistake that is often made is organizations focus on fixing "random" vulnerabilities. We hear organizations all of the time stating that we are going to fix the low hanging fruit, or let's fix 50 vulnerabilities a month to show the executives we are making progress. When it comes to vulnerabilities it is a quality not a quantity game. The quality comes is when we remember that we do not care about a vulnerability by itself. We only care about vulnerabilities in which there is an actual threat. An organization is always going to have vulnerabilities, so trying to fix every vulnerability is futile at best, you will never succeed. We want to focus on and only fix the vulnerabilities in which there is an offensive danger. Translation, offense must guide and inform the defense.

Fixing random vulnerabilities is doing a good thing and will still get you compromised by the APT. The right thing to do is let threat drive the risk equation. Now we are only worried about and going to address vulnerabilities in which there is a real threat. Another way to look at this is defining risk as:

risk (of a specific threat) = threat × vulnerabilities (to a specific threat).

Threat becomes the starting point for looking at and calculating risk. We would identify the threat, determine there is a vulnerable, and calculate the risk. We would then use vulnerability to reduce the risk. In many organizations, they use vulnerability to calculate the risk and end up focusing their energy and effort in the wrong areas.

The next challenge in calculating risk is being able to determine which threats we should focus our energy and effort on. When calculating risk, we focus on threats that have the highest likelihood of occurrence and vulnerabilities that have the biggest impact to our enterprise. In most cases we do not care about threats that have a low chance of occurring. Hurricanes are absolutely a threat. If you live in Florida you will spend time and energy making sure that your house is properly protected from a hurricane because there is a high likelihood of that threat occurring. If you live in Denver, Colorado (in the middle of the US) you do not worry about hurricanes because the likelihood of having a hurricane is very low. The threat did not change but based on the likelihood of the threat, you would act differently.

Once we have a high likelihood threat, we want to focus on the vulnerabilities with the biggest impact. If you have a test server, with no data on it and it gets compromised you are not very concerned because the overall impact is low (assuming it is on an isolated segment and cannot be used as a pivot point). However if you have a database server with millions of critical client records and it gets compromised, you are very concerned because the impact is much greater.

When calculating risk, there are four critical components: threats, vulnerabilities, likelihood, and impact. However, the formula that we are using only addresses threat and vulnerabilities. How do we bring in the other two components? The way we bring in likelihood and impact is by plotting risk on a risk matrix as shown in Figure 4.3.

The risk matrix now includes impact and likelihood as the two axes in the chart. We are showing a traditional four quadrant matrix but based on the granularity of risk you are plotting, this could easily be expanded to additional quadrants.

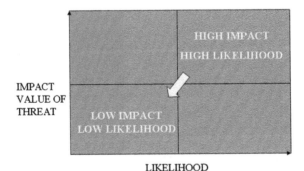

FIGURE 4.3 Mapping Risk to Impact and Likelihood. For Additional Granularity, the Quadrants can be Expanded to 8 or 12 Instead of Just 4

For most organizations, the biggest concern is the upper right quadrant the area in which you have a high likelihood and high impact, however that could change based on the specific business you are in. The goal of risk analysis is not to eliminate all risks, since that would essentially be impossible. There is no such thing as a risk free organization. The goal is to get all of your risks into the low left hand quadrant, where all of your risks are low likelihood and low impact.

Another common mistake when calculating risk is many organizations want to identify a high risk item and do everything possible in order to eliminate the risk. In some cases there is absolutely a reason where you would need to eliminate a risk but in most cases it is better to reduce the risk to an acceptable level. For example if you have an organization that has 20 high risk items. They could spend all of their energy and effort in eliminating five of the risks so they now have 15 high risks. The second option is to focus all of their energy and effort on lowering all of the risks. In this case they would now have 20 medium risks. While it does depend on many factors in most organization's it would be better to have 20 medium risks instead of 15 high risks.

INSURANCE MODEL

Since many people are new to taking a risk-based approach to security, it can be frustrating at times. We have even heard people say that no matter what you do you will not get ahead or win. In essence people are saying it does not matter what you do, your organization will be broken into. We have to be careful because this is like saying that no matter what we do, we are going to die so we should just play in the middle of a highway. Things are not perfect but by focusing in on the right areas you can be successful.

With regard to security being a losing battle, the author completely disagrees and has seen many cases where performing security correctly you can actually win. The best example to illustrate that managing security is not a losing battle is by looking at the insurance industry. If there was no chance of being able to calculate and manage risk correctly, every insurance industry would have gone out of business. The fact that insurance companies are making money shows that you can properly analyze risk. The big difference is the amount of checking and homework the insurance industry does. If you look at your traditional organization and ask them why they are spending money on this specific item, you will get a generic answer. If you ask them for the specific risk, you might get an answer. If you ask them to show the likelihood of the threat and impact of the vulnerable, there are very few who could provide answers.

Compare how a traditional company calculates risk to an insurance company. The next time you get a quote from an insurance company ask them how they calculated the quote. They will show you all of the paper work and analysis they performed to come up with that specific number. They perform calculations and gather information. The two most important pieces of information they use is your past history and information from others who are similar to you. If you do your homework correctly, risk is a winning game. The problem is many organizations do not do their homework. Very few companies can show me the same information that my insurance agent can show me. If we are both in the same business, we should both perform the same validation and analysis to be successful.

CALCULATING RISK

In calculating risk, there are two general formulas that are used: SLE (single loss expectancy) and ALE (annualized loss expectancy). SLE is the starting point to determine the single loss that would occur if a specific item occurred. The formula for the SLE is:

$$SLE = \text{asset value} \times \text{exposure factor}.$$

While the SLE is a valuable starting point it only represents the single loss an organization would suffer. Since many organizations suffer the same loss multiple times a year, you have to take the ARO (annualized rate of occurrence) and include it in the formula. This is done by calculating the ALE:

$$ALE = SLE \times \text{annualized rate of occurrence (ARO)}.$$

The ALE is what you always use to determine the cost of the risk and the TCO (total cost of ownership) is what is used to calculate the cost of a solution.

SUMMARY

When things go wrong in an organization and systems get compromised, it is easy to start spending money and buying more products. This might provide short-term relief but will not provide long-term protection. In order to properly defend an organization from attack, it is critical that organizations focus in on the right things to do. The right things are fixing the vulnerabilities that have the biggest impact that are caused by the threats that have the highest likelihood. Organizations that want to win must take a risk-based approach to security. While reducing a vulnerability is ultimately how an organization will lower a risk, threat must drive the risk equation. Risk reduction is a quality game not a quantity game. It is better to remediate five high priority risks in which there are high likelihood threats, than fixing 100 vulnerabilities that are easier and simple to fix.

While we have said it a few times it is worth repeating. Before you spend a dollar of your budget or an hour of your time on anything in the name of security make sure you can always answer three questions:

1. What is the risk?
2. Is it the highest priority risk?
3. Is it the most cost-effective way of reducing the risk?

Emerging Trends

II

The first section of the book addressed the growing problem of the APT. With the APT, an organization's focus needs to shift from dealing with the cyber common cold to cyber cancer. Based on the stealthy, targeted and data focused method of the adversary, many traditional security architectures are not effective against the new threat. New challenges require new solutions.

The second section of the book will focus on emerging trends that organizations who want to properly defend against the APT need to start doing. The following are the chapters that will be covered in section II:

Chapter 5: Protecting Your Data
Chapter 6: Prevention is Ideal but Detection is a Must
Chapter 7: Respond and Recover
Chapter 8: Technologies for Success

Traditional threats were more forgiving than the APT, which allowed organizations to make mistakes, overlook critical principles and not focus in on what is important. While the APT is not an insurmountable problem, it is if organizations do not change their approach to security. The chapters in this section redefine how to approach security to properly defend an organization against the next generation of advanced threats.

Protecting Your Data

5

INTRODUCTION

With everything going on in the world of cyber-attacks and organizations not always prepared to deal with the APT, it is easy to lose sight of what is important. The one fundamental truth of cyber security, it is and has always been about understanding, managing, and mitigating risk to an organization's critical information. While saying that statement is easy, understanding that statement is harder, but implementing it is even more difficult. We have many customers we work with who will nod their head in agreement when we state that security is all about your data or critical information. However, when we ask a simple question, what is your most critical information, they cannot always answer the question.

You cannot protect an organization, if you do not know what you are protecting. The first question is whether you can write down your organization's most critical information. If you can write down the list of your organization's most critical information, the next question is where does it reside and who has access to it. This was never an easy question but today it is much harder because our networks are more porous and our data is more portable. In the past, all information resided on a set of servers that were typically tightly controlled. All of the data resided on those servers and all access control was applied to the data residing on those servers. Today data might centrally be stored on a set of key servers but it quickly gets moved to other devices. Cloud and mobility are gaining a lot of attention on the security side because it changes the entire paradigm. Now information is available in many locations by many people and controlling access can be quite difficult. In addition, new information can be created instantly by anyone who has a portable device or any electronic equipment. The problem is in many organizations talking about data protection is futile at best, because they do not have a good handle of what their organization's most critical information is and where it resides.

The bottom line is you cannot protect information if you do not know what it is, where it is, and who has access to it. Therefore, data discovery and asset management is a critical component of protecting against the APT. Being on the offense is always easier than the defense. Even though that will always be the case, the unfortunate part today is that we have made it even easier for attackers. By having information on many devices (i.e. bring your own device—BYOD) and in many locations (i.e. cloud) means we have given the attacker many options to steal information. Since the APT is so effective at reconnaissance and scanning, the exploiting piece is almost trivial. The reason is that with the proper open source searching and intelligence, an adversary can locate and find most of the information they need publicly or at least identify the people who have it. Once this is done it takes a targeted attack to compromise and break into the organization. Once inside, since many organizations do not do a great job of data protection, the attacker just needs to find and extract the critical information they are after. Many organizations still take the M&M approach to security. They have a hard outer shell or perimeter but a soft gooey center. When DMZ systems were being targeted this approach had some merit, creating a robust strong perimeter. Today where the internal user is being targeted and the attacker can easily get inside, the gooey center means the house of cards collapses pretty quickly. By more strictly controlling information and limiting where it resides, can make it much harder for the attacker.

The other important misconception to point on when talking about data protection is the word data theft. Every organization is concerned with theft of their information but theft is not the right word. Theft implies someone stealing an object and you no longer have the benefit or use of that object. For example, theft of a car implies that someone took your car and you no longer have access to it. With traditional theft you can visibly tell that your car has been stolen. It is easy to detect and know that it happened. The problem with data theft is it is not theft, it is really data copying. In most cases when someone steals your information, they copy your information but it is still available to you. The good news is that you did not lose use of that information, like you would with traditional theft. The bad news is that you have no easy way to tell that your information has been stolen. This is one of the reasons why the APT can be so stealthy. The threat is data focused, but once it identifies the critical information, it makes a copy and leaves. Since there is nothing visible, it is hard for organizations to detect that anything is happening or did happen. Remember our key rule, prevention is ideal but detection is a must. We also have to remember that attackers will often use encryption to bypass our traditional detection measures so behavior patterns, not signatures need to be examined to detect data theft.

DATA DISCOVERY

While it sounds like a painful exercise, understanding, discovering, and controlling your data is a critical component to properly defend against the APT. When I was growing up there where no cell phones or pagers and when you left your house for the evening there was minimal communication with your parents. To help promote child protection and safety, there would be commercials run in the evening that would come on and show the current time and then state it is 10:05 do you know where your children are. Today with mobile computing and the cloud, they should start running similar commercials; it is 10:05 do you know where your data is. The scary part is most organizations do not. We have focused so much on availability of information, allowing it to be accessible from any location, we forgot about least privilege tied with need to know which requires only giving people the access they need to do their job, when they need it and all other access should be cut off.

If you are not convinced that this is a problem, identify a user in your organization and determine what information they need access to in order to perform their job. Once that is done, take their laptop and list all of the information that is contained on their laptop. I will almost guarantee that there is at least 40% more information on their laptop than what is needed for them to be effective. All of the extra information is just an accident waiting to happen.

In a perfect world, we would want to track and control all information. However, this is not practical so when we discuss data discovery we let threat drive the train just like we did with calculating risk. What is the information that, if it was compromised, would cause significant damage to your organization? Once that information is identified, all locations in which it resides need to be identified. If it is sensitive information, hopefully all of the location are internal, but external and mobile devices should also be checked to make sure there is a full understanding of the exposure. Once a list of all of the locations the information resides is created, create a list of where it should reside based on risk. Compare the two lists and identify any location where the information represents too great an exposure. In a perfect world, we would remove the information from those locations. However, in the real world there could be situations where the information needs to reside in a certain location even though it is too high a risk. In those cases, proper risk mitigation measures should be put in place to minimize the exposure to an acceptable level.

The bigger problem with data discovery is removing information from locations where it should not be stored. Simply deleting it off of a server is not enough, backups and local storage also have to be considered. The more difficult piece is sensitive information that is found on the Internet. Depending on where it is stored, in some cases it is almost impossible to remove information from the Internet. Therefore an organization should remove what it can but more importantly determine how it got there and put a process in place to make sure it does not occur again in the future. Even if the information cannot be fully removed, understanding that sensitive information is exposed allows an organization to put together an appropriate defensive response. Knowledge is power and knowing about a problem is better than thinking everything is fine and not realizing how exposed you really are.

PROTECTED ENCLAVES

Many organizations have focused a lot of energy in security on implementing network security products, but they have not focused as much energy on building a secure network architecture that can withstand an attack and minimize data exposure. From an Internet perspective, many organizations have done a good job with data segmentation limiting exposure from the Internet, see Figure 5.1.

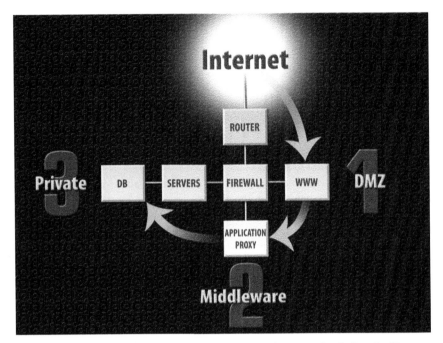

FIGURE 5.1 Creating a Network Architecture with Proper Segmentation is Required to Protect Critical Data

From a traditional threat perspective, the focus primarily has been on protecting information on servers from compromise from the Internet. This model is effective if the organization follows three critical rules:

1. Any systems accessible from the Internet reside on the DMZ and DMZ systems never contain sensitive information. DMZ systems should be considered high risk and low trust based on their exposure and potential chance of being compromised.
2. Any systems with sensitive data should reside on the private network and private network systems are never accessible from the Internet. Based on their limited access and separation from high-risk networks, private network systems are considered to be high trust and low risk.
3. The only way DMZ systems can communicate with private network systems is by going through an application proxy on a middleware tier. While DMZ systems do need to access information from the private network, you never want a high-risk systems directly communicating with a low-risk system. By going through an application proxy that makes two separate connections, this can be accomplished.

This architecture is called a n-tier architecture. While the number of tiers can be expanded, Figure 5.1 shows a traditional three-tier architecture, which is the minimal number of tiers you always want to use. This is the starting point for building out a secure infrastructure that allows services to be offered from the Internet. It is also important to point out that a three-tier architecture is a starting point. You can add more tiers but you should never go with less. If the risk is to great of only having one level of protection between the untrusted and trusted networks, additional middleware tiers can be added in. This would create a four-, five-, or six-tier architecture. You can add in more tiers to increase the overall security. The balance is that the more tiers there are, the more security and the more complexity. The goal is to have as few tiers as possible (without going below three) but have the maximum number of tiers for a proper level of protection.

Creating and building this infrastructure is critical to protect our servers but the problem is the threat approach has changed. However, it is critical to still keep a robust infrastructure with regard to Internet facing systems since attackers will utilize whatever works. One of the reasons why not as many attacks go after DMZ systems is because of the amount of time that has been invested in securing these systems. They are harder to break into for most organizations. While the APT will still target servers utilization zero-day attacks, typically the easier way into an organization is the client.

One of the main reasons that the client is targeted is because it resides on the private network and many private networks are fairly flat and open. This gives the attacker direct access to the information they need. By compromising a system on the private network, this gives the attacker a pivot point to extract information and create a command and control channel within the victim organization. As a simple check, pick any client on your network and see how many servers they have access to. Compare this to the list of servers they need access to do to their job. If you are like most organizations, internal users or anyone with a node on the private network can access more information than they should. Attackers recognize and take advantage of this weakness.

Once critical data is discovered, it needs to be protected with secure enclaves. If you go back to Figure 5.1, the three-tier architecture was created to protect the data when DMZ systems were being attacked. This was created out of necessity when an organizations Internet facing systems started to be targeted. Today the target is now the end user and the same architecture needs to be created to protect the new targets, the client. Using Figure 5.1 as a guide, replace the DMZ with the user enclave. Based on the APT, the client is now the target and your critical information needs to be protected from them. All client systems need to be put on a client segment which is high risk and low trust. All critical systems based on data discovery need to be put on a separate segment which is high trust and low risk. The only way users should be able to communicate with critical data is through an application proxy on a private middleware tier. By doing this if a user system gets compromised it can be controlled and contained. In addition to the three rules we have for servers on the DMZ, the three rules we have for clients when dealing with the APT are:

1. All client workstations and laptops should be on a private client network and client systems should contain a minimal amount of information. Utilizing thin clients or virtual machines can help contain and minimize the amount of information stored on the client system. For extra protection, the client workstation

network enclave can be further subdivided to minimize overall exposure. For example if 10,000 clients are on one network and it gets compromised, the malware can take over all 10,000 systems. If we put 100 systems each on separate firewalled segments, the amount of damage will be controlled. Finally, it is a good idea to put tablet systems and smartphones on separate segments based on the potential risk and exposure. Limiting the data that is kept on a smartphone is usually a little harder. However, there is a trick you can do. Most people do not use their phone as their primary computing device. They only utilize it when they are not in the office and away from their computer. Therefore they only need the information for a short period of time. One trick is to have the device securely wipe all information every 24h. Now if a device gets stolen you only have 24h worth of information not 6months. Remember security today requires you to look at the problem differently. When we first say this to executives they push back, when they try it, they realize it works.

2. All critical servers need to be on separate protected enclaves or networks. The networks should be broken up by the sensitivity of the information. A simple example is many organizations struggle with PCI compliance. The reason is that they try to make their entire network PCI compliant. By identifying all servers that contain PCI information and putting them on separate enclaves, reduces the scope and makes PCI compliance much more straightforward. Just like organizations would create a PCI zone to protect PCI compliant systems, organizations should also create an APT zone to protect systems that have a higher risk of being targeted. This allows extra security to be put around those systems, not the entire network.

3. The only way users can access critical information is by going through application proxies. Think of these as gateways that can control and monitor everything going in and everything going out. Not only does this increase security by limiting exposure, it gives an organization more visibility into who is accessing what information. Now if one client system is trying to access large amount of information from several servers, this could easily be caught and the damage detected early, to minimize exposure.

One of the key themes of security in general and dealing with the APT in particular is knowledge is power. You cannot protect what you do not know about. By designing and building a network infrastructure that properly segments and protects critical information can go a long way in defending against the APT.

EVERYTHING STARTS WITH YOUR DATA

Today there are many attacks vectors that could impact your organization. Recently we have seen the rise of hactivism, targeting financial and other critical organizations with denial of service attacks and persistent worms. While there will always be a variety of reasons why someone would target your organization, this book is focused on the APT. The APT is mainly concerned about an adversary targeting an organization to access and extract information. Remember the primary characteristics of the APT are stealthy, targeted and data focused. If you want to control and track the APT, you have to control and track your data. Today with security and dealing with the APT as a primary threat vector, controlling and managing your data is critical.

No single measure is going to protect an organization or its data. Therefore a defense in depth approach as depicted in Figure 5.2 is used.

The most important piece of the puzzle is an organization's data or information. Encryption, classification, need-to-know and other methods should be applied to keep an organization's information protected and controlled. No matter how much protection is put in place, it can still be bypassed. Therefore everything that accesses the data needs to have security wrapped around it. The way information is accessed by an organization is through applications or business processes. From authentication to stored procedures, a variety of security can be put in place at an application level. Applications are software and do not exist on their own. They need to reside on a computer which contains an operating system. Operating system security and host level protection need to be put in place. Computers do not typically exist by themselves. They are connected via a network. Network level security needs to be deployed to protect the flow of information. It is important to notice the order in which we protected our organization from the APT. We started from the center, the data and worked our way out. Most organizations approach to security starts at the outer ring of the network. Organizations implement a variety of network level protection and stop there. They claim they have defense in depth because they have implemented five different levels of network protection. While that was 1995 defense

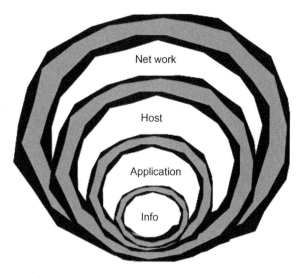

FIGURE 5.2 Defense in Depth Approach to Data Protection

in depth, it is not defense in depth today. Today defense in depth needs to be applied across all four levels. Actually it is five if you include the user, but they are so special we are going to deal with them separately. In order to test out how well your defense in depth approach is to the APT, take your existing network and answer the following questions:

1. What solutions and how many solutions do we have in place to protect and control our critical information?
2. What solutions and how many do we have integrated into our applications that access and store our critical information?
3. What solutions and how many do we have securing and protecting our hosts and severs that access and store our critical information?
4. What solutions and how many do we have securing and protecting our networks in which our sensitive information traverses?

If you are like most organizations, you will have a good answer for question four with a large number of solutions and for the other questions you will have a small number or zero. In a perfect world you should have a handful of solutions across all four areas. For every ring in Figure 5.2, there needs to be multiple levels of protection in order to properly defend against the APT. Remember that for each area, you should have a mixture of inbound prevention and outbound detection.

CIA

Most of the focus of data protection has been around preventing or controlling the disclosure of an organization's critical information. While the focus of the APT is on your data and stealing data is usually high on the list, we have to remember that there are three things the APT can do with your information:

1. *Disclose*—access information that they should not be able to access.
2. *Alter*—modify or change information so that it is no longer accurate.
3. *Deny access*—make information not available to those who need it.

While these are the goals of the attackers, the focus of defending against the APT means an organization needs to identify information and preserve the following:

1. *Confidentiality*—prevent, detect, and deter the unauthorized *disclosure* of information.
2. *Integrity*—prevent, detect, and deter the unauthorized *alteration* or modification of information. It is also important to point out that integrity deals with data consistency.
3. *Availability*—prevent, detect, and deter the unauthorized *denial of access* to information.

The trick is trying to find the balance of all three in implementing security across your enterprise. All three are always going to be important but in most organizations, one usually has a higher priority. It is important to figure out which one is more critical and prioritize the protection around those areas to make sure you are using your resources appropriately. In many cases, since the APT is targeting organizations that have sensitive information, protecting against disclosure is usually near the top of the list for the APT. However, it is always important to take a holistic approach to security and make sure that proper analysis is done across all three areas of security.

For example, if you work in a classified environment or a commercial entity that has sensitive, critical information that needs to be protected, confidentiality would be your primary concern. To emphasize this point if you look at the definition of top secret, it states that disclosure of this information would cause grave damage to the nation. The word disclosure is the first word in the definition.

With regard to integrity, this is usually one of the primary focus areas of financial institutions and banks, with availability being a very close second.

Availability is usually a primary focus of e-commerce sites that make most if not all of their money with online sales.

While all three are important to an organization, prioritizing and knowing which area would most likely be targeted by the attacker will make sure you put resources in the right areas. For example, instead of splitting your budget 33%, 33%, and 33% across all three, it might be better to put more toward confidentiality if you know the threat is going to try and disclose sensitive information.

DATA CLASSIFICATION

All of the methods we have talked about so far in this chapter are useful but at the end of the day if you want to protect your information from the APT, you must have a robust data classification process in place. All of the security in the world is not going to be effective if you do not understand the level of sensitivity of your information, where it resides and what the level of protection it requires. One of the problems with controlling the APT is it usually wants to extract information from your organization. You cannot stop all information from leaving an organization. It is required for your company to function and if you block all access in and all access out to the Internet, while it will provide a high level of protection, most likely you will go out of business. The trick is only allowing non-sensitive information out that is needed to accomplish the mission of the organization and block highly sensitive information from leaving. If you have two files, one is public information and one is confidential and there is no classification or labels, and they both are sent out of the organization, how are you going to detect that you have an information leakage problem. Only with proper data classification in place with digital rights management (DRM) tied closely with a data loss prevention (DLP) solution can an organization now control and manage the flow of information.

The following are the general steps of a good data classification process:

1. Identify the administrator/custodian.
2. Specify the criteria for how the information will be classified and labeled.

3. Classify the data by its owner who is subject to review by a supervisor.
4. Specify and document exceptions to the classification policy.
5. Specify the controls that will be applied to each classification level.
6. Specify the termination procedures for declassifying the information or for transferring custody of the information to another entity.
7. Create an enterprise awareness program about the classification controls.

Anyone who tells you that data classification is easy is lying to you. However organizations often make mistakes and make it a lot harder than it needs to be.

Data Classification Mistake 1

Organizations often start off with too many levels of data classification. We have seen organizations that create very complex data classification schemes that contain 12–15 different levels of classification. We had one client that created a 15-level data classification scheme. In one meeting they spent 35 min arguing over which level a certain file should be. People where debating on whether it should be a level 11, 12, or 13 and they went back and forth for over a half hour. Finally when I could not take it any longer I raised my hand and asked them how many files they had in their entire organizations. My point was that if it took them 35 min to classify each file, they would never get done with classifying all of their information. The method was way to complex and would not provide enough value if it would take 5 million years to implement the scheme.

Data Classification Rule 1

Based on this mistake, the first rule of data classification is to start with two levels of classification public and private. You can use different words but we start with two basic levels. Information that can be shared with the public and does not represent any risk to the organization is in one category and any information with any level of sensitivity is in a second category and is protected or private information. Once you have all of your information classified into those two categories, if you want to take your private information and break it into additional categories you can, but you always start with two. Now remember, do not go crazy. If you want to take your private or classified data and further subdivide it, it is recommended to stick with three. Remember at a general level, the federal government can get away with three general categories of classification: confidential, secret, and top secret, therefore you should be able to do the same.

It is also important to keep in mind that you only should have different data classification levels if you have different remediation or mitigation measures you are going to put in place. For example, if you have eight different levels but three of the levels are the same risk with the same remediation measures to protect it, then it should be level one not three. The trick here is keep it simple and try to get away with the smallest number of classification levels possible.

Data Classification Mistake 2

Often when organizations begin a data classification program, they start to go through their data and classify any information that is sensitive. The approach is assuming that the default level is public or unclassified. You would then go through and classify the information that needs to be protected. The problem with this approach is since all of your information is unclassified by default, if you make a mistake or do not get a chance to classify it, your information is vulnerable and not protected. This approach is error prone and if it takes 3 years to classify your information, it could be in an unprotected state for that period of time.

Data Classification Rule 2

When classifying data (unless there are rules that do not allow you to) the default state of all data should be classified. Only information that needs to be public should then be declassified but all information is protected and private by default. When you decide to begin your data classification program, on day one all of your information is classified. Now you do not have to worry about information leakage or data not being protected. As you go through your data, you would only declassify or make public the minimal amount of information that is required. This approach puts you in a position of strength where the chance of information leakage is minimal.

Data Classification Mistake 3

After organizations create and decide to implement a data classification scheme, the obvious place to start is with their existing data. The problem is new data is created all of the time, so if you start with your existing data the new data will continue to grow. We have one client who had 23 terabytes of information and they spent 4 months classifying 3 terabytes of information. Basic math would tell us they would now have 20 terabytes left. However during that 4 month period the organization created five new terabytes of information. They started with 23 terabytes worked for 4 months and they now have 25 terabytes of information to classify. By starting with existing data, the information will grow out of control.

Data Classification Rule 3

Instead of starting with existing data, you always start a data classification program focusing on the new data. If you start a data classification program on a specific day and start focusing in on all new information that is created, the existing data is now bounded and will not grow or get any larger. Now if each month you slowly work on existing data, it will not grow larger since all of the existing data is already taken care of. Another trick is to determine how long the data classification program will take and the useful life of each piece of information. If the data classification program will take 3 years to implement and half of the data has a useful life of 18 months, do not bother classifying it and put it at the end. By the time you get done with your program, it will already have expired and you will only have to worry about classifying half of your information.

The reason many companies do not implement a data classification program is because it takes a significant amount of time and resources to do it correctly and in the past it was not required. With the traditional threat you could get away without having any data classification, with the APT you cannot. However, by following the three core rules we outlined, data classification can be a reality.

The APT is not after public information, they are usually after sensitive information and with highly sensitive information, it should never leave your organization. By putting a robust data classification process an organization can track, control, and block that sensitive information from leaving the organization and impact the ability of the APT to cause damage.

While data classification is important and a critical foundation piece to protect against the APT, the other critical piece that is often missing is DRM (digital rights management). DRM is the ability to tag and apply digital watermarks to all critical files so that the classification cannot be removed or changed without destroying the file. The starting point of data classification is to classify servers based on the information they contain and put those systems on protected enclaves where all information coming in and out of that network segment is properly protected. This will work if the information is carefully controlled and the access is properly managed. The next step is to put headers and footers on all files specifying the classification. This allows DLP (data loss prevention) and other technologies to be able to track and control the information. This method is OK but it does not protect against someone who wants to deliberately bypass or extract information from an organization. Since the headers and footers can easily be modified, it does not provide a robust level of protection. Many organizations are not there yet but if you are looking toward the future and want to protect against APTv2, digital rights management is critical. Hopefully we have learned our lesson that reactive security does not work against the stealthy, advanced threat. We have to be more proactive and predictive. In this spirit of Wayne Gretsky who stated you have to skate to where the puck is going, not where it is, the puck is moving toward even more porous networks with more portable data, which means the first two approaches will be less successful. As we start to lock down the current vectors that the APT uses, it will adapt and the next version APTv2 will be able to bypass most data protection. Therefore if you want to get ahead of the curve DRM is a critical piece that is needed to protect and control information no matter where it goes. Once data classification is in place and all files are properly marked with digital rights management, the final piece is to use data loss prevention (DLP) solutions to be able to track, control, prevent, and alert any suspicious movement of sensitive information.

With digital information, it is so easy to collect and store as much information as possible but when it comes to APT and data protection, less is more. Someone cannot break in or compromise information that does not exist. Plus the defenders job becomes easier because you do not have to protect what you do not have. A key theme of dealing with the APT is to reduce the surface space or the amount of information you have. We have to continue to make it harder for the attacker and easier for the defender.

ENCRYPTION

If the APT is ultimately after an organization's critical information, encryption plays a key role in helping to protect the data from compromise. While encryption does play a key role in securing an organization, it is not a silver bullet. Encryption must be properly implemented and managed in order for it to provide the proper level of encryption. One of the things we hear all of the time is that an organization's critical information, that was encrypted, was stolen. The fundamental mistake that is made is encryption is like a lock. A lock is only effective if the keys are properly protected and controlled. Many organizations implement encryption, but they do not manage the keys and if an attacker can acquire the keys, they can decrypt the information and the encryption is completely ineffective.

> *The golden rule of encryption is the secrecy of the ciphertext is based on the secrecy of the key not the secrecy of the algorithm.*

While encryption is important, as important if not more important is key management. If you do not control and manage the key, all of the encryption in the world is not going to protect you. To assess the effectiveness of your encryption, ask three questions:

1. Where is the key?
2. Who has access to the key?
3. How is the key protected and managed?

One of the big problems many organizations have when it comes to encryption is the keys are stored with the data to make it easier or more transparent to the user. That would be like keeping a copy of the key under the doormat of your house. You can have the best, most secure lock in the world but if the key is not protected and an intruder can look under your doormat and find a copy, the lock is not going to keep your house safe. In order for a lock or encryption to be effective, the key needs to be protected and controlled. A critical part of encryption that is often overlooked is good key management.

The second common mistake with encryption besides not protecting the key is utilizing proprietary algorithms, instead of validated well-trusted algorithms. When it comes to encryption there is no way to prove an algorithm is secure. It would be great if there was a series of mathematical tests that could be performed to determine an algorithm is 100% secure, but unfortunately there are not. The question is how do you prove an algorithm is secure? You cannot, the only thing you can do is try to break it and if you are not able to break it, you then have a high level of confidence in its security. The way this is done is with cryptanalysis. These are people who specialize in trying to break the algorithms and find vulnerabilities or flaws in the cryptography. If after many, many years the cryptanalysis is not able to break the algorithm, we have a high level of confidence in its overall security. This brings up two critical points. First, the algorithm must be in the public domain in order for it to be tested and validated. If the algorithm is never shared or made public, how can it be analyzed? The one exception is of course NSA. If you are NSA, since they employ some of the best cryptanalysis people in the world, they do not need to follow this rule since they can perform testing internally, everyone else needs to follow this rule. Therefore, when it comes to cryptography, never ever trust proprietary. While the mathematics behind encryption can be straightforward, the devil is in the details. Let's look at an example to illustrate this. DES was built in the 1970s by NSA and IBM. Because NSA was involved everyone thought there was a backdoor embedded into the algorithm. People looked high and low and could not find a backdoor. The only strange thing that was found was how they created the S-boxes. The S-box is how you break-up the information in order to encrypt it. The way DES broke the data up into S-boxes was very strange and unusual. Everyone thought that might be a backdoor but no one could prove it. Twenty years after DES came out, a new method for breaking encryption was discovered called differential cryptanalysis. Differential cryptanalysis was able to break many algorithms but it turns out that the version of DES written by IBM and NSA was not vulnerable due to the strange S-boxes. The bit shift of the S-box was the difference between a secure algorithm and a vulnerable algorithm. The math is relatively straightforward but building a secure algorithm is extremely difficult and the chances of a proprietary algorithm being secure are very, very slim. Bottom line, it is not worth the risk. Remember a key rule of security, never ever underestimate your adversary, let your adversary underestimate you. Even though a vendor might think their proprietary algorithm is secure, it is only a matter of time before the APT will find a vulnerability or a way to exploit it. Play it safe and use the well-trusted algorithms.

Building robust cryptography is very difficult and the chances of getting it right the first time are fairly slim. Vendors who use proprietary encryption within their software, typically have flaws that are broken by an attacker. Since we are betting a lot on the encryption we use, never trust or use proprietary algorithms. The second piece is when a new algorithm is created and publicly released, we have minimal confidence in the overall strength of the algorithm. Only after it is tested and validated for eight years or more do we have a level of confidence in its security. Therefore never trust or use brand new algorithms because they have not been fully vetted. If you look at all of the robust encryption that you use today, you should notice something they all have in common. All of the algorithms have been out for a long period of time. Most of the algorithms we use today have been out for 15 or more years.

The other area of focus when implementing encryption is the length of the key. A cryptographic key is essentially a string of binary numbers. Therefore just like passwords it can be brute forced. While it depends on the specific algorithm, in general the longer the key, the harder it is to brute force and the shorter the key the easier it is. The general rule of thumb is that the key length has to be long enough so by the time someone can brute force the key, the useful life of the information has expired. Based on this logic many people focus solely on large keys and forget that there are many other aspects that are needed in order for the encryption to be secure. You can have the largest keys in the world but if the keys are not protected, the long key is not going to help you. Many organizations that deploy database encryption for very sensitive information deploy very large key lengths. However the keys are stored with the information and the attacker is able to compromise the keys and the data at the same time. Essentially the encryption is providing a false sense of security and providing minimal value because encryption without secure key management equals no security. The following is the checklist that needs to be used when implementing encryption:

1. Is the key protected and controlled?
2. Is the key a sufficient length based on the useful life of the information?
3. Is the algorithm not proprietary?
4. Has the algorithm been out in the public domain for a sufficient period of time to be fully vetted?

If you follow these core rules you are off to a solid start. The next thing to remember is you are only as strong as your weakest link. While protecting and controlling the keys and testing the algorithms are critical, you must make sure that your data is protected at all levels which includes protecting your data at rest and in transit. When using cryptography, you must always protect all three:

1. Data at rest.
2. Data in transit/in use.
3. Managing and controlling the keys.

This is a game where there is no partial credit. If you protect your data at rest and in transit but you do not control the keys, an attacker can obtain the keys and decrypt your information. If the keys are protected and your data is protected in transit but not at rest, an attacker can break into your local system or server and compromise your information. In security you must protect all three areas for your information to be protected from the APT.

TYPES OF ENCRYPTION

Encryption is a complex topic and there are entire books written on the subject; however, we need to briefly understand some of the core components of encryption in order to make sure an organization's information is properly protected from the APT. Often people think cryptography or encryption is all created equal when in reality there are different methods based on the problem you are trying to solve.

Encryption is part of cryptography which is part of a larger science known as cryptology, see Figure 5.3.

Cryptology is the art of science of building, testing, and validating algorithms that are used for the protection and control of critical information. Cryptology is broken down into two areas: (1) cryptography focused on the building and implementation

FIGURE 5.3 The Core Areas of Cryptology

of the algorithms and (2) cryptanalysis focused on the testing and validation of the algorithms. Cryptography is the art and science of building algorithms that can take information, encrypt it by running it through a mathematical transformation and creating random data known as ciphertext. The ciphertext can be run through a decryption algorithm and to obtain back the original information. The problem with encryption and decryption algorithms is that there is no way to prove an algorithm is secure. The way you validate the strength of an algorithm is with cryptanalysis. As pointed out earlier in the chapter, this is the art and science of trying to break algorithms to determine their overall strength.

In talking about cryptography there are three general types of algorithms:

1. *Symmetric*—symmetric encryption or secret key encryption is one key crypto. You use one key to encrypt the information and the same key to decrypt the information. The benefits is that it is very fast but since both parties use the same key, there needs to be a secure channel for key exchange. In symmetric encryption, the secret key needs to be protected and controlled.
2. *Asymmetric*—asymmetric or public key encryption is two key encryption. There are two keys a public and a private key. Whatever is encrypted with one key, can only be decrypted with the second key. Typically the public key is distributed via digital certifications that are signed by certificate authorities (CA) and anyone can have someone's public key. The private key is kept secure and protected and should only be known by the person who the key belongs to.
3. *Hash*—hashing performs a one-way transformation of the data that is irreversible. Both symmetric and asymmetric are reversible encryption, you can encrypt your information into ciphertext and decrypt it back to the original plaintext message. Hashing is irreversible encryption because once you run a piece of information through a hash, it is impossible to get back the original information, it performs a one-way transformation. Given the output of a hash it is impossible to get the original information. What makes a hash so powerful is that a hash will take information of any length and produce a fixed length output. Given an output there is no way to determine what the input was.

GOALS OF ENCRYPTION

Now that we understand the three core algorithms, let's look at the four goals of encryption:

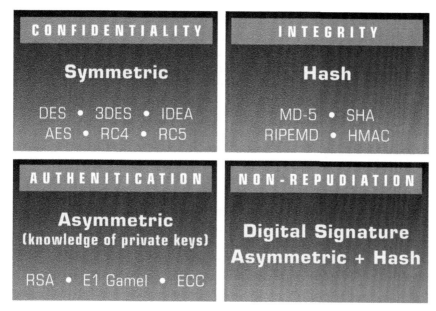

FIGURE 5.4 The Four Goals of Cryptography

1. *Confidentiality*—prevent, detect, deter the unauthorized disclosure of information.
2. *Integrity*—prevent, detect, deter the unauthorized alteration of information.
3. *Authentication*—proving that someone is who they say they are.
4. *Non-repudiation*—proving in a court of law that someone agreed to a contractual arrangement. Non-repudiation is essentially integrity and authentication together.

Figure 5.4 shows how we use the three algorithms to accomplish the four goals of encryption.

Figure 5.4 is an easy reference chart that will show you which algorithm and implementation you would use to accomplish the four goals of cryptography.

DATA AT REST

When protecting data at rest, there are essentially two options available:

- File folder level encryption.
- Full disk or on the fly encryption.

Each has pros and cons that need to be managed. With file/folder level encryption each file or folder is protected with a separate set of keys. Typically you would set up different folders for different projects and each one would be controlled and protected separately. With folder level encryption, you would use one password to login to the system and a separate passphrase to open the virtual safe that stores your keys for each folder. The benefit of file folder level encryption is you can create separate folders for different projects, each with different keys and protection. Now even if someone leaves their system logged in or someone compromises their system password all of their data is still protected and controlled. The drawbacks are you need to be very disciplined on where you store your information. If you accidentally save a sensitive file to the desktop instead of the proper folder, it will not be protected. It is also critical that you remember different passphrases for each folder. If you make them all the same or write them down, your information could potentially be compromised.

Full disk encryption is what many organizations use since it is easier for the user. Essentially all data and information written to the hard drive is encrypted. It does not matter which folder it is written to and therefore users do not have to be as disciplined. The drawback is that some full disk encryption solutions are tied to the user login credentials and transparent to the user. Therefore if the user's password gets compromised or their system is left logged in and they walk away, all information is potentially exposed. The other issue is some people do not always shut down their system, they just hibernate or shut the screen on their laptop to shut it off quickly. If not configured correctly, some laptops when you start them back up after hibernation, will not require a userID or password. This means if someone is traveling, hibernates their system and it gets stolen, an attacker could potentially turn on the system and get full access without requiring any passwords or credentials.

DATA AT MOTION

While protecting information at rest is important, it is also critical to protect any information that goes over an untrusted network. Utilizing VPNs when data is sent over an untrusted network is critical to make sure the information cannot be intercepted or compromised. While many organizations typically do a pretty good job of making sure their laptops have VPN clients installed when they communicate over the Internet, the area that we see organizations have trouble is with untrusted clients. More and more people are accessing and connecting to corporate resources from the Web using an untrusted client. Two of the most common examples are personal computers from home and computers at international airports. Many executives travel internationally and many airlines have lounges where people can wait between flights. To make it easier for them to check email or work, many airlines often have computers that can be used to make it easier so someone does not have to turn on their computer between flights. The problem in these cases is the communication is usually encrypted with SSL but there is no protection of the data at rest. When users use the Web and SSL to access sensitive information, information it is often saved to the local hard drive of the untrusted system without the user realizing it. Since the system is untrusted someone else could potentially use the computer and access the sensitive information that the user inadvertently saved to that system. Therefore to provide both data in transit and data at rest protection, SSL VPNs are often used. An SSL VPN is an SSL connection that creates an encrypted RAM drive on the untrusted computer and all of the activity with the session is stored in the encrypted RAM drive. Now any file or information that is saved is in an encrypted area and because it is in memory, it is removed when the system is turned off. Now by using SSL VPNs an organization can ensure that their information is protected when it is going across an untrusted network and when it is stored on an untrusted computer.

ENCRYPTION—MORE THAN YOU BARGAINED FOR

With all of the concern people are having with data protection, encryption seems like a viable solution to help protect an organization's most critical information. In security we have to avoid the extremes. Too much of something can be just as bad as too little. An area that organizations sometimes go overboard with is encryption. One big problem we often forget is encryption does not just stop an attacker from reading our information, it stops anyone from reading any information. If encryption is not deployed correctly it can actually weaken our security. If too much encryption is used, it could actually prevent certain security devices from working, Figure 5.5. If you implement layer 4 encryption, most of your network security devices like IDS (intrusion detection systems), IPS (intrusion prevention systems) and DLP (data loss prevention) become ineffective. Many network security devices actually need to read the payload of a packet in order to make a decision. If your upper layer protocols and

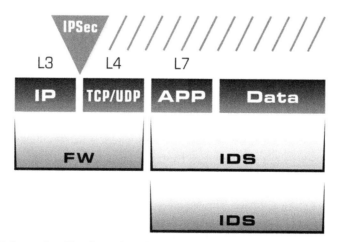

FIGURE 5.5 Encryption Often Stops Security Devices from Being Effective

data are all encrypted, many network security devices will no longer work. You cannot protect what you cannot see.

We had a client that wanted to implement internal, point to point encryption for all communication. Every packet leaving any computer was going to be fully encrypted with no unencrypted information traversing the network. While we did not think it was a good idea, we did not fight them, we just presented all of the information so they could make the best decision for their organization.

In order to be successful in security and defending against the APT, it is important to play the role of being an honest broker. Often with security we want to pick a side and argue and defend it. The better option is to clearly describe all options so the organization can make the best decision.

In this case I did not tell the client no, I just asked for 15 min to describe and analyze what would happen if they implemented point to point encryption. We put up a slide that showed the organization's network 5 years ago. Each slide we showed the next year and displayed what new network security devices they deployed and how much money they spent on security. At the end we had a slide of the current network architecture displaying all of the security devices and had a total of $4.9 million spent on security. The last slide displayed what would happen if they implemented point to point security for all devices. In doing this 90% of their entire network security devices had an x on them and $4.1 million of their $4.9 million investment would be useless by doing this. The reason is most network security devices need to read the packet and payload and if it is encrypted they cannot do their job and are ineffective against protecting against the threat. Too much security can be just as bad as too little security. Encryption is a very critical part of an organization's security arsenal but it must be designed and implemented correctly.

NETWORK SEGMENTATION AND DE-SCOPING

Whether it is dealing with the APT, meeting compliance or just increasing the security of an organization, one of the big themes is to reduce the complexity. Back in the 1990s when organizations started building out their networks, many had a good initial design. However, technology has taken us by storm and many organizations just kept adding new technology to their network, without a conscious decision of what the best design should be and the proper way to control and protect the environment. After all of this technology was added to their original design, they realized it needed to be secure. Security devices where added on after the fact and without even realizing it, many networks today are very large, very complex, and very difficult to know what is happening and occurring. These current networks are an attackers dream. What we need to do today is take the attackers dream and turn it into their biggest nightmare. The way this is done is with network segmentation and de-scoping.

For any programmers reading this book, one of the technologies that was very popular for building and deploying software is object oriented programming. The idea of object orientation is you build small, simple objects which are easy to test and validate. By putting multiple objects together you can build a complex program, but since it was built off of smaller, well-tested pieces, the overall stability and security is higher. This is the general idea of network segmentation. Instead of having a big flat network in which anyone can access any resource, we need to segment the network into smaller, self-contained groups that are easier to verify and validate. Trust is not what it used to be. Just because someone logged onto a system or authenticated does not mean they are trusted. By breaking a network down into smaller self-contained pieces not only makes it easier to verify and understand what is happening on a network, it also contains and controls damage. Since we know attackers are targeting the end user system, by segmenting out a network means that now if an attacker is able to compromise an internal system, they still have minimal access because all of the servers and critical data are on a separate segment. In the spirit of making things harder for the attacker and easier for the defender, network segmentation is a key ingredient to success.

The other key ingredient in creating an environment that can properly defend against the attacker is to de-scope the size of the problem. At some level everything in your organization needs to be protected and secure but not at the same level. The problem that we see with organizations is that they try to make the entire organization have the best or top level of security and that is just not practical. An organization needs to figure out which information is going to be targeted by the APT and/ or cause the most damage if compromised. That information should then be put on a separate segment and that one segment should be given a high level of security, not the entire network. By de-scoping the focus of an organization allows and organization to focus in on the areas that matter. The key component of de-scoping is identifying an organization's most critical information and isolating it on a separate network segment so additional protection can be implemented. Essentially you need to combine de-scoping with network segmentation. While you will get some benefit from each by themselves, putting them together is where you get the real value.

ENCRYPTION FREE ZONE

In order to succeed, win, and properly defend against today's advanced threat, we have to be willing to break the glass and develop creative new ways to solve security. Sometimes we get so comfortable in doing things a certain way, we resist change and criticize alternatives because they are different. We have to accept that what we are doing today is good, but not good enough to properly defend our organization. We also have to remember that there is no perfect solution. Every solution does not fit every organization, but you constantly need to evaluate solutions by asking yourself two simple questions: (1) what do you gain and (2) what do you lose. If the gains are worth more than the losses, then we should look at it as a potential solution in our organization.

One of the problems today is organizations implement a large amount of internal encryption and have minimal network visibility into what is happening. The APT is focused on turning our strengths against us. One of the common tactics of the advanced threat is it will trick a user to click on a link or open an attachment in order to compromise a system on the private network. Since many organizations have a fairly flat network, the APT now has access to critical, sensitive information. Once it identifies the critical information, it needs to extract it from the organization in a stealthy manner. If it just sent the information out in its current form, DLP and other network security devices would detect that there was a problem. Therefore, after compromising a system the common tactic of the attacker is to create an encrypted outbound connection out of the organization, often known as the command and control channel. By using an encrypted outbound session, the attacker can slip under the radar of most network security devices and not get caught. One common reply to this is that many network security devices have the ability to decrypt traffic and information. The problem is that these devices can only decrypt information in which they have the keys. If you are deploying an organization-wide encryption solution, your company has the keys they can load on the system. If an attacker is using their own encryption, your organization does not have the keys and therefore cannot decrypt the data. They have used technology that was meant for good and turned it to be used for evil.

Therefore one of the tricks that we have implemented for clients is to create an encryption-free zone. This is an internal segment of the network, typically where client systems reside in which not only is encryption not used but no encryption is allowed. All traffic is unencrypted and crypto detectors are installed that allow encryption to be detected. Each of these encrypted-free zones have all of the network security devices installed so now they can see, analyze, and provide proper security for all traffic. These zones are broken down by sensitivity levels and have gateways to control all information coming in and all traffic leaving. Traffic leaving can be encrypted at the gateway if it is going over an untrusted network. By doing this trick, not only does it improve security but it now allows an organization to detect a compromised system in seconds.

The typical approach today is an attacker compromises a system and creates an outbound encrypted channel. Since encryption is allowed anywhere on a network, this traffic looks normal but slips under the radar and is not detected by any of the traditional network security devices. A system could now be compromised for months without anyone detecting it.

The new approach has all client systems, which are often targeted by the attacker, on an encrypted-free zone. Now when the user opens an attachment, infects their systems, and creates an outbound encrypted channel, it can be detected instantly. We have now taken the attackers greatest strength and have turned it into their biggest weakness. Since we know that no traffic is supposed to be encrypted and we know that the attacker will encrypt their information, we can instantly detect a compromised system and contain the damage.

In using this approach, we have taken organizations that have had systems compromised with the APT for months and the organization is now able to detect and remediate a compromised system in minutes, greatly reducing and containing the amount of damage the threat can do to their organization.

SUMMARY

If an organization wants to do better in dealing with the APT, they need to focus on what the attacker is ultimately after—the data. Taking a data centric approach is critical to having a secure environment. The more an organization can control, manage, and minimize the amount of information they have, the harder it is for the attacker to cause harm. It is also critical to make sure we do not give ourselves a false sense of security by implementing pain killer security. Many organizations buy data protection solutions like encryption and believe they are secure. If an organization does not properly protect their data at rest and in transit and manage and control the keys, all of the encryption in the world is not going to help. You are not fixing the problem and if you do not fix the problem, you might have short-term relief but you will not have long term protection.

Protecting an organization's data begins with data identification and discovery. You need to understand and know what your critical information is and where it resides in order to protect it. Many organizations will think they are secure, deploy encryption and DLP but if the critical information has not been identified and determined where it is located, the organization will still be impacted by the APT. You cannot protect what you do not know.

Once the critical information has been identified, a robust data classification process needs to be put in place and enforced with digital rights management (DRM). While DRM is something that many organizations are not doing today, in the spirit of proactive/predictive security it needs to be on the security roadmap. The reason is things are not going to get any easier in the future. With cloud security and mobilization, data will continue to be more portable and networks will be more porous. If all of an organization's information is kept on a set of servers, placed on a separate VLAN with isolation and protection, they might be able to provide appropriate security without data classification and DRM. However with data moving to the cloud so it can be accessed anywhere from any location and mobilization increasing at a rapid pace, robust data classification with embedded classification via DRM is becoming a necessity.

One of the many reason why the APT is so devastating is organizations did not plan for the future and it caught them by surprise. With traditional threats, waiting for the attacker and reacting to what they did was effective because the attacker was visible. Today with stealthy, targeted, and data focused attacks, reactive security will not work. Not only do we need to plan and defend against the current APT, but more and more threats will emerge and APTv2 will be a different exposure. We do not know how future attackers will break in but we do know what they will go after, the data. Therefore all efforts involving data protection will be time well spent because it will protect and control what the attacker is after. Planning ahead is critical and it is important to plan for the future than be surprised.

Prevention is Ideal but Detection is a Must

6

INTRODUCTION

We are at a very interesting time in security; the fundamental way we look at security has to change. In any area or sport but especially with security, offense is always easier than the defense. In order for the offense to be successful they only have to find one vulnerability or group of vulnerabilities. In order for the defense to win they have to find all of the vulnerabilities and fix them before the offense attacks and breaks in. While identifying and finding all of the vulnerabilities was never easy, in the past with proper planning and threat analysis organizations had a chance of keeping their organizations secure. In the 1990s while it was very difficult it was possible for organizations to not have any breaches or compromised systems, unlikely but possible.

Today based on the sophistication of the adversary and the persistence of the attack we have to accept the fact that we are going to be compromised. Any organization of reasonable size has to recognize that they have been compromised and will be compromised again in the future. While this statement can be daunting and depressing as we have talked about previously in the book, this is no different than how we approach everyday life. Everyone is going to get sick and everyone is going to die. This does not mean that we can still not live a happy life and be healthy most of the time, but we must always be aware that something could happen. Every day of our life we must be careful and always try to exercise and be healthy to minimize the chances of an illness occurring.

We must keep this same positive aspect when we look at cyber security. While we do have to recognize that organizations have been and will be compromised, that does not mean we are going to lose. Think of any professional sports, the team that wins almost always gives up points. Just because the offense scores does not mean you lost the game. You just have to minimize and manage the offense and be willing to give up certain plays to control the amount of points they will score. At the end you can still win a game, even if the offense scores. This is the approach we need to take with security. It is perfectly ok if we understand and know how the offense operates and how the APT is going to cause damage and we properly control and manage it. Saying we have no clue on the state of our organization is a dangerous place to be. However stating that we have a well-segmented network, we have a high trust and confidence in our most high worth systems and while some of our low worth systems might be compromised, the overall damage will be minimal, is an acceptable approach. Knowledge is power in this game. If an organization is ignorant of the APT, they most definitely will lose, but if you understand the exposures and carefully control and manage them, the amount of overall impact the APT will have will be minimized.

One of the common mistakes that is often made by executives is stating that security professionals have been overhyping the problem for years and creating a bigger problem than there really is. A common remark is that you have been stating that organizations have been compromised and we have had no compromises for the last several years. A statement like this can be very dangerous if we do not define the parameters of what constitutes a compromised system. In most of these organizations, what the executives should be stating is that there have not been any visible attacks that they have seen. The problem is they are still in a year 2000 mindset in which most attacks were visible. With that mindset they are correct. Today there are very few visible attacks and most organizations are doing a good job in preventing visible attacks. The problem is that is not what you need to be concerned about today. This mindset would be equivalent to someone stating I never need to go to the doctor since I feel fine. I will only go to the doctor if there is a visible sign of a problem. While this approach will work and scale if we are concerned about the common cold; however if we are concerned about cancer this approach will not work. As we know, if you wait to have a visible sign with cancer in order to go to the doctor, it will be too late. Preventive measures are not enough with a really serious illness, you must constantly look for and detect problems when they are small.

This same approach applies to security. Only looking for visible signs of an attack will work with low-level attacks. However with advanced attacks like the APT, reacting to visible signs will prove futile and will not work. Today we need to educate our executives that just because everything looks fine on the surface and there are no visible signs, that does not mean we are secure and protected. In many cases that will give you a false sense of security.

Prevention is ideal and will work with visible style attacks. Prevention will have less value against stealthy, targeted, and data focused attacks. With the APT timely detection is critical. Now we have to be careful to remember that prevention is still important. One mistake that we often see made with the APT is forgetting about prevention and focusing solely on detection. The slightly good news is that are some attacks that can still be prevented. If we can prevent an attack, that is ideal. However we must augment our detection with timely prevention. What we cannot prevent we must detect in a timely manner. We also have to remember that prevention can also slow down the attacker, giving an organization more time to detect an adversary.

If you look at recent breach data it will become clear that organizations are focusing all of their efforts on prevention with minimal effort on detection. When you see breach statistics like 15 million records stolen, it only means one thing, there is no detection. If there was any detection being done at all the number would be a lot smaller. The reason is simple. If a company was able to detect an attack they would have found the attacker and stopped them at 500 or even 1000 records. The fact that the attacker could keep taking records and no one stops them shows that there is zero detection. Most networks today are configured that if someone can get past the prevention there is no stopping them. Therefore in this chapter we will examine the fundamental approach for dealing with the APT. Prevention is ideal but detection is a must.

INBOUND PREVENTION

Prevention technology focuses in on identifying and stopping an attacker before any damage occurs. Prevention means stopping someone before it starts. As you can imagine, in a perfect world prevention is ideal. With the traditional style attack in which a large number of organizations were targeted over a long period of time and the attack started off gradually and did not change, prevention was successful for a large number of attacks. The logic was that we could catch attacks early since they were visible and determine a pattern to look for. This signature could then be loaded on all systems and the specific vector could be prevented for future attacks. Since the attack ramped up slowly, the initial attacks would be successful but all future attacks would be prevented. Plus the attack did not change so once we knew about it, all future attempts could be successfully prevented.

In addition, servers were the target of the attack. To break into a server required three items, visible IPs, open ports, and vulnerabilities in the services. By controlling and locking down the system, could also minimize the chance of an attack being successful.

While preventive technology is not as effective against the APT because it is stealthy, targeted, and data focused—aka the cyber shoplifter—it still has value and is still a requirement. We have to be careful of how we approach security with the APT and how we analyze the data. Even though most organizations that were compromised had preventive technology and other core security in place, we cannot conclude that this technology is useless and should not be used.

With the APT, even though traditional defenses are not 100% effective, things would have been a lot worse if key technologies were not in place. New attacks require a new way of thinking to protect against them, but this does not mean that traditional measures should be replaced. Replacement means that the current technology has no value. It is almost a guarantee that firewalls and IPSs have dropped and blocked packets which means they are catching attacks. Removing them from the network would be very dangerous and now all of those attacks that are being caught would be allowed through. Instead of replacement, with the APT we have to think augmentation. The current technology we have is not enough but it does have value, therefore we have to augment it with additional technology to make it more effective.

While preventive technology is not enough, the solutions still have value and need to be understood. Some of the traditional prevention technologies that organizations have deployed are:

- *Firewalls*—network-based firewalls are traditional inline devices. This means they are a router with a filtering rule set. They have the ability to look for certain types of traffic and either allow or block the traffic. The value of a firewall is based on its configuration and what it is looking to block. Firewalls were originally used to protect the perimeter of an organization. It typically resided between the Internet and the organizations internal network. While perimeter-based firewalls are important, boundary-based defense is more critical in protecting against the APT. The problem with a traditional perimeter based firewall is that it creates a strong outer shell, with a soft center. Essentially it means that if an attacker gets around the perimeter firewall, they have full access to all of the servers and critical information. Today, we need to segment an internal network into trust levels and deploy internal boundary-based firewalls between those areas. Now even if a perimeter firewall is breached, the internal boundary firewalls will still provide protection and make it harder for an attacker. What is important to remember is that a firewall or series of firewalls can provide protection or at least provide another level of security against the APT. The reason why they have provided minimal protection is based off the fact that they were only located at the perimeter and not always properly configured. By deploying multiple firewalls within an organization makes it more difficult for the attacker. Another option to maximize the effectiveness of a firewall is to have different firewalls (from different vendors) with different rule sets. Having multiple firewalls that are all exactly the same with the same configuration provides minimal value. This is because once an attacker figures out a way around one firewall, it could be used against all of the firewalls. While having firewalls from different vendors with different configurations makes it more difficult to manage and control, what you have to remember is it is still easier and cheaper than catching and dealing with a successful APT compromise. Drastic times require drastic measures. Things that we would not do in the past because it required too much effort, is a requirement today. While they still require considerable effort, the effort is still a lot less than the effort it would take to deal with a successful compromise. The other complimentary component of a firewall is to augment network-based firewalls with host-based firewalls. Not only must the network be protected but the hosts also need to be secure.
- *Intrusion Prevention Systems (IPS)*—Intrusion prevention systems are inline devices but were originally designed to be intrusion detection systems (IDS) that could block traffic. One of the values of an intrusion detection system (IDS) is that it can be more aggressive than a firewall because it has the ability to have some level of false positives. However as IDS technology become more mature some signatures were tuned to the point where they had zero false positives. Since these signatures were always correct, the idea was to block the

traffic instead of just alerting on the traffic and requiring someone to take manual action on the attack. IPS systems have matured where they now can block additional payloads and traffic indicative of an attacker so if properly tuned can also look for indicators of advanced threats.

- *Data Loss Prevention (DLP)*—While IPS is meant to look for indicators of an attack and prevent those attacks from entering an organization, DLP focuses in on the data. The purpose of DLP is to understand and recognize the critical information to an organization, track and control where it is going, and prevent or detect unauthorized use. While DLP systems have a lot of value, many implementations focus on keywords to flag critical information. While this will catch a successful attack, since it is based off of key words, a malicious insider or deliberate attacker could easily bypass or get around these measures. As with many of these technologies, one of the most powerful tools of the attacker is to utilize encryption. By encrypting the information, it can bypass most DLP solutions since the key words are no longer visible. For DLP solutions to be successful, first there needs to be a robust data classification program in place. If there is no classification of the data, the DLP solution will be based on key words which have a limited chance of success. A critical requirement for dealing with the APT, all data must be properly classified and protected. While data classification is important, it is critical that the labels cannot easily be removed. If all of an organization's information is classified but it is simply done by placing a label in the header and footer of a file, a malicious insider or attacker could easily remove it. To complement data classification and make it more robust, it must be tied with a digital rights management (DRM) solution. A DRM solution will embed the classification into each file so it cannot be removed or changed. This is critical because all of the classification in the world is not going to help if it cannot be protected and controlled.

Each of these technologies deal with a different potential problem and work best when integrated together.

While each technology has weaknesses, together they provide a stronger solution for protecting against attacks.

These technologies are what we call foundational security. While they are not enough to stop and deal with the APT, they are required as a foundation in order for the more advanced technology to be effective. One of the common mistakes that organizations make is that they are so focused on deploying advanced technology they ignore and forgot about having a solid foundation. We all know that you can have the most beautiful house in the world but if it is not built on a solid foundation, nothing else matters.

Cyber security especially in dealing with the APT follows the same logic. While all organizations want to get to the point where they are defending against the APT, make sure the foundational items are in place first. If an organization has a poorly configured firewall, that is not designed or configured correctly, you can have all of the behavioral analysis you want but it will have a minimal overall impact. Security is only as strong as the weakest link and it is important to always identify and fix those weak areas as soon as possible.

Now that we understand the core solutions, let's look at the technologies that they are based off of:

- *Rules*—rules are a list of conditions and when a condition is meant a certain action is taken. Rules are very common with firewalls where you would list what type of traffic is allowed and what type of traffic is denied. As with any technology, rules are only as good as the level of detail that is covered in the ruleset and how knowledgeable the person is who is writing the rules of the environment they are protecting. It is also important to remember that there is too much traffic to be able write an individual rule for every piece of information or packet that the rule set sees. Therefore there has to be a default rule. This rule is used if all of the other rules are searched and there is not a match. The two general approaches are default allow and default deny. Default allow says anything that does not match a rule and makes it to the bottom of the rule-set is allowed. Default allow is not recommended because it is too permissive and will allow too much traffic through. Default deny is recommended. This states anything that does not match a rule is automatically dropped or denied access.
- *Signatures*—signatures are also known as pattern matching. This is where the system looks for a match against a pattern of activity. This is the technology that traditional anti-virus software was built of and used in many IDS systems. Signature detection works very well against known attacks that it has seen before. Once it sees an attack, it can create a signature for the attack, put it in the system and when it sees the signature again, it can flag it as an attack. Signatures work very well against attacks that are known and do not change very often. For example, worms that start off going after a small number of systems, slowly ramps up and does not change, signatures are very effective at catching. However, signatures do not work as well against the APT. The APT is always changing and stealthy so once a signature is pulled, it most likely will change or be different for each system. With the APT each site is unique and typically has a specially crafted attack that was created just for that organization. Signature detection is also based off of a default allow stance which is not very robust. With signature detection, the system has a list of known attacks. Anything that matches the attack is stopped or alerted on. Anything that does not match a signature is allowed through. While this will work with some attacks, it is not very scalable against the APT.

These technologies while important to have implemented on a network, will not be 100% effective against the APT. The main reason is they are focusing in on typically what is entering the network or a host and stopping anything that is suspicious. In essence, they focus in on visible and static attacks. The premise behind these technologies is that we understand how the adversary works, we know what to look for and it does not change. These characteristics are usually not true for the APT, however there are aspects of it that will still work today. For example, one of the common methods the APT deploys is to spoof an email address to look like it is coming from a trusted person within your office, i.e. your boss or an executive. While the source email address is someone within your organization, the email is actually originating from outside your organization. Therefore a preventive measure could be to examine the source address of an email and if it is from someone within the organization but originating from outside the network, it should be blocked. While this technically will work in some cases, the APT is very adaptive and as soon as an organization figures out how to block an attack, the threat will figure out a way around it.

The other big challenge with preventive technology is traditional preventive technology is fairly rigid. It will either always block or always allow. It is making the assumption that something is always bad or always good. Unfortunately today, that is rarely true. While our traditional preventive measures can still provide some value, we have to adapt our technology. Remember that almost all organizations that were breached by an APT had preventive technology in place.

Today, we have to move towards more intelligent preventive measures that are adaptive. This means the technology will gather more information and constantly adjust and change what is or is not allowed. With a worm that does not change for 9–12 months, blocking a specific port or IP address is an effective way to deal with the threat. Since the current threat is persistent and will continue to try to break in, what works today will not work tomorrow, so we have to continuously adapt our technology. This represents a fundamental paradigm shift for many security professionals since they are configuring a security device and unless there is a required change, they do not modify or update the system. Today's security requires constant analysis of the threats and updating of the defensive measures to keep pace with the attacker.

Three of the common adaptive, preventive technologies that provide increase protection against the APT are:

- *Application aware devices*—Traditional preventive technology focused on using information in the protocol headers to make a determination on whether traffic or applications should be permitted or denied. Typically these devices utilize layer 4 ports to determine whether a given service is allowed through. For example, allowing TCP port 80—HTTP (hyper text transfer protocol) would enable web traffic and blocking TCP port 25—SMTP (simple mail transport protocol) would stop email. The problem with this approach is it is assuming that everyone is playing by the rules and only using the default ports for the well-known services they are supposed to run on. However, you could literally run any service on any port. Well-known ports are used to make it easier to find a given service. Think of how complicated the web would be if you had to determine what port a given web service is listening on. Instead, your browser will automatically connect to TCP port 80 when you put http in the url field. There is no reason I could not run email or even IRC (internet relay chat) over port 80. Therefore these traditional devices only check a port and perform no validation of the service. Therefore a clever attacker could easily tunnel any service they want through those ports. Since almost every site allows users to make outbound web (TCP 80) and SSL (TCP 443) connections, a clever attacker after they compromise a system would make an outbound encrypted channel over TCP port 443, the traditional firewall would assume it is SSL, perform no validation and allow the service through. While this provides some level of protection, it is very dangerous because it makes assumptions and those assumptions are not always true.

Application aware devices will actually check and monitor the traffic and make sure it really contains the traffic that is supposed to be sent over a port. Now if you allow HTTP, an application aware device will examine the traffic and confirm it is actually web traffic. What is important to remember is that any given technology in the hands of a clever attacker could be bypassed.

While there is no such thing as perfect security, it is important to remember that the power of these technologies is to use them all together to provide a comprehensive level of protection. You often read articles how security testers will show how they can bypass any device making the claim they are not secure. Give any smart person a single technology and they will be able to bypass it. The trick goes back to our theme that prevention is ideal but detection is a must. There is no value in proving a technology is not 100% secure because that is true of every device. The trick is proper configuration and integration of multiple devices together to achieve a proper level of protection against the APT with the goal of containing and minimizing the impact. With the APT an organization will get compromised, but there are measures an organization can take to minimize the impact and the extent of the compromise.

- *Behavioral monitoring*—It sounds like a cliché but computers do not break into systems people do. Even with worms or automated scripts, it is ultimately humans that wrote the code or scripts that broke into a system. Instead of looking for signatures, it turns out that there are distinct behavioral characteristics that differentiate a legitimate user from an attacker. From a purely analytical standpoint the legitimate user and the attacker have to have behavior that differentiates from each other. If their behavioral patterns are always the same between a user and the APT, that means all users are evil or APT is harmless. We know neither of those statements is true. Therefore by looking at behavior patterns of the amount of traffic, and where information is flowing, differences of how the APT acts can be picked up on.
- *Anomaly Analysis*—Understanding behavior patterns is very helpful but the value for finding the APT comes into play when you tie it with anomaly analysis. What we want to do is build profiles of what the normal user looks like. Anything that deviates from that normal user profile is deemed an attacker. While this activity is helpful, the other beneficial type of anomaly analysis is to build behavior characteristics of how the APT operates and look for those patterns. The problem with many systems today is they pick one method or the other. The real value is to use both methods together to provide a robust level of detection. While anomaly analysis can be used to prevent attacks, because

the patterns have to constantly be adapted, the real benefit is in detection. Remember to catch a shop lifter you have to look for and track the points of deviation. This means they have to do the harmful action before you can track it, which means it only has value for detection not prevention. The APT is similar in that we have to wait for malicious or harmful actions to be taken before proper validation and detection can be performed.

While preventive technology provides a base level of protection and needs to continue, it needs to be enhanced with more adaptive technology that is focused on preventing indicators of the APT. The bottom line to remember is that while there are some things that can be done to prevent certain aspects of the APT, many APTs cannot be prevented and must be augmented with detective technology.

OUTBOUND DETECTION

Most of the security technologies that are used today where built and developed to deal with the traditional threat. With a traditional threat the main approach was look at what is coming into an organization and prevent/stop bad traffic. If you know what is coming and you know what to look for the best way to protect against an attack is inbound prevention.

Prevention is ideal because it stops an attacker before they cause any damage. Stopping damage is the best way to minimize and take away the impact of an attack. While prevention is ideal, it is not always possible with stealthy, targeted, and data focused attacks. The problem with most organizations security is they have bet everything on being able to prevent all attacks. If they are not able to prevent an attack, the adversary has full access to their network and minimal security impairing them from causing damage and exploiting any system they want. This is evident based on how much data is being stolen from organizations. When you see millions of records being stolen it shows us that organizations have no detection in place. If an organization had any detection you might see a few thousand records stolen, the organization would detect it and stop the attack. When the number of records gets in the millions, it is clear that there is no detection and once an attacker gets into the organization, they can do anything they want.

To combat and deal with the APT, organizations need to enhance their security posture by putting more focus on outbound traffic and detection. If you own a store and you are worried about someone stealing from your store, you do not watch and inspect customers entering your store, you watch and inspect what they are doing while they are in your store and most importantly, you watch and track when they leave to make sure they paid for everything they are taking with them. Since one of the main overall concerns today is data theft from the APT, data theft does not occur when someone enters, it occurs when someone leaves. Therefore while we talk about prevention being ideal, it is critical that we remember detection is a must. What we really are referring to is inbound prevention and outbound detection, see Figure 6.1.

FIGURE 6.1 Defense in Depth to Deal With the APT

The more we can do to limit, track, and control what is leaving an organization, the more effective we will be with the APT.

When detecting shoplifters in a store, one of the areas you focus in on is called the point of deviation. When a legitimate customer and a shoplifter enter a store, they look identical. There is no way to differentiate or prevent a shoplifter from entering a store. However, if the one person is really a legitimate customer and the other person is a shoplifter, at some point their actions will have to deviate. For example, the normal customer will put an item in their shopping cart, the shoplifter would put the item in their pocket. If the shoplifter acts like the legitimate customer the entire time they are in the store, including when they leave, guess what; they are not a shoplifter they are a normal customer. A shoplifter can be very clever and tricky but at the end of the day, their entry pattern looks identical but their exit pattern has to be different, otherwise they would not be committing a crime.

The same holds true with the APT and is the fundamental problem why so many organizations and people have difficulty with it. Cyber security has been very accustomed to preventing and blocking attackers and focusing in on what is entering an organization. However, with the APT because at point of entry they look like legitimate traffic, that approach will not work. Very important note—this does not mean that traditional security is ineffective or dead, it just means it was built to deal with one type of threat and the APT is a new threat. The key lesson is the APT is not the only threat today. The traditional threat is still alive and well. This is not a replacement but an augmentation, where there is just another threat that we have to deal with. Therefore we must keep/maintain our inbound prevention but we need to focus more energy on outbound detection.

Today to deal with the APT we need to assume that the attacker is in the network already and energy needs to put against looking for the points of deviation in terms of what is leaving your organization not what is entering. Some initial points of deviation to look for is to focus on clipping levels.

In using clipping levels we are stealing a page out of the play book of credit card companies. Credit card companies are very concerned about fraudulent transaction. In an ideal world, they would inspect every transaction as being fraudulent and investigate each one. Unfortunately, they do not have enough staff or budget to perform this activity. Therefore they utilize clipping levels. The idea of a clipping level is to identify activity that is bad 80% of the time. Instead of looking at a large list of transaction trying to find the small percent that are bad, we focus on a smaller list where 80% is bad, see Figure 6.2.

Using clipping levels, allows for resources to be more focused and have a greater chance of success. In a perfect world you would suspect every transaction or packet and investigate it. However this would require a ridiculously large staff which no organization can afford. Clipping levels allow you to focus in on more suspicious traffic.

You have probably tripped a clipping level without even realizing it. Have you ever made a transaction that you thought was legitimate but 5 min later you receive a phone call from the credit card company saying that they have noticed unusual activity. Whether you realized it or not you tripped over a clipping level. Now notice they did not say that they detected fraud because what they found is 70–80% of the time bad but that means 20–30% of the time it is good. Therefore, they are just investigating it to make sure.

Since we have limited resources on the cyber security side, we want to take this same approach to looking for the APT. In an ideal situation every packet would be investigated as a compromise but we would need a huge team and enormous amount of resources. Therefore we look for items that are bad 70–80% of the time to reduce the amount of space we need to search.

As introduction to outbound detection using clipping levels let's look at some brief examples. It is important to remember that activity called out by clipping levels are not 100% bad otherwise they would be signatures and signatures are too rigid and not flexible enough to deal with the APT. When you look at the clipping levels it is common for people to say that they can think of some cases where the clipping levels would trip normal traffic. In reality you should be able to think of

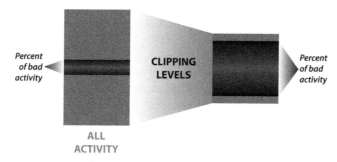

FIGURE 6.2 Clipping Levels Reduce the Amount of Information That Needs to be Searched

20–30% of the cases where this is true. Second thing to remember when talking about clipping levels is that every organization is unique and different. The clipping levels that we listed are meant to work for most organizations. Based on the unique requirements for your enterprise, the clipping levels might have to be adjusted.

The following are clipping levels that we found to be most effective at looking at outbound traffic to detect the APT:

1. *Destination IP address vs. domain name*—most legitimate users utilize domain names for outbound connections and most attackers utilize pure IP addresses. Some attackers do utilize dynamic DNS but this would typically fit under the 30% exception that is acceptable with clipping levels. For all outbound traffic, take the destination IP address and see if there is an entry in the DNS cache. If there is, this mean the connection started off as a domain name and is more indicative of a normal user and is OK. If there is no entry in the DNS cache, this means the connection started off as a pure IP connection and is more indicative of an attacker and the clipping level should be flagged.

   While it was not part of the original design, IP addresses are positional. That means you can tell where in the world the endpoint of a connection is coming from by looking at the IP address. Therefore, if you know what countries your organization should be doing business with and you notice outbound connections to an IP address in a foreign country that is not on the list of approved countries, the connection could also be flagged as anomalous.

2. *Length of the Connection*—Normal users connections are relatively short for most activity like web surfing. Attackers, however, create outbound command and control channels which are often long so the attacker can extract information from the organization. For this clipping level look at the length of the connection. If it is shorter than 5 min it is most likely normal traffic and is OK. If the connection is longer than 5 min it is more indicative of the APT and should be flagged. Remember that every organization is different so the clipping levels might need to be adjusted for each organization. For example if you have applications that make connections for 8 min, it might have to be adjusted to 10 or 15 min to be effective.

3. *Amount of Data*—Normal users when they make outbound connections send a small amount of information out of the organization and receive a large amount of information back. Attackers, especially with the APT, send large amounts of information out of the organization which looks quite different from normal traffic. For this clipping level if the amount of data per connection is under 5MB it is normal and OK. If the amount of traffic is greater than 5MB, it trips the clipping level and an alert should be sent off. With regard to the APT and damage, this clipping level usually proves to be the most useful because it gets at the heart of what is so damaging about the APT—extraction of critical data from an organization. However, for this clipping level to be useful it is critical that it is tuned for each organization, because data flow is very dependent on the business that is being performed.

4. *(Optional) Number of Packets*—Tied to the length of the connection is the number of packets. Normal users make a small number of requests outbound and receive a large number of packets back. The attacker when they compromise a system to use it as a command and control channel send a small number of packets inbound and a large number of packets outbound. If the number of outbound packets is under 500 it is normal traffic but if the number of packets is over 500 for a given session, the clipping level should be set off. This one is listed as optional because it has the most variance associated with and prone to false alarms. Traditionally when we work on analyzing outbound traffic for the APT, we usually do not use this clipping level. However to be thorough, we included it in the book for completeness.

What is important to point out about these clipping levels is that they are quite different than most normal approaches to security. Most of our traditional security relies on the ability to be able to see and analyze the payload for the security devices to make an appropriate decision. One of the favorite tools of the APT is to utilize an encrypted outbound connection. By making the outbound connection encrypted renders most traditional security devices useless and allows the APT to fly stealth under the radar. If you look at the clipping levels closely you will notice that encryption does not matter. Even if the payload is encrypted, these clipping levels will work perfectly fine. In order to defend against the APT, we need to understand how the attacker works and turn their greatness strengths into their biggest weaknesses.

This hopefully gives you an idea of the new way we need to approach security to deal with the APT. One of the rules we always tell our clients, is try out the techniques before you critique them. The above clipping levels seem very straightforward by they are highly effective. For example, we had a client that had over 130,000 endpoints and they received calls from a third party that their information was being extracted out of the organization. They spent over three weeks trying to find the compromised systems and did not have any luck. They had teams working around the clock but there was just too much information. We came onsite and went through their data using the three primary clipping levels discussed above and created a top ten list for each of those clipping levels. We then compared the three lists to see which systems are on all three lists and there were six systems listed. After detailed analysis it turned out three of the systems was the primary compromise that they were concerned with. Two of the systems were actually a separate compromise extracting information to a different country that they were not even aware what was happening. The last system turned out to be an online video store that a rogue administrator was running out of their data center that no one was aware of. The only word we had when we found the illegal video store was awesome. It makes you really wonder and shake your head of how little organizations know about what is happening in their organization. The point of this example is they spent significant amount of resources for a month and was not able to find the compromised systems because there was too much data. By utilizing clipping levels to reduce the search space we were able to find the system within a few days.

Organizations need to move from doing good things, looking at all of the traffic, to do the right things which is looking at the traffic that matters. To catch the APT it is a quality game not a quantity game.

The next question to ask is how does this get implemented? One common methods is to use event correlation tools like Splunk that can correlate all of the information, analyze clipping levels, and produce the information of value.

While Security Incident and Event Management (SIEM) tools can be used to perform the clipping levels in can also be done at a network level via NAC. NAC or network access control is a very underutilized technology. Many organizations use it when a device first connects to the network and NAC goes to sleep. However with proper monitoring, NAC can be used to do continuous monitoring because it typically works at a switch level and switches see everything going in and out of an organization. Instead of just having NAC perform an initial check when a system connects, NAC can build profiles for each user and with scripting track the clipping levels. When a clipping level is exceeded it can either drop the system to a lower trust level to contain and control the damage or send off an alert to an administrator so additional action can be taken. While the latter method of performing alerting will work, one of the reasons why organizations are losing the battle is because they are still performing manual-based methods. While some techniques with the APT are manual, one of the main reasons APT is so effective is that the threat performs enough analysis to be able to automate the actual attack and extraction of information to increase the chance of success, reduce the exposure time and be more stealthy. Therefore as defenders we must fight fire with fire and utilize automation as a way to be able to effectively keep pace with the attacker. This is the reason we prefer having a network configured with different network segments or VLANs based on trust and access and when traffic exceeds a clipping level, the system is dropped to a lower trust segment.

NETWORK VS. HOST

The original philosophy of security was to keep attackers as far away from the systems and data as possible. Therefore blocking at attack at a network entry point is better than letting the attacker get to the host and blocking them on the system where the data resides. Today we do not have that luxury. Attackers are going to make it to the host. Also, with the increased mobile technology that organizations are utilizing, it is critical that security be pushed out to hosts and not reside just on the network.

In addition, portable devices such as laptops continue to have very large hard drives and often get plugged into untrusted networks. Robust network security is of value when computers are plugged into a private network. However, what happens when that laptop gets plugged into a hotel or coffee shop, now all of the network security is gone and the system becomes a big target. Once again we cannot forget about network-level security, but it must be complimented with robust host-level protection.

When we talk about host-based protection it is critical to remember two important points:

1. *All devices must get proper protection*—many organizations when they approach security let the form factor of the device dictate the security. In reality, the data that is present on the device is what dictates the risk and should drive the level of security, not the size of the device. We often have organizations who we have built robust security policies that cover laptops and desktops, ask us to develop a security policy for mobile devices. We often tell them that since the same data will reside on both devices the policy for laptops would also apply to mobile devices. They get a strange look on their face and say we cannot have 15 character passwords that change every 90 days on our mobile device. The real question is why not? If these devices have the same information, similar risks and are often easier to steal then a desktop, why would they not be protected in the same why. Data should drive security decisions not the portability of the device we are using. This philosophy not only holds true for security policies, it also holds true for end point protection. Very sensitive information should have a series of protections that are required in order for the data to exist on a device. For example, any critical data should only reside on devices that have full end point protection both preventive and detective measures. In addition, since new vulnerabilities are being discovered all of the time, proper patch management should also be running on the host. The response we get from clients is that these new mobile devices do not have full end point protection or patch management available. The answer might be that these are not ready for the enterprise. An enterprise ready device is not just about functionality, it is about functionality and security. If a new device represents an unnecessary risk to the enterprise, maybe the device is not ready to be used within the organization. Letting functionality drive business decisions was maybe OK ten years ago, but it does not work today. Today security is about making hard decisions, not easy decisions. As we tell our clients, you are going to have to pay; you either pay now or pay later. Making a business case that a new device is not ready for the enterprise today might be painful, but putting it on the network without proper security will be much more painful after a breach occurs.

2. *All operating systems require end point protection*—many organizations will read this previous statement and say that all of their Windows systems are protected with endpoint protection. That is a good starting point but it is not all operating systems. People often make the mistake that only Windows systems have vulnerabilities and exposures. Therefore attackers only go after Windows systems. Building operating systems is hard and all operating systems have vulnerabilities. The bottom line is there is no perfect operating system and all operating systems have vulnerabilities and exposures that will allow them to be compromised. Bottom line is all operating systems need end point protection.

The real question is if this is true and all operating systems have exposures, why is there so much more focus on Microsoft than other operating systems? It is important to remember that while all operating systems have vulnerabilities, attackers are going to go after the target that has the highest return on investment or the best chance of getting in. Translation, they are going to focus in on the most popular operating system. Since Microsoft has approximately a 90% install based on traditional computers, this is often the target. To help put these numbers in perspective we have to look at the exploit to vulnerability ratio. Remember a vulnerability is a weakness in a system. Just because there is a weakness does not mean that there is any easy way to break in. An exploit is a threat that takes advantage of a vulnerability and uses it to compromise a system. Since Windows was so popular if you go back ten years, the ratio of exploit to vulnerability for Windows was 1/2—this means there was one exploit for every two vulnerabilities. Approximately ten years ago the ratio for Linux and Apple was 1/47. This means that if there were 200 vulnerabilities found for an operating system there would be 100 Windows exploit but 4 Linux or Apple exploits. Since organization typically track exploits as a way to measure security, Windows looked a lot worse.

However, the winds of change are upon us. Based on the high initial focus of attackers going after Windows system, organizations put a lot of energy and effort into securing them. Today most Windows systems are locked down and fairly secure. The chance of getting into a Windows system today is much harder than it was in the past. However since many organization did not see Linux and Apple systems as a major threat many of those systems did not have proper endpoint security installed. Now from an attackers perspective would you go after the 90% that have end point protection or the 10% that do not. Therefore we have seen the exploit to vulnerability ratio for Windows stay at a 1/2 but the ration for Apple and Linux switch from 1/47 to 1/9 showing that more attackers are focusing their energy effort on other operating systems. The contributing factor is if you change the percent from traditional desktop to tablets and all of the new computing devices the percent of Apple and Linux boxes are also increasing.

Bottom line, any device that has critical information and data on it needs to be protected and locked down. In the past if you only focused on the high percent items, you might have a chance of being successful. Today, the APT is extremely thorough and they will always find the weakest link. If you have several operating systems in your environment all with sensitive information and some are left unprotected, that is what the attacker is going to go after. Odds might be something you want to try if you go to Vegas, but when it comes to security the odds are never in your favor and you will always lose.

MAKING HARD DECISIONS

When I started working in security for the government, I remember being trained back in the 1980s by a very senior security analyst. He put his arm on my shoulder and said son, let me tell you how we do security. We are going to attend meetings and the first time someone asks you whether they can do something in the name of security you always say NO. At that point most of the people will go away. The second time they ask you the same question and ask whether they can do it in the name of security you say NO again. Most requests you will never hear from again. If they come back a third time, you say that we will analyze it and we will then look at it very closely to see if it makes sense for the business.

The approach of saying no to security might have worked over ten years ago but today it does not work. Today if someone asks if they can do something in the name of security and you say NO, they will just not invite you to the meetings and treat it as a covert operation. In many cases, by the time you find out about it, they already received funding and you cannot stop it. Saying NO does not work today. You need to make sure security is engaged through the entire process and from the very beginning, understand and assess the risk and make sure key business decision makers understand the impact to the business.

Technology is necessary for companies to be successful today. If security says NO, the organization will think that security does not understand the business and security will continue to be ineffective. The APT understands the business and will constantly exploit new technologies that organizations are going to deploy. If security does not engage with these new technologies but the APT is tracking and exploiting them, you are going to lose. Security needs to act like the APT, continuously tracking new technology, recognizing they are going to be deployed within an organization and seeing how it can be done in a secure manner.

In addition to not saying NO, security has to change their role from picking a side in a fight to being an honest broker. This new role to be effective in security involves thinking more like a business person than a pure technologist. Instead of saying an idea is to high a risk and saying no because the technology does not make sense. To deal with the APT, the security professional needs to present both sides of the story, showing what you gain and what you lose by pursuing a new idea or new technology. Both sides need to be presented to the executive so they can determine whether they want to except the risk or not but the executives need to be fully aware of the exposure.

This sometimes requires thinking outside of the box and challenging the way we traditionally do business.

Let's look at an example. One of the common ways that the APT exploits an organization is by sending a well-crafted and targeted email to an individual at an organization with an attachment that looks legitimate. The user is tricked into opening the attachment that contains malicious code, exploits the system and creates a pivot point for further exploitation. An obvious way of minimizing and stopping this particular APT is to block all attachments coming in from outside of the organization. If we perform this with the old security hat on where we go into a meeting and say we must block all attachments coming in from outside addresses, everyone will look at you like you are crazy. Senior executives will say that security does not understand the business and this will be too big an impact to the organization. When you pick a side in a fight you will often lose because no one likes change. The big problem is people like the status quo and will usually fight any change. The main issue is that they see blocking all attachments as having a big impact to the business and assumes that the way they are doing things today is perfectly fine and represents no risk at all to the enterprise. As we all know, the way things are being done today is absolutely not secure but by picking a side in the fight, the executives will never see this. It is better to be the honest broker. Go to the executives and present both sides of the story, this is the problem today, this is an alternative, which decision would you like to make?

Let's use a recent client who was having a major problem with the APT and the security team kept picking a side in the fight, losing and the threat continued to cause significant harm. Our approach was to change how they looked at the problem and shift the security team from a fighter to an honest broker. We went to the executives and presented the two main options:

- *Option 1*—Continue doing what you are doing and allow all email attachments into the organization. However based on analysis over the last year this will cost you approximately $2 million per year based on stolen intellectual property and damage to the organization.
- *Option 2*—Block all attachments from coming into the organization from external addresses. By performing analysis based on productivity of employees, frustration and impact to customer communication, this option will cost you approximately $600k per year.

By performing this analysis, the executives now had a clear picture of what the impact would be to the organization. The problem with the old approach of saying we must block attachments is they saw this as hurting the business but assumed that what they were currently doing today was fine. They did not realize the amount of impact the current way of doing business was having on the organization. To put these options another way, do you want to lose $2 million or $600k. You are going to lose money, the question is how much. By always presenting both sides of the equation, with potential monetary loss, now helps put the solutions and decisions in perspective.

While these options are a good starting point, they are typically the extremes and while they do work in some environments, they are usually not the best choice. The choice for many clients including this one was super secret option number 3:

- *Option 3*—Allow attachments only from trusted organizations or clients and block everything else. When being the honest broker in security and thinking like a business person, starting with the two extremes is a solid starting point, but often the best solution is a middle ground or compromise. In this particular case, the client had a large amount of historical email in which we could determine which external entities needed to send them attachments and created a white listing application that allowed those applications through and nothing else. Ideally utilizing digital signatures to verify the authenticity of the originator was the ideal solution, but this required additional time to setup and configure. The important thing to point out with this approach is we changed the traditional way of thinking about security which was looking for bad and blocking it. Now the organization was looking for good and blocking everything else. When attacks first starting happening, organizations would look for and spot signatures or patterns of attack, block those and allow everything else into the organization. With traditional threats this approach has some chance of success. With the APT, because it looks and acts like normal traffic, this approach of looking for bad does not scale. Today we need to determine what is good and block everything else.

While option 3 is a good short-term solution, the real solution is Option 4 which is to utilize digital signatures to verify all entities sending emails with attachments or links and dropping any emails that have an invalid or no digital signature. Since this requires installation and use of specialized software and close coordination with all customers who will be communicating with email, it often takes more planning to be successful. While the APT will try to adapt, when an organization utilizes robust cryptographic authentication via digital signatures to determine what is legitimate and blocking everything else, makes it very difficult for the APT to be successful.

When putting dollar values on loss and performing quantitative analysis, it is important to remember that risk is the probability for loss which means there is uncertainty involved. These are not exact numbers. If you could with 100% certainty determine the monetary loss a threat was going to have it would no longer be risk and therefore no longer be security. We have to do what the insurance industry does and based on historical information and what is happening to other similar organization, make a determination of what the impact will be to the organization. Remember that while quantitative analysis is more valuable for business decision-making it takes too long to come up with exact numeric values for every risk. With security it is often better to perform qualitative analysis, narrowing down the high-risk items and performing a limited quantitative analysis, just on those high-risk items. The more you can think and act like the executives from a business perspective, the more successful you will be overall in security.

Another example of showing how security has to switch from saying NO to being the honest broker is with the cloud. If you say no to the cloud you will lose, because in tough economic times you cannot argue with cost savings. The better approach is to be the honest broker. Present both sides of the equation showing what do you gain and lose by going to the cloud and allow the business decision makers to make the best informed decision.

Organizations often view cloud activity as a binary yes or no decision—either do everything in the cloud or do nothing in the cloud. Neither of these options is a smart choice. Exposing all company data to the cloud infrastructure poses unnecessary and foolish risks. On the other hand, preventing all information sharing in the cloud eliminates opportunities for major cost savings. Instead, as part of building a transition roadmap, business processes, services and applications should be systematically assessed, risk evaluated, and compartmentalized into three security categories:

Cloud Ready (existing applications that are good to go; information that is acceptable for public consumption), *Potential Cloud* (sensitive information; may be okay in the future following some sanitization and/or executive approval to increase risk level), and *Never Cloud* (information that should never be publicly available based on defined control, risk, and exposure levels). Establishing this logical decision-making criteria secures critical information and assets, and enables acceptance, buy-in and accountability for an optimized cloud strategy from the business units responsible for enterprise cloud management. In order to properly segment applications on whether they are cloud ready or not, information needs to be properly classified so appropriate risk decisions can be made. It is always important to remember that while the cloud does have cost savings, it can also be targeted by the APT to more easily steal information.

If we are not careful, the cloud changes the traditional paradigm. Instead of targeting one organization, finding a method of exploitation and breaking in and stealing one organization's critical information. The cloud could allow the APT to target one organization, a cloud provider and now have access to thousands of organizations critical information.

IS AV/HOST PROTECTION DEAD?

One of the debates that we often hear is when threats are released or new challenges are presented to an organization, i.e. the APT, that bypass or minimize the impact of a certain device it is easy to say that a given technology is dead or useless. Before we dive directly into this issue we have to remember that there is no silver bullet when it comes to security. There is no single technology that if we deploy will instantly make our network security and protect against all threats. Therefore any single technology in the hands of an expert can be bypassed or have weaknesses found with it. This is the whole reason why we always rely on a defense in depth strategy to implement effective security because no single device by itself can provide proper protection. Let's imagine for a second that there was a technology that would make a network 100% secure. Would we want to use it? The answer is absolutely not and the reason is simple. If there was a single technology that was used to provide all of the security, how many devices would an attacker have to bypass, compromise, or find a vulnerability with to get into your network? Just one. That would be too easy for the attacker. Therefore we always want to have multiple layers of prevention and detection so if one layer fails another layer will take over.

It is easy to take a single technology in a lab setting and find attacks that the APT can use to bypass and get around those technologies. With a given advanced attack, a given technology might be less effective than it once was but that does not mean it is dead. Dead means it has no value or usefulness. The question I always ask when people imply a technology is dead is look at what it did for the last week and see if it caught, prevented, or detected any attacks. If it did, it is not dead, it is just less effective against certain attack vectors.

One of the areas that often get criticized is whether host-based AV or IDS is dead because many of the tactics that the APT uses is meant to look like a legitimate user and bypass AV software. However before we say it is dead, run a report across your enterprise for the last month and look at how many viruses the AV software detected. If it is like most of our clients that number is several hundred and for large networks several thousand. A technology that costs around $30 per client and catches hundreds of pieces of malicious code does not sound dead to me. The real concern when people say a technology is dead is the temptation is to remove or uninstall it from a system. As you can see with the case of AV software, that would be a very dangerous thing to do.

The analogy I like to use when saying whether AV is dead is to compare it to household aspirin. Aspirin was developed in the 1950s and when it was first developed it was used to help with a large number if alignments. Over the years more powerful pain killers came out and aspirin is used for a lot less issues than it was in the 1950s. However if you go to most people's home and ask for an aspirin, you can find it in most medicine cabinets. It is easy to say that aspirin is used a lot less and there are other more powerful drugs available, but the reason people still have aspirin because is it is cheap, accessible, and it works, so why not. That is the same analogy that I used with traditional AV software. It does not catch watch it use to but it still catches enough items and based on the cost, why not. There is no such thing as 100% security so it should not surprise us that a smart person can study a specific security solution and find ways to bypass it. The better question to ask is not whether it is dead but where does it work well and what are its weaknesses. For the weaknesses make sure other technologies are used to complement it. Since AV is not very effective against the APT, other technologies absolutely have to be used but remember, the goal of security is to protect against all attacks, including the APT, not just a single threat vector.

SUMMARY

As the APT continues to evolve we have to recognize that traditional measures of defense are no longer going to work. Traditional attacks were not persistent and went after the low hanging fruit as a way to compromise an enterprise. If you fixed the big items and applied patches you would be fine. Today that is not true. While we always hope to prevent attacks, we have to recognize that some attacks will sneak in and our golden rule has to be prevention is ideal but detection is a must.

An ancient Chinese curse threatens, "May you live in interesting times." When it comes to cyber security this statement is definitely true. We cannot go a day without hearing about another organization being compromised. No one is spared. Government, commercial, universities, and non-profits are all being compromised. The APT has changed the game forever and therefore our mindset has to change from pure prevention to one of always hunting and looking for the attacker. For many organizations it is a very frightening, frustrating and scary time because the old tools and methodology that we have used in the past to properly defend our networks no longer works. That does not mean we should stop what we are doing or get rid of our traditional security. We just have to augment and keep changing our defense measures in the same way that attackers are changing their offensive measures. Organizations are spending tremendous amount of money, energy, and effort on security and they are still getting compromised.

One executive pulled me aside during a consultant engagement and said be honest with me, is trying to secure an organization helpless and should we just give up. The good news is things are not hopeless and you can get ahead of the curve but we have to change our way of thinking. As Albert Einstein said, "We cannot solve our problems with the same thinking we used when we created them." We must change our thinking from a purely preventive mindset to one that recognizes we can be compromised and focuses on timely detection. This initially is hard to swallow but we have to recognize that we are going to be compromised and the question now is containing and controlling the damage.

The threat has changed dramatically over the last three years, but our approach to security has not changed. Traditional threats were treated by using reactive security. With today's threats increasing and becoming more stealthy, targeted, and data focused, reactive security no longer works. Predictive, proactive security is the answer. We need to stop looking for signs of an attack and get inside the mind of the adversary and understand how they think and operate.

Incident Response: Respond and Recover

The game of security has changed and you cannot be successful if you do not understand the rules. Think of how difficult it would be if you showed up to a game thinking you were playing rugby but in reality everyone else was playing soccer and no one told you. It would be extremely frustrating when you started tackling people, receiving penalties and not knowing why. Before you embark on an endeavor, it is always important to understand the rules of engagement. Security is no different, if you do not have agreement on your job and you start doing x but the executives believe you should be doing y, it will be very frustrating because you will not understand what you are doing wrong. First and most important, it is critical to make sure executives understand that networks are going to be compromised. If they view a compromise as a sign of weakness and you understand that based on the risk posture and resources that compromises are going to occur, you will be setup for failure. It is critical to make sure everyone understands the current threat landscape and is in agreement with what could and will happen.

While it might seem like a simple question, what is your job in security? Many people say to keep the organization safe, which is partly true. In reality security is all about making sure the organization understands and manages risk at an appropriate level. A key rule to be successful in security is no surprises. Everyone in the organization should understand the threat-level and associated risks and if bad things happen, they should be prepared, not caught off guard. This means that we have to accept that compromises are going to occur. Many organizations state that if a breach occurs security has failed and did not do their job correctly. That is absolutely and completely wrong. Every organization needs to take risks in order to accomplish their mission. As soon as you accept a risk that means that compromises can occur. For example, an owner of a store can prevent shoplifting and theft by locking all of the doors and all of the Windows, not allowing anyone in or anyone to leave. While this will work to prevent the threat, the store will also go out of business because no legitimate customers would be allowed in. Therefore every owner of a store has to recognize that shoplifting will occur and accept the risk. Store owners know that items will get stolen but they structure the layout of their store and complement it with video surveillance to reduce the risk to an acceptable level, but there is a still a level of risk that has to be accepted. In an organization, the same level of logic has to occur. We have to recognize that there is always some risk, determine what the acceptable level of risk is and accept with recognition of what that means. It means that a compromise could occur and there could be loss to the organization. If a compromise occurs against a risk that the organization was aware of and decided to accept the risk, security did nothing wrong. That is the cost of doing business. We have to recognize and make sure that everyone in the organization is aware that the rules have changed. The old rule was any compromise is a bad thing. The new rules are compromises are a part of doing business and the goal is to make sure all critical risks have been identified and mitigated to a level consistent with corporate culture.

It is always interesting when giving a keynote presentation to watch people's expression when you make the statement that no matter how hard you try or what you do, your organization will be compromised and most likely is compromised already. Based on the facial expressions that people make you can tell that they are surprised. This means they fully expect their organization to be 100% secure. Many organizations assume that if you perform security correctly, you will never ever be broken into and all attacks with be stopped. While you could argue that statement was never true, it is definitely not true today when we are dealing with the APT. Just like saying that you will never get sick is naïve, saying you will never get broken into is just as naïve. It is not a matter of if an incident is going to occur but when.

One of the key underlying themes of this book that highlights this fact is the statement prevention is ideal but detection is a must. In this day and age, any size and type organization is going to have breaches and incidents occur, the question is how quickly can you detect it and how fast you can react to minimize the impact to an organization? Two main problems with the APT emphasizing the importance of incident response:

- *APTs are often detected by a third party*—as we have talked about throughout this book, many organizations are deploying solutions that are not effective for dealing with the APT. One of the common themes that occurs when we work APT incident response is that the client was not the one who actually detected that they were compromised. When we are contacted by a client they often tell us that that they have just been contacted by a third party such as law enforcement or a cloud provider telling them that they have found the organization's sensitive data on systems on the Internet, where the information should not be located. While this chapter is focused in on incident response with the APT, we have to recognize that if an organization is not able to detect the APT, how are they going to be able to respond to a compromise? *Organizations usually do not detect an APT for 6–9 months after compromise*—based on the idea that most organizations are not able to detect when they are compromised, it should not be surprising that organizations are often compromised for 6–9 months before it is detected. While incident response is still important to be performed at any time in the lifecycle of an attack, the real benefit is to perform it during an incident to minimize the damage, not perform it after all of the information has been stolen. With that said, even 6 months after the attack, incident response is still critical because the goal of the APT is often to have access to a system for the next several years so they can continue to monitor and extract information from the site. While incident response being performed 6 months after a compromise is not great, it is still critical to control and minimize long-term compromise. The general rule is sooner is better; 6 h is better than 6 days which is better than 6 weeks which is better than 6 months which is better than 6 years.

There is a lot of focus, energy and effort put against incident response today, but what we have found is not everyone is using the same definitions. Therefore in order to make sure that we are using consistent terminology, the following terms will be used throughout this section:

- *Event*—An observable occurrence or activity that is being performed. The easiest way to think of an event is an entry in a log file. Logs typically store events and become the key evidence in proving what has happened on a system. This is the reason why protection and control of the log files is so important is because they contain the events.
- *Incident*—An adverse event resulting in harm or the threat of an adverse event that could cause potential harm to computer systems or data. Anything that impacts or could impact a system falls under an incident. It is important to remember that intent does not matter. Both an APT breaking into a system and a pipe breaking and flooding your data center would be considered an incident.
- *Incident Response (IR)*—Actions taken subsequent to an incident to understand the incident and take remedial action. The key theme of security is prevention is ideal but detection is a must. Incident response focuses in on once an attack is detected, assessing the damage, responding and recovering back to normal operation. If normal operations are interrupted when an incident occurs, IR focuses on recovery and getting the organization back up and running.
- *Computer Forensics*—The science of analyzing, finding, and presenting digital evidence in court. One of the key steps of incident response is to figure out what happened. Discovering evidence is critical to determining what happening and for making a case in court to prove your side in order to get a favorable ruling. Forensics focuses in on making sure you have the information you need to determine and prove what happened.

THE NEW RULE

The original rule that we have been using in this book is prevention is ideal but detection is a must. We are going to expand the rule in this chapter to be prevention is ideal but detection is a must, however detection without response is useless. What is the point of detecting an attack if you are not going to do anything about it? We also have to remember some of the key aspects of our defensive measures:

- *Prevention*—The main benefit of a preventive measure is that it stops an attack. This means that it is able to stop any damage *before* it occurs. As we have discussed, this is ideal to stop all damage before it happens. However this is not always possible and with very sophisticated attacks, there is always a chance they can defeat or get around any defensive measure. Since before any damage occurs is ideal, this is where the first part of our statement comes from, prevention is ideal.
- *Detection*—If an attacker is able to bypass a preventive measure and attack an organization, the goal is to minimize the damage by detecting them as soon as possible. Because detection is occurring *during* an attack, reaction time is critical.
- *Response*—Incident response is dealing with the damage *after* it is detected and one of its goals is to fix the problem, make sure it does not happen again and recover the organization back to a normal state of operation.

Preventive technologies like firewalls and IPS are very well understand in most organizations. What is nice about a preventive technology is once it is configured, setup, validated, and tested, it can perform it jobs without the manual assistance of a human. Once a ruleset is in place, the firewall will block all traffic and perform its job with no human interaction required. Systems absolutely need to be maintained and updated, but the main function of the device is meant to be automated which makes it scalable.

Detection is a different beast. The perfect example of a detective device is an alarm system in your home. In order for the alarm system to be effective, what are the two requirements: (1) 24/7 monitoring and (2) timely response. If someone is not monitoring the system and available to respond, the system will not be effective. The basic premise of an alarm system is that the detection and reaction time will be much shorter than the time it takes for harm to be caused. Typically it would take someone 1–2 h to rob your house. With an alarm system, the alarm will alert and be verified within 3 min and the police will show up within 15 min. There will still be some damage but it is contained and the robbers are caught. How effective would an alarm system be if it took 5 h for the alarm to be verified and the police to show up? The answer is not very effective because by the time the police showed up the robber was gone and all of your items were stolen. Incident response would still be needed to contact insurance and make sure you do not get robbed again, but detection would have been less effective in that particular case. Therefore in our environments the value add of detection is how quickly can incidents be detected and responded to. This is a common area of mistake for organizations. We had one client who installed an IDS on their network and said that they will review all alerts from 1–5 pm every Friday. That would be like you hiring an alarm company to monitor your house, but they are not going to monitor 24/7, they will only review the alerts once a week. A robber would break into your house on Tuesday, steal all of your items and leave. On Friday, the alarm company checks and sees that you have been robbed and calls you up on vacation and tells you that you have been robbed on Tuesday. You can imagine that would not be very helpful. An alarm system requires timely, manual intervention. If an IDS sets off an alert and no one is available to take action, what happens? The attacker just keeps causing more and more damage. The other important point to bring up is detection implies that a preventive measure failed. In a perfect world we should prevent all attacks. If an attack was detected, it means the prevention was not effective and we should look at ways to make it more effective. While it is ideal to prevent all attacks we have to remember that some of the sophisticated types of APT, are so stealthy that while prevention is ideal, detection is a must and sometimes the only chance of containing damage.

Since detection is during an attack, this means there is some damage to your organization and security was not effective as it should be. In those cases, incident response is critical to repair the damage and recover the organization. Since previous chapters covered preventing and detecting the APT, this chapter will talk about incident response.

SUICIDAL MINDSET

While incident response is a necessity since all attacks cannot be stopped, it is not an ideal state to operate in. In a perfect world we want to reduce and minimize the number of success attacks. Purely from a business perspective having an incident or a breach should not be considered a good thing. While the previous sentence is absolutely true—an organization does not want to have a breach or a compromise—it often amazes me that some security staff will say the best thing that happened to them was that they had a breach because it finally got everyone's attention and they started listening to the security team. As we focus on incident response, while they are a necessary evil, they are not something that people should want or be viewed as being good for the organization. When someone says the best thing that could happen to us is we have a compromise is very concerning. If you have a friend that says the best thing that could happen to me is if I get hit by a car, that would be concerning to you. That is bordering on a suicidal mindset and if you really cared about that person you would take action and help them. The fact that many organizations today are in a suicidal mindset is concerning and means they need help.

If the best thing that could happen or the best thing that did happen to your organization was a breach because finally the executives understand that security is important, it is essence means security is not doing their job correctly. I know some people might get mad with that statement but remember the goal of security is to make sure everyone in the organization understands and recognizes the risk. Having a breach is one way to show an organization that the risk is real but that can be done without having a breach. There is enough information and data available that with careful analysis the same points can be made to the executives without have to experience loss to the organization. It is critical to make sure that the executives and security team are speaking a common language and there is a understanding of the risk posture and current exposures the organization faces.

In order to be successful in security and especially to be successful with the APT it is critical that risks and exposures are properly communicated to the executives. This is done by having clear metrics that can be tracked to grades so executives are fully aware that a high risk low scoring system has such as high chance of a compromise occurring that it is equivalent to a compromise. If you can get to the point where you have built up enough confidence with the executives that they trust the accuracy of the metrics and grades that are assigned to overall risk, business decisions can be made against the scores.

One way to track and create metrics is by using the SANS 20 Critical Controls:

1. Inventory of Authorized and Unauthorized Devices.
2. Inventory of Authorized and Unauthorized Software.
3. Secure Configurations for Hardware and Software on Laptops, Workstations, and Servers.
4. Continuous Vulnerability Assessment and Remediation.
5. Malware Defenses.
6. Application Software Security.
7. Wireless Device Control.
8. Data Recovery Capability (validated manually).
9. Security Skills Assessment and Appropriate Training to Fill Gaps (validated manually).
10. Secure Configurations for Network Devices such as Firewalls, Routers, and Switches.
11. Limitation and Control of Network Ports, Protocols, and Services.
12. Controlled Use of Administrative Privileges.
13. Boundary Defense.
14. Maintenance, Monitoring, and Analysis of Security Audit Logs.
15. Controlled Access Based on the Need to Know.
16. Account Monitoring and Control.
17. Data Loss Prevention.
18. Incident Response Capability (validated manually).
19. Secure Network Engineering (validated manually).
20. Penetration Tests and Red Team Exercises (validated manually).

The Critical Controls aims to begin the process of establishing a prioritized baseline of information security measures and controls that can be applied across federal and commercial environments to deal with various threats to include the APT. The consensual effort that produced this document identifies 20 specific technical security controls that are viewed as effective in blocking and detecting currently known high-priority attacks as well as those attack types expected in the near future. Each of the 20 control areas includes multiple individual subcontrols that specify actions an organization can take to help improve its defenses.

The control areas and individual subcontrols focus on various technical aspects of information security with the primary goal of helping organizations prioritize their efforts to defend against today's most common and damaging computer and network attacks. Outside of the technical realm, a comprehensive security program should also take into account many other areas of security, including overall policy, organizational structure, personnel issues (e.g. background checks, etc.), awareness, and physical security. The guiding principles used in devising these control areas and their associated subcontrols include the following:

- Defenses should focus on addressing the most common and damaging attack activities occurring today, and those anticipated in the near future.
- Enterprise environments must ensure that consistent controls are in place across the organization to effectively negate attacks.
- Defenses should be automated where possible and periodically or continuously measured using automated measurement techniques where feasible.
- A variety of specific technical activities should be undertaken to produce a more consistent defense against attacks that occur on a frequent basis against numerous organizations.
- Root cause problems must be fixed in order to ensure the prevention or timely detection of attacks.
- Metrics should be established that facilitate common ground for measuring the effectiveness of security measures, providing a common language for executives, information technology specialists, auditors, and security officials to communicate about risk within the organization.

INCIDENT RESPONSE

In developing a strategy for dealing with the APT it is critical that it is multi-tiered, covering Prevention—Detection—Response. Incident response is focused on attacks that have not been prevented and after it has been detected, recovering and minimizing the chances of it occurring again. Incident response is very similar to EMT (emergency medical technicians) because they both involve an area called first responders. A first responder is often the first person on the scene after an incident or accident and they have to assess the situation and take action to prevent further exposure. In being a first responder across EMT and cyber, there are three things that are in common:

- *High stress situation*—when organizations are losing money or if someone is injured, people are not happy and very stressed. Typically during an incident there is a lot of chaos and confusion because everyone is running around trying to solve the problem. Usually during an incident there is not a good plan so while there are many people very busy, in some cases they are causing additional harm which also leads to increased stress. From an executive perspective if a large number of people have been working for many hours and things are no better off than they were before, that adds continuous stress to the organization.

- *Time is not on your side*—during an incident normal operations are interrupted which typically means an organization is losing money. This means the longer your organization is impacted the more money you are losing.
- *Mistakes are very costly*—Since time is not on your side the temptation is to go very quickly, however because it is a high stress situation there is a greater chance of mistake. During an incident any mistake could actually cause more harm and have a greater impact than during normal operation and therefore a minor mistake could compound into a major mistake during an incident.

In looking at these three characteristics in could seem like you have a dilemma in what to do during an incident. If you go slowly it is better but time is not on your side and you are losing money. If you go fast, you can get back up and running quickly but since it is a high stress environment there would be a greater chance of making a mistake. Since recovery is the ultimate goal and mistakes are very costly, it is better to do it right than rush and make mistakes. The best way to think of this is from the perspective of an ambulance driver. If you are driving an ambulance, your lights are on, the siren is going, and you are heading to an accident, what do you if you get to an intersection and you have a red light? In most jurisdictions you have to treat it as stop sign or at least slow down and proceed with caution. The comment that most people say is what if there are seven red lights between the firehouse and the accident, this could take an additional 10 min to get to the scene which could be the difference between life or death of the accident victim. While this is true they have determined it is better to go slow and arrive. Otherwise if you go fast you might get to the accident quicker but there is also a greater chance of someone who has a green light not seeing the ambulance and getting into an accident. It is better to go slow and do it right, than rush, safe a few minutes but run the risk of getting into a bigger accident. When you work on an incident think of the ambulance driver, slow and steady wins the race.

Many people who have not worked on incident response before underestimate the impact stress could have on performing a task. People look at what has to be done during an incident and comment that backing up data and running commands is something they do every day so why do we need to practice. The reason is things that are easy to do during normal operations can be very complex and difficult when you add stress to an equation. To illustrate this think of fire fighters; walking into a building is easy, walking into a burning building is completely different. Think of the following task, walking across a room being timed with a stop watch and wearing a heart monitor. Walk across the room timing how long it took you to go across the room and what your average heart rate was for performing this task. Now put on a 30lb backpack and perform the same task once again recording your time and heart rate. Now randomly place tables in the room and perform the same task. Now fill the room with smoke and perform the same task. Finally light the tables on fire and perform the same task. You are still only walking across the room but in the latter case when you have added in a lot of items to increase the stress it will take you a lot longer, it is a lot harder and your heart rate would be a lot higher. You are still performing the same task but when you change the environment and mental variables, it could have a huge impact on the overall difficulty. This is why training is so critical in being part of an incident response team.

In dealing with the APT we actually take a multi definition approach to what incident response is:

Incident response is an action plan for dealing with (1) an adverse event to an organization or (2) the threat of adverse event to an organization.

When something damaging or impactful occurs to an organization you need to take action to minimize exposure and try to prevent a similar action from occurring again in the future. There are many important parts to this definition that we need to cover. First, what is an event? An event is an observable occurrence or an entry in a log file. All incidents are composed of events but not all events are an incident. The goal of incident response is to take the log files and/or other data and determine what happened.

An adverse event is anything that interrupts normal operation. Clearly if you look at the first part of the definition of an incident that is obvious. Anything that does interrupt normal operations is an incident and needs to be dealt with. The important thing to remember with an incident is anything that interrupts normal operation is an incident but intent does not matter. Many people associate incident response with catching an attacker that is breaking in from half way across the world to steal government secrets. While hacking is definitely one part of incident response, anything that interrupts normal operations or causes the organization to not behave correctly would still be classified as an incident. What is important to remember is that while incident response would cover a wide category of incidents, it is important to categorize the incident based on the risk to the organization. Think of a fire house. When someone calls 911, the incident is classified and the appropriate personnel are deployed. Some 911 calls a single truck is deployed, some calls the entire firehouse is sent to the fire. The mistake that is often made is some organizations only classify high risk items as an incident and ignore everything else which ends up causing a lot of damage and impact that could have been avoided. Anything that interrupts normal operation is an incident, but not all incidents are dealt with in the same manner.

If you look at the first part of the definition of an incident it is dealing with an organization after an attack has occurred. Looking at our 5-step process that attackers use to break into a system, the following shows where part 1 of the definition fits in:

1. Reconnaissance.
2. Scanning.
3. Exploit:
   – Traditional incident response
4. Create backdoors.
5. Covering tracks.

Anytime an attacker exploits a system or causes harm, it absolutely is an incident and needs to be dealt with. Since proactive is always better than reactive, wouldn't it be nice if we could detect and deal with a threat before an attacker causes harm. The second part of our incident response definition deals with this: the threat of harm to an organization. What we are now doing is changing the model to being proactive as seen below:

1. Reconnaissance.
2. Scanning:
   - Threat of occurrence—proactive incident response
3. Exploit.
4. Create backdoors.
5. Covering tracks.

By utilizing part two of our definition we can actually deal with a problem before it causes harm. Many people looking at this definition will come back and say according to this definition a port scan would be an incident and the answer is yes. Some people might say that in their environment, this could be problematic because we are a university and get port scanned constantly. Before you get to upset remember that there are different categories of an incident and this might be a category that requires logging, with no action required. The reason a port scan is an incident is to remember a simple fact, normal people do not port scan a system before they connect to it. Therefore if someone is port scanning your system they are on step 2 of the 5-step process. While this is true the counter argument is that while proactive is better than reactive, there are going to be a lot more attempted attacks than successful attacks. For traditional attacks, the ration looks like the following:

1. Reconnaissance.
2. Scanning:
   - 50,000 attempted attacks.
3. Exploit:
   - 5 successful attacks.
4. Create backdoors.
5. Covering tracks.

Therefore the argument is it is easier to deal with 5 attacks than 50,000. While that might be true it is important to remember that the 50,000 attempts are going to be a lot cheaper than dealing with the 5 successful attacks. In addition this ratio is true for the traditional attacks. However because the APT is persistent, the more proactive you can be the better because if ignored the APT will eventually get in.

EVENTS/AUDIT TRAILS

It is important to remember that all incidents are composed of events. Events are entry in the log files and log files or audit trails become your evidence. No logs, no evidence, no clue of what happened. Therefore keeping and storing logs is critical in making sure that an organization knows what is happening. While there are some space requirements in keeping and storing logs, from a security perspective it is always better to store more than less. I have worked on many incidents in which I was in a cold dark data center at 3 am trying to figure out what happened and we were struggling because the organization did not store enough logs. I would look towards the heavens and say I wish they would have stored more logs. This has happened on many occasions. Many organizations do not store enough logs and it ends up making incident response much harder than it needs to be. With that said, there has never been a single incident, not even one in which I said I wish the organization had less logs, why did they log so much. I could always search through what I do not need but cannot create what I do not have. From a security perspective, do not be afraid to overdo it, when it comes to logs the more the better. However there is a potential issue that you need to be aware of. From a security perspective, logs are a good thing because they provide evidence of what occurred and can be used to find and track the attacker, figure out what they did and improve any organizations defensive measure. Logs can also be a bad thing because they could show evidence or wrong doing by the organization in legal proceedings.

One of the main questions we often receive from users is how long should we keep the logs for. The real question is how long is it going to take you to detect an attack. The logs need to be kept long enough so you can go back to before the attacker broke in and figure out what they did. With regard to the APT, since many organizations are not doing a great job detecting the APT and can be compromised for 6–9 months before they detect it, our recommendation is to keep the logs for at least 9 months. While there are absolutely storage requirements with keeping the information for a long period of time, the other piece that is often missed is the legal implications. Security likes to keep logs for a long period of time so they can go back and determined what happened. It is important to remember that logs are technically evidence that can be used against an organization in a court of law and therefore, the law department typically wants to keep logs for a short period of time. Life is about balances and it is important to coordinate with them. We just wanted to give you a heads up that in many organizations while you will push for keeping the log files for a long period of time, you could meet some resistance from the legal department.

Now that we understand the importance of logs, let's look at some examples of events:

- Ecole logged into the network.
- Ecole cd to a directory.
- The system is rebooted.
- An executable runs when the system starts.

When analyzing events it is important to never take a single event and make a decision of whether it is an incident in a vacuum. You always need to put it in perspective and look at the big picture. Any single event can either be good or bad depending on the context of what occurred around it. Junior incident handlers often make the mistake of looking at a single event and jumping to a conclusion that might not be correct.

For example, we had a client who had a junior incident response team member who would come into work at 7 am each morning and review the logs. One morning he saw in the logs that one of the critical database servers was rebooted at 3 am in the morning. He remembers reading about a new type of attack that would break in after hours and reboot the system in order to activate the malware. Without perform any other verification and using a single event of a serving being rebooted, he made the conclusion that they suffered a major breach and needed to institute the incident response plan. To make a long story short, after they pulled the system from the network and started costing the company significant money, they realized that the system had maintenance performed the previous night. The maintenance was approved by the change control board and as part of the process, the system needed to be rebooted which occurred at 3 am. Now because a well intentional but ill-informed incident response team member thought they had an incident with no validation and pulled the server, they cost the company significant money. If they would have looked at all of the logs or checked with the change control board, they could have easily determined that this was normal activity and not an incident. It is important to always validate whether a single event is an incident by looking at the facts, which are the other events in the logs. Jumping to conclusions can be very dangerous and should be avoided at all costs.

SAMPLE INCIDENTS

While the focus of this book is on APT, it is also important to understand the premise of incident response and look at a few examples to understand the depth and breadth of incidents. While understand and knowing about APTs with a plan for prevention, detection, and response is critical, it is important to make sure that you still take a holistic approach to security. One of the mistakes we have seen organizations make is they get so focused on the APT, they lose sight of other types of attacks, get breached with non-APT attacks and still have harm caused to the enterprise. The APT is critical and important but protecting your organization is what is ultimately important. In order to keep the organization secure, all incidents must be detected and dealt with to include the APT. We just need to make sure we do not miss the forest through the trees.

To make sure we have a comprehensive plan for dealing with incidents, let's look at a few examples:

- *IIS being exploited with a buffer overflow attack on a Windows 2008 Server—* this first example is very straightforward. IIS is a www server that runs on a Microsoft operating system such as Windows 2008. This is clearly an incident because it is an adverse event in which a vulnerability and threat are connecting which means a compromise is occurring and damage is being caused on the system. Since this is a DMZ system and most likely the buffer overflow is either public or going to be public which means the chance of being attacked by multiple adversaries is very high. Therefore incident response is critical in order to react in a timely manner to prevent further damage from occurring.

- *IIS attempted exploit on a RedHat Linux server*—at first glance this scenario does not seem as straightforward as the first example. In this case IIS is a Windows service that does not run on a Linux operating system. Someone is trying to utilize a Windows exploit to break into a Linux server. At quick glance it is tempted to say that the attack will not be successful and therefore it is not an incident. That conclusion is not correct because if you look at our definition, success is not one of the two criterias for classifying an incident. Clearly this does not fit the first definition because it is not an adverse event. However, if you look closely this is clearly the threat of an occurrence so would definitely fit our second definition and is absolutely an incident. To help understand this, let's look at this more closely. The main question to ask is why would someone run a Windows exploit against a Linux system. There are two answers: (1) they are morons or stupid; (2) they do not care. Trust me it is option 2. Most likely it is a worm that does not care because it knows that if it connects to enough systems it will eventually find a Windows system and break in. Many worms work in a similar fashion. The real question to ask is whether your organization has any Windows servers. In most cases the answer is yes. Therefore you have two options. Option one, ignore this and do not treat it as an incident, wait for the attacker to compromise your Windows system and deal with an incident after there is damage. Option two, is to treat it as an incident, proactively fix the Windows system so by the time the worm connects to the Windows system, it is already protected and there is no damage. In most cases, option two is the best way to go and illustrates why it is important to always treat the threat of an occurrence as an incident. By doing this allows you to switch from a reactive to a proactive approach.
- *USB Backup drive containing sensitive information is copied by an unauthorized user*—reading this example, it is absolutely an incident. The million dollar question is whether you can detect and tell whether this happens. You cannot react to an incident if you do not know it is occurring. If someone walked into a facility, took a drive, made a copy, and put it back a few hours later would you be able to detect it. This is one of the driving themes with performing APT incident response. It is great that there is a long list of what types of incidents you need to detect but the real question is whether you have the proper security in place to detect indicators of the APT, so you can react and perform incident response to minimize and control the damage.

Now that we understand some of the types of attacks, it is important to cover some of the golden rules of incident response:

- *Integrity*—the integrity of the data must be maintained starting with proper preservation and handling through analysis and reporting. One of the biggest mistakes that are often made is failure to think litigation and protection of the evidence. Even if your organization never plans on prosecuting a case, it is better to have proper evidence and not need it, than need evidence and not have it. As new laws continue to evolve, it might not be your choice on whether a case goes to court or not. Either way, accurate evidence is needed to determine what occurred and to properly remediate an incident.

- *Approved Methodology*—it is critical that you follow an approved methodology to make sure all of the proper steps are performed. Remember that an incident is a high stress environment, time is not on your side and mistakes are very costly. Therefore "winging it" is prone to mistakes and errors. Having a robust methodology will make sure that you can recover from the incident as quickly as possible.
- *Approved Tools & Techniques*—in writing code and using programs your results are only as good as the validity or trust you have in the programs that you use. If you use a crappy program or one that has unreliable results, the tool is useless. It is better to not perform any analysis than to use a tool that provides inaccurate information. During incident response it is important and critical to only use trusted and validated tools. While trusting the tool is important, you have to remember that if the evidence is going to go to court, you have to use tools that have been approved by the courts, otherwise the results will be questioned.
- *Custody / Data Integrity (e.g. Hashing)*—depending on the type of incident you are involved with, there will be people (i.e. the attacker or malicious insider) who will not want you to figure out what occurred. Therefore if you do not preserve and protect the information, someone might be able to tamper with the evidence and you would then be fixing the wrong problem. In addition, if you need to present the evidence in court and you cannot prove the integrity of the evidence, it will be brought into question and make it hard, if not difficult to

```
Command Prompt                                                    _|□|×|
E:\>dir case_ERIC290905_disk1_image.img
 Volume in drive E is DATOS
 Volume Serial Number is 2533-B511

 Directory of E:\

11/03/2006  01:49       665.387.008 case_ERIC290905_disk1_image.img
               1 File(s)     665.387.008 bytes
               0 Dir(s)      606.785.536 bytes free

E:\>md5deep case_ERIC290905_disk1_image.img
2c65ab703ce06daf29426dc35a4bbc64   E:\case_ERIC290905_disk1_image.img

E:\>type case_ERIC290905_disk1_image.img | md5deep
2c65ab703ce06daf29426dc35a4bbc64

E:\>sha1deep case_ERIC290905_disk1_image.img
504937b1a993f986a3023975fc9cf421f2e071f6   E:\case_ERIC290905_disk1_image.img

E:\>_
```

FIGURE 7.1 Cryptographic Hashing is the Best Way to Prove that the Evidence has not been Modified

win your case. The only valid way to prove the authenticity of the evidence is to use a cryptographic hash of the information, see Figure 7.1.

- *Documentation*—Preserving evidence is critical but it is important to remember that documentation is a type of evidence. It is critical that all activities are recorded accurately to be able to prove and show what you did in investigating the incident. While preservation of digital evidence is critical, it is also important to track everything that the incident response team did to be able to make a determination of what happened on the network.
- *Authority*—It is important to know your job and do not overstep your authority. Remember you are the technical person working on the case; you typically are not an attorney or law enforcement. While the components involving both attorneys and law enforcements are often critical parts of an incident, it is not the technical person's job to perform these activities. Not only do they not have the proper authority but in many cases they do not have the proper training and therefore can make mistakes and cause more harm than good. Working with other people on your team during an incident is critical but it is always important to make sure you play your position and only play positions in which you are properly trained and authorized to do so.

6-STEP PROCESS

In order to increase your chance of success, it is critical that we always follow a set process when handling an incident. The following is the industry standard for handling an incident:

1. *Preparation*—since time is not on your side during an incident, preparation is concerned with making sure you have everything you need in order to handle the incident in an efficient and timely manner.
2. *Identification*—in order to make sure the incident response team can respond in a timely manner means that we need to have a way to be able to identify an incident quickly. If it takes an organization 4 months to identify that there is an incident, the fact that the team responded within 2 h is not relevant to the amount of damage that is caused to the environment. It is important that all employees are trained and understand what they need to do if they see something unusual.
3. *Containment*—after an incident has been confirmed, the first step is to stabilize the environment and make sure the problem does not get any worse. Included as part of containment is to make sure the attacker is no longer in the network performing damage or harm.
4. *Eradication*—during an incident it is critical to figure out what happened, how the compromise occurred and to improve the overall security to minimize the chance of a similar compromise from occurring. Having an incident is bad, having a re-occurrence or re-infection could be disastrous.

5. *Recovery*—the ultimate goal of incident response is recovery to get operations back up and running. Once the problem has been identified and fixed, you want to get the systems back up and running again. Recovery includes not only rebuilding the systems but also restoring all data and information back to the servers.

6. *Lesson Learned*—whenever you are dealing with a high stress environment mistakes will be made. There is no such thing as a perfect incident. The idea of incident response is constant improvement. Also included in lessons learned is putting together an report to executives covering a postmortem of what occurred and what can be done to minimize it from occurring again in the future.

Each of these steps will be covered in more detail in this chapter but Figure 7.2, shows how all of the pieces fit together. What is important to note is even though incident response is a 6-step process, it is really a continuous process making sure an organization is prepared to perform timely response.

It is important to remember that every organization is unique and different and therefore the process needs to be adapted to each organization. While the process can be adapted, you must always follow all six steps. The six steps are non-negotiable but the specific details within each step can be modified. To help understand the specifics, we will cover each step in detail in the next sections.

Preparation

Preparation is one of the most critical steps in incident response but it is also one of the steps that is most often looked. The reason why organizations overlooks this step is because no one ever thinks that bad things happen to them, bad things always happen to other organizations. To illustrate the point, let's look at a simple question—what is the number one reason why someone installs an alarm system? After they or someone they know very well had their house robbed. Once something hits home, people take it seriously. No one wants to spend the $3,000 on an alarm system because they think

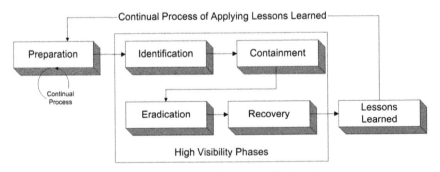

FIGURE 7.2 The 6-Step Process and How All of the Steps Fit Together

it is a waste of money. However, after your house is broken into and it costs a lot more than $3,000 in time, replacement cost and stress, people realize it is a bargain.

Organizations look at preparation with incident handling the same way. No one thinks an incident is going to happen to them and keep pushing off the preparation stage. Properly preparing for an incident keeps getting delayed and delayed until eventually they have an incident and because no one knows what to do, it turns into a disaster. Similar to the alarm system example, one of the number one drivers of why organizations will develop an incident response plan is after they have an incident and realize how much simpler and easier it would have been if they would have just properly prepared. One of the things we always say when it comes to incidents, is you either pay now (prepare for an incident) or pay later (have an incident with no plan). Both are going to cost you money, but it is going to be a lot cheaper and easier to prepare for an incident, than to have no plan at all.

The reason why preparation is so important is because the ultimate goal of incident response is timely recovery and response. If you have a plan that has been practiced, you can react quickly with minimal mistakes. If you do not have a plan, figuring out what to do takes valuable time and since you are figuring it out on the fly, the chance of mistakes is very high which will also add to the overall time and cost of handling the incident. The old saying is it is better to be prepared for an incident and not have one, than not have a plan, suffer an incident and not be prepared. In dealing with the traditional attack there was a chance that you would not have an incident. Today with the APT it is a guarantee that you are going to have an incident and therefore having a plan is critical in terms of timely recovery.

One of the first key phases of incident response is agreeing on the rules of engagement with the executives. Often when an APT incident occurs you have to react quickly and the executives are not always around. Even if they are around, getting agreement across the executive team on how to handle an incident and the approach your organization should take could take hours, days, or even weeks to decide. Having all of these meetings before there is an incident and having a clear plan of action decided upon prior to an incident occurring is critical. Waiting to be in the middle of an incident and having to get concurrence across all of the executives is wasting valuable time and just does not make sense. It is imperative to get everyone in agreement prior to an incident so the plan can be executed quickly.

Especially when dealing with APT incidents, a key phrase to remember is allows assume worse case and plan for the unexpected. One of the key areas to plan for is with communication. Most organizations when you bring this up state that they have robust communication via Email and phone. However if your entire network is compromised can you trust the use of Email. One of the mistakes that organizations made during 9/11 was that they assumed cell phone communication would always be available. During a critical incident not only might cell phones not be available but in some cases the cell towers could be switched to priority use so they will only be available to law enforcement or for critical communication. Regular organizations would not be able to communicate via cell phones. Based on those scenarios it is important to have alternative communications available.

Remember our key theme, it is better to have it and not need it than need it and not have it.

A critical rule of life is do not wait until you need a favor to build a friendship. During an incident it is often critical and/or desirable to seek assistance from law enforcement and outside council. Having relationships with these entities prior to an incident will make it easier to work with them and for them to be responsive. If you have a critical breach and you have to try and figure out who you need to call and build a relationship with them, it is going to take a lot longer to obtain assistance and the longer it takes the more damage that is being caused to your organization. Not only is building external relationships important, but also building internal relationships is just as critical. If you have a working relationship with the help desk manager, legal and public relations, asking for their assistance during an incident is going to be a lot easier and smoother to get it accomplished.

Ultimately the most critical part of incident handling is building and training your team. For any size incident, especially a large-scale incident like an APT compromise, having a well-trained team is critical to success. An important piece of information to remember when dealing with building a team is you want to "select" your team members. Often members of an incident response team are given to you, or it is based off of promotion criteria, which is heavily focused on technical skills. Technical skills are important but you can train anyone to learn the skills. More important than technical skills is having the proper personality. Personality is critical to success and if you have the wrong personality all the training in the world is not going to help. The two critical personality traits everyone on the incident handling team must have is: (1) being able to handle stress and work under pressure; and (2) being a team member and working as part of a team. Some of the smartest people I know make terrible incident handlers because they do not have the right personality. Pick personality traits not technical ability and you will have a successful team. Even if you have a perfect team, they will need to learn to work together which is done through training. Training is not only critical to make sure everyone is working together but since incidents are high stress and mistakes are very closely, training will help minimize any mistakes and allow the incident to be handled in a timely manner.

Identification

Preparation is an ongoing phase waiting for the phone to ring or something to happen. There will be some cases where identification is easy, for example a fire in your data center or a flooded data center. However with the APT it can sometimes be more challenging because you might receive a phone call from an outside entity indicating that your organization has been compromised. While that is helpful, you still have to go through your systems to confirm it and determine the scope of the compromise. Based on the complexities of the APT and the fact that during identification you have to determine what happened without making any changes to the system, means you often want to have your best incident responder handling the identification phase. The reason you cannot change anything is if it turns out to be an incident and you changed things during the identification phase, you could have potentially corrupted evidence or made it more difficult to figure out what the attacker did. The primary handler will often have a team working with them, but you want to make sure it is done properly, preserving all evidence. The lead responder would also be responsible to work with the forensic team to make sure, after a series of events has been declared an incident, proper forensics is performed prior to any changes being made to the system.

One of the challenges during the identification phase is proper communication with the executives. It is critical to make sure that you provide honest communication that the executives understand and it is presented in a way that they do not under or over react. We have seen cases where an organization thinks they have an incident, they tell the executives, everyone panics, and puts effort toward dealing with the incident, only to find out there is a reasonable explanation for what happened and that it is not really an incident. If you do that several times, the executives get desensitized and when there is a real incident no one believes you. Therefore it is critical to avoid the boy that cried wolf by honestly reporting what is going on. However, in some cases people are so concerned that executives will overreact, we have seen some organizations downplay or not say anything until they are 100% sure they have an incident. The problem with this approach is by the time you tell them you have an incident, things are so bad and now the executives are frustrated that no one said anything earlier. The trick to making sure identification is performed correctly is by performing proper executive awareness during the preparation phase. Executive need to understand that there are going to be some false alarms and just because someone says there is an incident does not mean it is true. Convince them you have a validated process and trust so as soon as an incident is confirmed, they will be notified immediately. The more they are made comfortable that there is a proven process, the more effective the overall incident response process will be. Most importantly during an incident everyone needs to understand their role and work as a team for successful recovery of the organization.

During an incident, communication can be a double edge sword. On the one hand you need to make sure that all of the key executives are aware of what is going on. However during the early stages you do not know if it is an inside job or how much access the APT has. Therefore you have to be very careful and limit communication to only those who are required and if possible utilize out of band communication. Accidentally tipping off the threat during an incident can make it much easier for them to cover their tracks and much harder to figure out what is really going on.

One of the challenges with identification is to determine who is responsible for reporting an incident within the organization. We have often heard technical people say that it needs to be their responsibility because the general population does not have the skills or expertise to detect and determine if there is an incident. While there might be some logic to this, this is as bizarre as saying it is the fire departments responsibility for finding a house that is on fire not the population. This would never scale. Bottom line is even though there are false alarms, the only way for fire safety to scale is to have the population responsible for reporting the fire and the fire department is responsible for timely reaction and putting out the fire. With traditional incidents, the approach has to be the same. The general population needs to be properly trained and made aware of what to look for and to call when there is suspicious activity and the incident response team is responsible for dealing with the incident.

While this does work, the problem with APT is it is so stealthy that organizations have not done a good job in detecting it. In many cases one of the most common forms of identification is an outside third party calling the company telling them that they have indications to believe that the company is compromised with an APT. Therefore having the population responsible for finding the APT does not always work. However before we dismiss this there are two reasons why this is the case. First, the APT is very stealthy and from a user perspective it is hard to detect once they are compromised. Second, they have not been trained properly to look for indicators of a compromise. In many cases the initial point of compromise does have a visual component that if the user was made aware of, could potentially be detected. This still will not fully scale but through proper training and awareness, they can do a better job than they are doing today.

Even with proper awareness, all APTs will not be properly identified by the population. Organizations need to deploy better behavioral detection technology so indicators of the APT could be found quickly and most importantly be detected before a third party has to call the company and let them know.

Containment

One of the initial steps of a first responder is to contain the problem and make sure it does not get any worse. A good example of this is an EMT (emergency medical technician). These are people who show up with an ambulance and provide assistance. If you look at an EMT, they are not full doctors and did not go to medical school. Their job is not to determine what is wrong with you and treat you to make you better. Their sole goal is to stabilize the patient and get them to the hospital in no worse shape. The incident responder's goal is similar, to stabilize the environment and make sure it does not get any worse. Actually the goal of containment is two key areas: (1) make sure the attacker is no longer in the network and can no longer cause damage; (2) contain the problem so whatever is wrong does not spread and get worse during the course of the incident.

The traditional way of doing containment was physical containment. This meant either physically disconnecting the system from the network or disconnecting the system and plugging in a hub or similar device so proper monitoring could be performed.

With physical containment, you are actually moving cables around and temporarily changing the physical topology of the network. While this is effective, it can also be high risk because networks are becoming so complex that if you start to change the cables, there is a chance the systems might not be plugged back in the same way. Therefore today, it is more common to perform virtual containment. This is done by performing two steps:

1. *Block all connections to the system from the firewall*—in order to make sure the attacker is no longer in the system, it is important to block all connections

going to the compromised system. Not only with this make sure the attacker is not still in the system, causing additional damage during the incident, but you can also set an alert on the ruleset so if attempts are made to the system it can be logged to better understand the attacker and how persistent they might be. During containment, some organizations will also go in and block all connections coming from the source IP address of the attacker. The problem with doing this only is that the attacker will constantly jump IPs when one is blocked, so this would typically have short-term success. One thing that we have found beneficial is to block both connections to the target systems and the source IP of the attacker. By doing both you not only have made sure that the attacker can no longer break into the system but by blocking the source IP of the attacker you are forcing them to try other methods of breaking in. Now by watching other attempted attacks to the target IP, you can start to build a profile of how the attacker works to build better detection measures down the road.

2. *Isolate the suspect systems on a separate VLAN*—depending on the type of incident but typically with an APT attack, the compromised system is used a pivot point to break into other systems across the network. Therefore it is important to isolate the system on a separate network segment to be able to stop the problem from getting worse or spreading to other systems across the network. With any attack, but especially with the APT it is important to always log all attempted connections trying to leave the system to better understand the extent of the compromise and what the APT is doing. On a large busy network, it is easy for the APT traffic to blend in with the other traffic and be very difficult to detect. However, once you find a compromised system, it is easier to isolate the system on a separate segment, capturing all outbound traffic. That traffic can be more carefully analyzed to not only build a profile of the attacker but to also see what other systems it is communicating with and what other systems might be compromised.

The immediate concern is that you are modifying configurations on key devices. While true, the big benefit of virtual containment is that you can back up all configurations before making changes. After the incident, you can restore the systems from the original configurations and perform cryptographic hashing against them to confirm that they are back in the original state. This type of backing up and verification cannot be done with physical containment. Therefore virtual containment tends to be safer in complex environments.

With the traditional attack we are assuming that we understand and know how the attacker broke in before we contain, which is critical in order to perform the next step which is eradication. However in some environments and especially with the APT you might not fully understand the problem. For example, if a third party or law enforcement calls your organization and tells you that you have a compromised system and they show you proof, that is strong evidence. The problem is that you have no idea what happened. Therefore if you contain and temporarily stop the attacker but have no idea what they did or how they got in, it will be hard to stop them in the future. Therefore in some situations an organization might decide to "watch and learn" instead of "contain and stop." With the traditional threat this was more the exception than the norm. Today with the increased sophistication of the attacker including the APT, this is starting to become more common.

The idea of watch and learn is to not make any changes to your environment or do anything that would tip the attackers hand that you know they are in the network and doing harm. Instead an organization would set up passive monitoring and watch everything the attacker is doing, trying to gather as much information as possible. The idea is to learn how the attacker is operating and build better intelligence to be able to better defend against the attack in the future. Remember the phrase if the offense knows more than the defense, you will lose. The idea of watching and learning is to allow the defense to know more than the offense and build better defensive measures. By observing and watching the attacker, an organization can learn exactly what the attacker is doing and how they broke in. This information can not only be used to fix the problem but also be used to build better profiles for detection in the future.

It is important to note that it is always important to work very closely with corporate legal on any decisions involving incident response. It is easy to get caught up in the details and lose sight of the exposure a certain decision could have to an organization. Watch and learn is a perfect example of an implied legal issue for an organization. By watching an attacker compromise an organization and allowing the actions to continue, could not only make it harder to prosecute, but if the attacker causes harm to another organization it could also cause unnecessary legal liability for your organization. Bottom line, it is always important to consult with the experts and with the increase exposure of APTs, legal and security should be BFF (best friends forever).

Eradication

A key part of incident response that is often overlooked is fixing the problem. During an incident an organization is losing money and the focus is often on getting the organization up and running as soon as possible to minimize any monetary impact to the organization. What is often forgotten is that if the attacker got in once, they will get in a second time. While having an incident is never pleasant, if handled correctly it can be a positive event showing that the team had a solid plan and knew what to do. No matter how you look at it, there is no positive way to spin a re-infection. While it does take time to determine how an attacker broke in and fix the problem, it is a critical step because if you don't, the attacker will come back in, perform more damage and be even harder to catch the second time.

Eradication, especially with the APT is not just about stopping the attacker. Remember the persistent piece in APT and while it is never pleasant there is no such thing as 100% security. An organization will never be able to stop all attacks. While stopping the direct cause of the attack is critical, the organization should also look at what other changes could be made to the environment to minimize future attacks of a similar nature. In addition, it is also important to look at detective measures that could be put in place to catch the attacker sooner and minimize overall damage and exposure.

Recovery

Once the cause of the incident has been determined and fixed, the next phase is to recover/rebuild the systems and data and put the systems back into production. It is critical to pay close attention during recovery to make sure that as the data is put back on the systems, that the attacker's code or point of infection is not reintroduced onto the system. We have seen organizations perform a great job on the incident response up to this point and without realizing it, re-infect the system when they recovered the information from backup.

The second important step with recovery is to monitor the systems after they are put back online to make sure the attacker does not successful get back into the system. With the traditional threat, normally the systems that are compromised are watched and they are normally monitored for a relatively short period of time. With APT since they are typically targeting an individual, usually the person that they target changes each time they try to break in. Therefore the monitoring with APT that is done during recovery should be broader and not watching a specific system but focused on the behavior patterns associated with the means and methods of the attack. In addition, normally when the APT targets a different entity it is not immediate. They wait a period of time so typically the monitoring is recommended to be performed longer with the APT since they will definitely come back and it is critical to be able to perform timely detection.

Lesson Learned

There is no such thing as a perfect incident. Whenever you are dealing with the duration and high stress level of an incident, in particular with the APT, mistakes are going to be made. The trick is to learn from the past and not make the same mistake over and over again. A key rule of incident response is to learn as a team. After each incident, the team should perform a lessons learned, figure out what could be done better, using this information to improve the overall processes and procedures.

During lessons learned the team should also put together a brief but factual executive summary of what occurred and what could be done to minimize this type of incident from occurring again. After an incident the team could sometimes be very frustrated but it is important to remember the executive report is not the time or place to vent. In many cases the report could be used as evidence in a legal case so it is critical to make sure it is concise and accurate.

FORENSIC OVERVIEW

While this chapter and book is on preventing, detecting and dealing with the APT, not forensics, it is still important to mention the importance of forensics in the overall context of incident response. If incident response is about recovery, it is important to know what occurred and what happened. Having evidence is critical to being able to figure out what occurred and make sure it does not happen again. Forensics is the key to making sure you have the details you need and that the evidence is admissible if the incident needs to be presented in a court of law.

The following is a high-level breakdown of the forensic lifecycle:

- *Verify the incident*—at the most basic level, if something unusual is occurring you need evidence to be discovered via forensics to determine what happened. Conclusions of what occurred should be based off of facts not hypothetical opinions. We have seen many companies spend a large amount of energy and effort on a really great story that was made up by guessing about what occurred. When all was said and done it turned out nothing really happening. Stories are good for bedtime, facts are required for incident response. During this stage, it is also important to understand and identify what type of information you are looking for so you can focus the team in the correct area and prioritize what they need to work on.
- *Gather a system description*—when buying a house one of the phrases that people always say is location, location, location. When working on an incident and performing forensics, one of the key phrases is documentation, documentation, documentation. You need to keep a clean and accurate record of the system you are working on and any relevant details. Some of the critical information you want to gather about a system include.
  - Date/time that the event was noticed.
  - Type of activity observed (e.g. Encrypted Tunnel).
  - Number of systems identified as being involved.
  - Location of the systems identified;
  - Purpose of the systems identified (e.g. Application Server).
  - Use of encryption on systems (e.g. BitLocker, PGP).
  - Type of data on the systems identified (e.g. PII).
  - Assigned or typical user base (e.g. Frank Jones or Sales).

- *Collect evidence, logs, reports*—one of the goals of forensics is to uncover and discover evidence to be able to determine what happened and depending on the type of case, be able to prove it in a court of law. What can be very frustrating in some cases is you can have evidence that shows 100% that someone performed a crime and is guilty but if the evidence was not gathered through legal means or cannot be proven to be authentic, it might be thrown out. Carefully documenting where the evidence was gathered is a critical first step, see Figure 7.3.

While showing how the evidence was collected is important, it is also critical to always be able to prove and preserve the chain of custody, see Figure 7.4.

Being able to maintain a chain of custody is critical and accomplished through the following steps:
  - *Attestation*—clearly documenting who collected the evidence. It is critical to make sure that whoever collected the information has the authority to take the evidence in question.

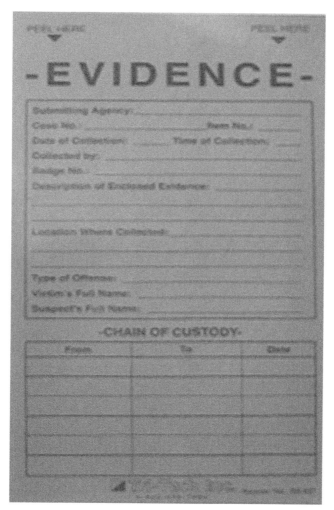

FIGURE 7.3 All Evidence Should Be Clearly Documented and When and How it was Acquired

- *Collect*—list what was collected, how it was collected, and where it was collected.
- *Ensure evidence is auditable*—keeping detailed logs allows you to be able to prove that the information on the evidence is accurate and you can prove that it has not been modified or changed.
- *Sign and seal*—as we illustrated above, it is important to sign for evidence to maintain the chain of custody and to clearly show that the evidence was protected and has not been modified.

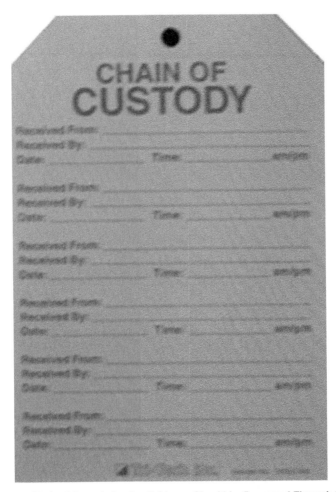

FIGURE 7.4 The Chain of Custody for Any Evidence Should be Preserved Through the Entire Process

- *Timeline creation*—in traditional crimes one of the main goals of forensics is to re-create the crime scene. By uncovering evidence and showing actually what occurred, you can solve the crime and if the evidence was properly controlled you could prove it in a court of law. With cybercrime, the goal is to uncover evidence to figure out what happened. To help determine what happened and see what additional information you need it is helpful to create a timeline showing when the initial reconnaissance/probing started, when the attacker moved to detailed scanning, the ultimate point of exploitation and the overall damage that occurred.

- *Media Analysis*—technology works very well from a functional perspective but very often there is evidence left on a system. When you run a program or open a file, it is loaded in memory and depending on the system, pieces of that information could still be found in memory several hours later. When information is written to a hard drive and it is deleted, the data is still on the hard drive and depending on the use and type of system, the information could be recovered for days or weeks. One of the key parts of forensics is the ability to go through all of the media and recover evidence to help fill in the time line and ultimately prove what happened. Proving what happened is critical but is it also important to always protect the chain of custody and gather evidence in a legal manner so it can still be admissible in a court of law.
- *Recover data*—depending on the amount of information involved in the incident, forensics could take several weeks or sometimes months to process all of the information. It is also important to prioritize the evidence so the most critical information is processed first. Even with prioritization, forensics can take time; however the longer an organization's systems are not available the more money they are losing. Therefore an organization cannot wait 2 months to put the systems back online. The normal process is for forensics to perform all of the binary backups and extraction of the evidence. Once the evidence has been acquired, you would recover the data, put the systems back online and once the systems are back online (to prevent monetary loss to the organization), the forensic analysis can continue.
- *Keyword search*—processing every single piece of information on a 4TB drive could take a very long time. Normally during forensics you have an idea of what you are looking for. Therefore as a starting point, it is usually a good idea to start searching the evidence based off of keywords to start narrowing down the amount of information that has to be initially analyzed.
- *Report*—once all of the evidence has been processed, you would create a factual based report, covering what information was found, including how it was analyzed and acquired. It is important to remember that any report produced could be used as evidence in court and therefore it needs to be written very carefully.

It is important to remember that while incident response and forensics are different activity, they are also complimentary efforts and not completely independent. Since both efforts support each other there is a overlap between some of the steps. While you would typically have an incident response team and a forensics team, they work very closely together continuously sharing and exchanging information throughout the entire process.

SUMMARY

No one likes to talk about the fact that they are going to get sick but we have to recognize that it is going to happen. Most of us exercise and try to be careful to prevent from being sick. If we know that someone is sick, we will not go to their house and will we avoid contact. Even though we all try to prevent getting sick, we recognize it is going to happen and have medicine in our medicine cabinet. The same approach needs to be taken with incident response. It always amazes me how people recognize that they are going to get sick but are surprised when you tell them that their networks and servers are going to be compromised. The question is not whether you are going to get attacked but how prepared are you to react in an efficient manner. Having an incident response plan is always important, but the more likely the attack the more important it is. With APT, compromise has become a guarantee. Therefore incident response has moved from a nice to have to a requirement. Having an incident response plan is important but it is important to remember that for it to be highly effective it needs to be part of a robust lifecycle:

PREVENTION – DETECTION – REACTION – RESPONSE.

Depending on your vantage point security can be one of the most exciting or one of the most frustrating jobs. There are always new challenges that make it exciting but nothing is more frustrating than after working really hard and spending significant resources, your organization still gets compromised. It is important to remember that no single measure is going to protect you and only by having an integrated, dynamic defense will your solution be able to stand the test of time. Incidents should not be a point of frustration, but a point of reflection. After an incident you should use the time to reflect on what went wrong, what can be done differently, and how to improve the overall defenses of your organization.

The most important thing to remember is that incidents are going to occur and having an incident is not a sign of weakness. However avoiding re-infection is critical. While an incident is never a pleasant situation, spend the time to do it right. In incident response there is no tomorrow, you have once chance to get it right so it is important to spend the time and make sure you do not get re-infected with the same problem.

Technologies for Success

INTRODUCTION

In order to win in any area including security you need to have both a strategic and tactical plan in order to be successful. It is important to remember that in dealing with any threat not all technology is going to work and some technology that was successful in the past might not be successful in the future. While changes might have to be made to your environment, that does not mean that you cannot be successful. It is important to remember that all threats will not be prevented and some attacks will sneak through even the best defenses that we deploy. While this is true it does not mean it was not worth the energy or effort. We have to remember that even the best sports players make mistakes. The top-rated quarterbacks still throw interceptions and the best baseball players still strike out. That does not mean that they are not successful, it just means they are not perfect. With APT we have to differentiate between perfect solutions and effective solutions. By nature of how the APT works, an organization will never be able to prevent 100% of all attacks. However, by having an integrated set of technologies, the organizations can scale for success.

This fact should not surprise or upset you because it is true in our everyday life. You as an individual cannot prevent all accidents and there is no such thing as a 100% safe life. No one can guarantee that an accident will never happen to them. However by managing risk and making wise decisions, many people can have a long successful life.

Just because there is no such thing as a 100% security, does not mean that a robust defense cannot be put in place. It is important to remember that there are three core tiers to effective solutions:

1. *Prevention*—Attacks that an organization knows about should be stopped and not allowed into an organization. Since prevention is before an attack, this is the ideal way to minimize or control damage to an organization. While it is ideal, the more advanced the attack the harder it is to prevent and stop the threat when it initial breaks into an organization. Prevention relies on having a trigger point or something visible that can be alerted on, caught,

and prevented before entering an organization. With advanced attacks, this does not always exist. In addition to having a visible component that can be acted upon to block, prevention can only stop indicators of an attacker that are always bad. If there is an activity that is bad 100% of the time, it can be blocked and prevented. However with APT many of the packets and tactics that are used are not always bad. Some of the time they are bad and some of the time they are good. This allows the APT to be stealthy and sneak into a network. In cases where a particular packet, connection, or piece of information is bad 99% or less, it cannot be prevented. The reason is anything below 100% means some of the time it is good and if that traffic is blocked you are impacting the business. If you ask any executive, what percent of legitimate traffic can be blocked in the name of the security, the answer will always be 0%. Even dropping 1% of all legitimate customer transactions or business is not acceptable.

2. *Detection*—While our ultimate goal is to prevent attacks, as attacks continue to be stealthy and covert and slip under the radar, many attacks will not be able to be prevented. It is always important to remember that prevention is ideal but detection is a must. Some organizations do not like where this is heading because this implies that your organization is compromised. Remember, if you are not able to prevent an attack, that means you have to catch the attack in progress. Detection means during an attack. Therefore if we recognize that prevention will not always work and that we must detect attacks in a timely manner, we are stating that our organization will be compromised. This is a theme we have pointed out in this book that any reasonable size organization with critical information, has already been compromised, the question is how long will it take to detect. With a common cold, if you ignore it, the body might heal itself and you might get better. With cancer, the longer you ignore it the worse it will get until it progresses to the point where it is terminal. With serious illnesses, ignorance is not an option, quick timely response is a must. Since the APT is cyber cancer and it will initially go undetected. Detection is our primary area of focus. There is some prevention that can be done with the APT, but since it is persistence, it will eventually break in. Since detection is during an attack, timely detection is critical. The quicker you can detect the less damage. As we have pointed out one of the primary problems with the APT is that organization put all of their energy in prevention and if prevention fails, there is minimal or no detection. This is evident by the fact that many organizations are often compromised for a long period of time and are ultimately notified by a third party that they have been compromised. It is very nice that third parties do this but it takes too long. Organizations need to recognize that with the APT, prevention is not going to always work and they must put in place robust outbound detection mechanisms focused in on protecting an organizations sensitive data.

3. *Response*—While detection is critical and important, detecting attacks that are in progress does not do much good without appropriate response. With

a typical incident that is detected quickly response is critical to control and minimize the damage of the active attack, but since the attacks tend to be short duration, if you do not detect and react the damage stops when the attack stops. However with the APT, the goal of the attacker is long term compromise. Typically there is an initial data that is targeted but in many cases it is long term access to an organizations data and information. Therefore response becomes even more critical. With a typical attack if you do not respond it stops. With the APT, the longer it takes an organization to respond the more damage and exposure to the organization.

These three areas tie directly in with our core motto for dealing with the APT:

> *"Prevention is ideal but detection is a must; however detection without response is useless."*

All three must effectively come together to defend against the APT. It is important to remember that with security there is no partial credit, either you do everything correctly or you do not. We often hear organizations saying we have solid prevention and detection but have to work on the response. We are still doing good because two out of three isn't bad. If you are writing lyrics to a song that might work, but in the real world you either do all three correctly or you fail. It is really all or nothing. As I like to say there is no "E" for effort when it comes to security. Even if organizations spend a lot of money on security but they do not do the right thing, it does not count.

INTEGRATED APPROACH TO APT

One of the areas that many organizations typical focus initial effort on is APT hunting and forensics. Hunting for the APT is important because the APT can bypass and get around most current defensive measures. This is a natural start since many organizations typical architecture was built to defend against the traditional threat. The way current technology is tuned, it is not very effective against the APT. Therefore it is very common that the APT can bypass most traditional defensive measures, compromise a network and go undetected for months. The way most organizations get acquainted with the APT is when a third-party calls them or they get notified that they have been compromised. Based on this scenario, hunting for the APT is the natural approach and the typical focus for an organization; however that is not the only approach. The more an organization can engage with the full lifecycle of the APT, the better prepared they can be.

By understanding and knowing how the APT works, technologies can be built and adapted to better defend and protect against attack. The APT will never be able to be prevented 100% so response that includes hunting will always be necessary. The key goal is to control, minimize, mitigate, and contain the APT as much as possible. By properly embracing technology, organizations can have a more integrated, scalable approach to dealing with the APT. The bottom line is in many cases an organizations security and architecture has to be rebuilt or reconfigured in order to properly defend against the APT. The things that worked in the past against traditional threats will not necessarily scale against today's new advanced threats. Three core lessons that highlight this point are:

1. *Vigilant monitoring for anomalous activity is critical to success*—Prevention will always play a key role in architecting a secure solution but robust continuous monitoring is no longer optional and critical for success. Base lining of activity must be performed and anomalies detected and reacted to in a timely manner.
2. *Threat analysis must drive defensive solutions*—We are no longer dealing with low hanging fruit attacks nick named "smash and grab" attacks where they all act very similar and can be dealt with in the same manner. Stealthy targeted attacks that will adapt if necessary to break into an organization are the norm. This means that the threat is always changing and must drive the risk calculation. Fixing random vulnerabilities is no longer enough. Today organizations must only fix vulnerabilities in which there is a real threat that has a high likelihood and impact.
3. *Users are the target; social engineering is at the heart of most attacks*—Attackers are recognizing that breaking into systems that contain sensitive data is too difficult. Organizations over the years have done a great job with segmenting and isolating critical servers making direct compromise from the Internet very difficult. Today the user is a much easier target. Not only is it simpler to break in but once a client system is compromised, they have full access to almost all data and information on the network.

HOW BAD IS THE PROBLEM?

Based on the stealthy nature of the APT, the way organizations became aware of the threat is after many successful compromises of large organizations. Ideally we would like to get to a state where organizations can detect and respond to the APT themselves, but many organizations are not there. Since the APT has not been properly addressed and ignored by many organizations for a long time before we begin the prevention and timely detection process, an organization needs to make sure they are not compromised.

One of the comments we often receive from our clients is that we are not targeted by the APT and it is not a concern in our environment. My response is that since you do not think it is a threat and it has been ignored and you have not been looking for it; based on the stealthy nature of how it operates how would you know? You very well could be compromised and not know about it. Therefore before we talk about technologies that would help effectively deal with the APT, an organization needs to assess their environment, see if they are infected and see how bad it really is.

For most organizations they need to assume they are infected and ask three key questions:

1. *Are we currently infected by APT?*—The test many organizations run to determine if they are compromised is looking for something visible on their network. This works OK for the traditional threat but is completely ineffective against the APT. With most advanced threats there will never be a visible sign of an attack and in cases where there is a visible sign, by the time it appears it is to late—all of the information has been compromised. Therefore to detect the APT requires proper planning. An organization must have a proper baseline of their network traffic, logs, and systems so they can spot and track anomalies. The problem is if you have never created a baseline and you are concerned you are attacked, you have nothing to compare it to. Second, when you take a baseline you need to examine it very closely to make sure that during the time the baseline was run the network was not compromised. If the network is compromised during the baseline, attack traffic will be learned as normal and it will make the results less accurate. While network baselines can be difficult for the above reasons, system baselines are typically more straightforward because an organization should have proper configuration management and know how the original system was built. With proper change control all changes to the baseline should be tracked so a comparison can be performed against the current system and the known good baseline, looking for any anomalies. Any changes should be examined to look for indicators of a compromise. While the APT is very advanced, how they compromise systems are similar so proper indicators of a compromise can also be examined and used to determine if a system or network has been compromised. Bottom line is when it comes to the APT, signatures and visible signs are not going to work. Only by having the ability to spot deviations from a norm or an anomaly, will an organization be able to know harm is occurring to their organization.

2. *How do we react if we are infected?*—Two of the common methods (and mistakes) that organizations make when they determine they are infected are (1) fix a random problem and not perform proper root cause analysis; and (2) rebuild the system and not remediate the problem. First, many organizations after they find out they are infected focus on doing something so they can justify that they dealt with the APT. The number one response after an organization is infected is to purchase a new security device. It seems that if a breach becomes public and the organization can show that significant money was spent on a solution, it will show that the organization handled the compromise correctly. What is scary is this approach often works. If you do not determine the root cause of a problem and address it, an organization will continue to lose money. One of my friends was complaining that he always gets sick and is constantly going to the doctor. My response was, what is the cause or reason you are getting sick so often? Based on his facial expression, it was like I was talking a different language. He would go to the doctor, get

medicine, very often treat the symptom but he never ever asked why. If you are OK with constantly dealing with a problem address the symptom, if you want to address a problem and minimize re-occurrence fix the root cause.

The second common problem is if an organization does put the energy and effort to determine which system was compromised, the approach is to pull the system off of the network, rebuild it, and put it back online. The justification is that we are rebuilding the system from a secure build, therefore the system will be secure. The problem is that the system was originally built off of a secure build and the attacker found a way in. Therefore if you rebuild the system back to the original build that was compromised, what do you think is going to happen—they are going to break back into the system again. Maybe an organizations secure build is not as secure as they think. Not preventing reinfection with the APT is a common problem and because the threat is stealthy, many organizations are re-infected and do not even know it because there is no visible sign or impact that a compromise occurred.

3. *How did the infection occur so we can prevent it in the future?*—With a typical compromise you identify how the attacker broke in and fix the problem so that they cannot break in again in the future. The problem with the APT is the distance in time from when a compromise occurred to when an organization detects it. With a traditional attack, if you detect it within a week or two you go back into the logs for the last month, see how the attacker broke in and fix the problems. With the APT, since many organizations do not detect it for a long period of time, they might need to go back through 9 months worth of logs to see what happened. First, many organizations do not keep detailed logs from all of their systems for that long so the information is not available. Second, even if all of the logs were available, going back through 9 months worth of logs takes up a lot of time and energy and it is a very difficult task. Since the organization does not know exactly when the compromise occurred, it is like looking for a needle in a haystack. They have to systematically start going back in time, look at every single log entry trying to figure out when the adverse activity occurred. This can take a long period of time and often organizations are not very successful.

Ideally the best way to deal with an incident is to contain and eradicate, this is not always possible with the APT since the information, details, and logs needed to do this is not always available. Therefore while not ideal, in some cases with the APT, "watch and learn" is the only option. This means that the organization must carefully monitor what the attacker is doing, figure out how they exploited and gained access, and use that information to build more robust defensive measures moving forward. While this is sometimes the only option with the APT, legal counsel should be consulted since there are legal implications with knowingly watching and allowing an attacker to cause to harm.

The ideal way of dealing with the APT is prevention, which will be covered later in the chapter. If prevention is not successful, then timely detection is critical. In order for detection to work, it has to be timely, the problem has to be contained, and the root cause of the compromise has to be fixed. Containment, eradication, and recovery are the keys to success. Once again if you know what to do and have formally tested and validated processes in place, security can be straightforward and dealing with the APT can scale across an organization. The problem is, it is all or nothing. If you only contain and recovery without eradicating the problem, re-infection will occur and your organization will be worse off because you have a false sense of security. A false sense of security is actually worse in some cases to having no security. If you have no security, an organization knows they are exposed and are often careful and the executives are nervous because they know a compromise can occur at any time. While not ideal, at least with minimal security organizations are aware they have a problem. With a false sense of security, an organization thinks they are secure because they spent money on a problem. Therefore they will let down their guard thinking everything is OK. The issue is they fixed the wrong problem and the actual issue is still present on the system. Now they think everything is fine, they let down their guard, when in reality they are just as bad as if they have no security but they are not aware of the problem.

While performing this analysis at the beginning of dealing with the APT is ideal, it is really an ongoing effort. Since the APT is very stealthy organizations must perform continuous monitoring of what is coming in but most importantly, what is leaving an organization. Early in the book we compared the attacker to the cyber shoplifter. As we have discussed, you cannot prevent shoplifting you can only detect shoplifting by performing outbound detection. The way you perform timely detection with someone stealing from a store is by looking for points of deviation. At point of entry a shoplifter looks just like a legitimate customer. At some point while they are in the store their activity will have to deviate from that of a normal shopper. If the activity of the shoplifter and the legitimate customer are exactly the same the entire time they are in the store, guess what, they are not a shoplifter they are a legitimate customer. At some point if someone is going to steal, there activity must deviate from the activity of a normal person. By tracking and catching those deviation points allow you to minimize overall damage. What is another word for deviation points? Anomaly detection. By performing a baseline of normal activity and looking for a deviation from that baseline will allow an organization to catch and track the APT. The logic is simple. If the APT does exactly what a user does with no deviation at all, either the APT is not dangerous or your normal users are dangerous, but they cannot both act the same way but have different impact to your organization. While the point seems so simple, continuous tracking of a baseline and looking for deviation is a very effective way of catching and dealing with attacks in an enterprise.

TRYING TO HIT A MOVING TARGET

In the past and with the traditional threat, security was all about hitting a target. Organizations would perform threat analysis, identify what the adversary did and how they operated, and would typically create a ruleset to block it or a signature to detect the attack. Since the attack did not change that often, this method worked extremely well for viruses or worms. With these methods of attack, an adversary would create a piece of malware, launch it at a larger number of targets and see how many systems it broke into. Even though there were some polymorphic worms and malware that could change or modify how it worked, essentially it was software that was ultimately breaking into system. Though the software might try to morph and change, it still operated in a predictable manner and if the defense was able to obtain a piece of the malware they could reverse engineer it, figure out how it behaved, and still be able to write rulesets and signatures to properly address the threat.

With the APT, it is a completely different threat because very often it is an individual or organization breaking in, not an automated piece of software than can be reversed engineered. We now have a moving target that is constantly changing, constantly adapting, and morphing on how it behaves. Remember that in the past, when we used the word advanced to refer to a piece of malware, we were referring to the advanced nature of the attack and how the code worked. If it had obfuscated code so it could not be reversed engineered and constantly recompiled to change the signature, we would say the code was advanced. However today with the APT, the "A" is referring to the advanced nature of the adversary—the entity actually launching the attack. If you are dealing with an advanced adversary they will always try the simplest, most effective way of breaking in, constantly changing, so you cannot detect it and always trying to stay one step ahead of the attacker. With the APT, not only are you dealing with a moving target but you are dealing with an invisible target. Therefore with APT, the method of attack switched from software to an individual. In order to defend against it we have to switch from using software to our primary defense to human-based controls. Now we have to be careful. The adversary still uses software and automation to be as effective as possible. The more we can think and behave like the adversary, the more effective we will be overall.

It is actually a very interesting problem when there is now a human mind behind the attack as opposed to a predictable piece of software that will always operate in the same manner. This is the reason adaptive solutions work the best against the APT. Since the adversary is always changing, we have to constantly change our defensive measures. By looking at behavior patterns and tracking anomalies, we have a much better chance of success than looking for and tracking patterns.

While the APT is an invisible moving target, there are some common ways that it operates and behaves.

The common goals of the APT, at least for today are relatively steady state. Most APTs have the following similar characteristics:

- *Collection of information*—many traditional attacks typical move directly to exploitation of the system. The APT performs a very large amount of reconnaissance of open and closed source information to increase the chance of success to almost 100%. What is interesting is typically reconnaissance and open source information gathering does not touch or do anything directly against the individual or organization that is being targeted. Therefore it is very stealthy and hard to detect. With a typical attack that directly tries to break it, it is often not successful on the first try because the attacker has limited information. Therefore if you watch the firewall logs you can see a high number of failed attempts which is detectable and can be acted upon. The APT takes a completely different approach. It performs a high amount of information gathering to determine the most successful vector and when it launches an attack, it has a very high chance of success, with minimal noise and very difficult to detect.

- *Targets an individual (typically via email)*—Traditional attacks typically target servers because that is what runs the business and where the data is. However the APT has learned that servers are locked down and typically much harder to break into. Therefore it is easier to target the entities that have access to the information, the users. With proper research and validation, tricking the user to open an attachment or click on a link is so easy and almost guaranteed that it has become one of the methods of choice. This has become such a common target of attack that some people jokingly say that the APT stands for average phishing technique. What is important to remember is the adaptive nature of the attacker. They are using direct emails against individuals as the primary way because it is easy and works. We need to be aware of this but do not get locked in that this is the only method used by the APT. As soon as this method no longer proves viable, they will quickly move to a new method very quickly.

- *Initial entry is to create a pivot point*—The APT is very patient and very focused on the ultimate goal, however they realize that gaining direct access to the server that has the information they want is not only very difficult but not very scalable. Therefore their goal is to create a pivot point on the network that they can use to access any server or piece of information they want. The ultimate information that the APT wants changes over time, therefore one of the objectives is to get into a position where the adversary can easily access the information whenever they want. The information an adversary is after today might change in a few months, so if they broke directly into the server with the information they want today, they would have to break into another server in a few months. Gaining access takes time and is high risk. Therefore creating a well-positioned pivot point to allow access to the entire network, puts the attacker in a position to do more long term damage and ultimately extract information. Also, once the pivot point is set up in a stealthy manner, it has a greater chance of going undetected.

- *Maintain long term access*—The APT typically wants long term access to your organization. Essentially that want to continuously monitoring the enterprise, track what you are doing, always looking for information that could be of value to them. The APT is the ultimate cyber stalker. Depending on the goal of the attack they do not always want to steal a piece of information and be gone, they sometimes want to cause long term harm.

- *Exfiltrate information from the organization*—Ultimately the reason for the APT and behind the APT is to steal information from the organization. There have been some case were the APT also modified information to impact the ability of an organization to be competitive or to provide misinformation to an operation, but ultimately the goal is disclosure of sensitive information to give the adversary an advantage. As we have been saying for the last 20 years, it is all about the data. Since the attacker is ultimately focused on the data, the more we can do to protect and manage the information, the better off we will be in defending against the attack.

While the common goals of the APT are usually very similar across many attacks, the specifics and details are always changing which makes traditional signature methods not effective. However, regardless of how stealthy they try to be, the ways an attacker works is different than normal activity and therefore the above information can be used as a preventive and detective method.

FINDING THE NEEDLE IN THE HAYSTACK

What makes the needle in the haystack problem so difficult is if you do not know what the needle looks like and there is a lot of hay. While the general problem will always be difficult, if you know what is the size, color, and general attributes of the needle and you can reduce the amount of hay you have to search through, the problem becomes a little more achievable. Ideally if you can understand the unique attributes of the needle vs. the hay and build a machine that can sift through all of the hay and the only thing that remains is the needle, the problem actually becomes very achievable. This is the general approach we need to take with the APT. There is so much traffic going across a network that searching through all of it is very difficult. In addition, since the APT is targeting a specific organization and is different for each entity it targets, an organization does not always know what to look for. However by studying similarities of how the APT operates, there are some ways that you can differentiate between normal and attacker traffic, reducing the amount of information that has to be identified and allowing the anomalies to bubble to the top of the search space.

While the APT is stealthy and hard to detect if you do not know what you are looking for, the bottom line is if the APT matched legitimate traffic 100% and there were no differences, it would be legitimate traffic. At quick glance attack traffic might appear to look normal, if you examine it closely and look for the right properties, it is reasonable to find, remediate, and even prevent.

In order to be able to differentiate and find the bad traffic from the good, we have to understand what is normal in a given environment. This is one of the things that doctors have done over the last several decades is build up a large knowledge base of the human body, tracking what is normal so they can identify problem areas. The reason a doctor can take a sample and determine if it is benign or cancer is because they have the properties of cancer which allow them to differentiate good from bad.

We need to do the same thing with cyber cancer. Common attributes that can be used to prevent and detect the APT are:

Destination IP addresses that are being connected to—Organizations should constantly look at the destination IP addresses that are leaving an organization and sort them based on the country they are going to. Very rarely does a compromised system make an outbound connection to a country that the organization usually communicates with on a regular basis (unless you live in Russia or China). Even if they do, if you correlate the destination country that is being communicated with and tie it with length of the connection and amount of data, it is almost always different. While tracking destination countries for an organization is very valuable and usually provides enough information to spot anomalies, for organizations that are truly international, sometimes you have to track it down to an individual system. In almost all cases, if you look at the countries a computer normal goes to and the countries a compromised system connects to, there are distinct differences in the traffic. Once again this is where net flow analysis can really prove useful. Often clients tell us that there is too much traffic and too many packets to do this type of analysis. However, by graphically displaying the information on a map and showing all of the connections, unusual connections can easily be tracked, spotted, and remediated. The more organizations start tracking and watching their traffic, the easier it is to prevent, detect, and react to compromised systems. What is also very important to remember with this analysis is that the APT is very adaptive and will constantly change based on how the defense operates. Today, very few organizations are tracking the location an outbound connection is going to so the APT is not very stealthy in hiding where it is going. If no one is looking for it, why protect it. However, as more and more organizations perform this analysis, the APT will investigate common countries that systems communicate with, setup relays in those countries and make it harder to use destination country as a sole discriminator. This is why correlating with all of the below information will be of value. A doctor does not see if you have a fever and use it as a sole discriminator to determine what is wrong. They correlate it with other factors to get a complete picture of the problem. While today, using destination IP address by itself will be valuable, it is more scalable to constantly correlate the date across many different sources (Figure 8.1).

It is important to point out that an IP address can tell an organization which country or specific location an endpoint connection is coming from. However, it might not be the location of the actual attacker because it can be bypassed by a clever attacker with relays and secure tunnels. However, as we have pointed out today not many attackers are putting in a lot of effort to hide the country they are coming from since most defenders are not looking for this information. Be prepared, as more organizations use this technique to find the APT, the threat will evolve and make it harder for this technique to work by itself.

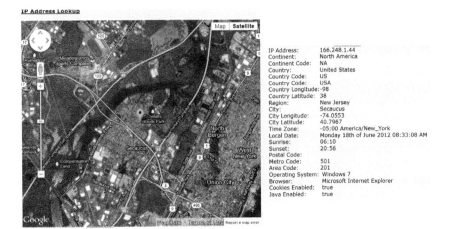

IP Address Lookup

IP Address:	166.248.1.44
Continent:	North America
Continent Code:	NA
Country:	United States
Country Code:	US
Country Code:	USA
Country Longitude:	-98
Country Latitude:	38
Region:	New Jersey
City:	Secaucus
City Longitude:	-74.0553
City Latitude:	40.7967
Time Zone:	-05:00 America/New_York
Local Date:	Monday 18th of June 2012 08:33:08 AM
Sunrise:	06:10
Sunset:	20:56
Postal Code:	
Metro Code:	501
Area Code:	201
Operating System:	Windows 7
Browser:	Microsoft Internet Explorer
Cookies Enabled:	true
Java Enabled:	true

FIGURE 8.1 IP Addresses can be Used to Determine Which Country and Location an Endpoint is Coming From While This has Value it is Important to Point Out that this Might not Necessarily be Where the Attacker is Ultimately Located

IP address tied to domain name—This behavioral pattern is a perfect example of one that use to work extremely well but as the adversary caught on to how the defense was working they started to hide and be more stealthy. While this measure is not as valuable as it was in the past, it is still important to mention since it still proves to be an effective secondary measure to look for. Most users when they make connections utilize domain names. For example if you send an Email or surf to a Website you are going to type www.syngress.com you are not going to type 69.163.177.2 into your browser. This means that the domain name will have to be resolved to an IP address (typically via DNS) before the connection is made. Most attackers preferable use straight IP address connections because it is easier, simplifier, and less overhead. Therefore if you take a destination IP address and look in DNS cache and there is an entry that corresponds back to a domain name, most likely that was a legitimate user. If there is no entry in DNS cache, it most likely is a direct IP connection which is very suspicious and means it is most likely an attacker and needs to be investigated. While this method will work to catch some of the threats that are out there, more and more APTs are using dynamic DNS to allow the relays and endpoints to be more dynamic, jump around and be harder to find. Therefore while this method could provide some insight, it is getting less reliable based on the adaptive nature of the APT. For example, Figure 8.2 shows sample network activity including the number of DNS queries a recent attack performed after it compromised the system.

What is interesting about domain names is that the original technique of seeing if there is an entry in DNS cache to determine whether the connection was a domain

4.e) attrib.exe - Network Activity

DNS Queries:

Name	Query Type	Query Result
www.worldcasino.to		
mail.fucuzzy		
mail.TIKTIKZ		
mail.telon-servers.net		
www.worldcasino.to		
mail.fucuzzy		
mail.TIKTIKZ		

TCP Conversation from 192.168.0.2:1067 to 64.86.133.5:80

Data sent:
```
4e49 434b 205b 5030 307c 4155 547c 3838    NICK [P00|AUT|88
3232 3530 3335 5d0d 0a                     225035]..
```

Data sent:
```
5553 4552 2058 502d 3533 3037 202a 2030    USER XP-5307 * 0
203a 5455 2d34 4e48 3039 534d 4347 3148    :TU-4NH09SMCG1H
430d 0a                                    C..
```

Data received:
```
3a6c 6f67 2e75 732e 7379 7320 4e4f 5449    :log.us.sys NOTI
4345 205b 5030 307c 4155 547c 3838 3232    CE [P00|AUT|8822
3530 3335 5d20 3a2a 2a2a 2059 6f75 2061    5035] :*** You a
7265 2070 6572 6d61 6e65 6e74 6c79 2062    re permanently b
616e 6e65 6420 6672 6f6d 2043 6973 636f    anned from Cisco
2028 6e6f 2072 6561 736f 6e29 0d0a 4552    (no reason)..ER
524f 5220 3a43 6c6f 7369 6e67 204c 696e    ROR :Closing Lin
6b3a 205b 5030 307c 4155 547c 3838 3232    k: [P00|AUT|8822
3530 3335 5d5b 616e 616c 7973 6973 2e73    5035][analysis.s
6563 6c61 622e 7475 7769 656e 2e61 632e    eclab.tuwien.ac.
6174 5d20 2855 7365 7220 6861 7320 6265    at] (User has be
656e 2070 6572 6d61 6e65 6e74 6c79 2062    en permanently b
```

FIGURE 8.2 Network Activity Including DNS Queries Made During a Sample Attack

name request or pure IP connection is getting less effective. However, if you look at the domain names that are being connected to, they are still suspicious. Therefore this detection method has been adapted to now correlate all of the domain name connections that are being made on a regular basis. Review the list, make sure the names are legitimate and baseline the list. Most people tend to go to the same base list of domains on a regular basis. If someone tries to connect to a domain name in which there have been no other connections to in the last month, an alert/email would be sent to the SOC (security operations center) to review. If it is something normal like www.cisco.com that would be added to the list. If it is a weird or unusual name, they would investigate and if it is not normal or a common domain name used by attackers, it would be flagged.

• *Amount of outbound data per connection*—Ultimately the goal of security is to protect and minimize the risk of exposure of critical information to an organization. While it would be nice if a system was never compromised, the really damaging part of a compromise is the theft or exfiltration of information out of the organization. If someone broke into a system, compromised it but did not make an outbound connection or send information out of the organization, consider yourself lucky. Since the real concern is compromise of information, looking at the amount of data leaving an organization is critical. While this sounds obvious, very few clients are actually looking at what type and the amount of information that leaves an organization. While looking at the overall amount of information leaving an organization is important for situational awareness, the real value in terms of catching the APT is to look at the amount of information leaving an organization per connection and per user. For example, with typical Web surfing a small amount of data typically leaves the organization in the form of a request and large amounts of information is downloaded to the client. If the connection is going to port 80 but is really a command and control channel being disguised as Web surfing, there might be a large amount of information leaving the organization and little coming back. For most client communication but especially Web surfing, there should not be 80MB of data leaving the organization. Once an organization knows what to look for, this pattern is very easy to detect, but you have to be tracking it in order to catch the APT. Hopefully what this section is showing is that we need to move beyond looking for signatures because they are too rigid and inflexible because they require the ability to read and process the content of a packet (which is not always possible). Instead, by looking at the amount of data that is going outbound per connection, not only is the data being protected but an organization is now containing and controlling the information. Normal user requests should have small amounts of outbound traffic and compromised systems have large amounts. It is always important to remember that there will always be exceptions to the rules. For example, if an organization is using cloud-based backup services for their employees, when there data is being backed up there would be a large amount of data leaving the organization which could fit the pattern of an attacker. However in those cases, these should be well documented, always going to the same location so they can easily be tracked and managed as an exception. The reason signatures no longer work today is because there is no 100% guaranteed way of catching an attacker. Therefore we have to recognize that there will always be some exceptions and analysis required. The goal is to reduce the size of the search space and make it easier to find the anomalies.

- *Encrypted information or channels*—A key goal of the attacker is to not get caught and maintain long term access to the enterprise. Most traditional security devices that are deployed on networks today (i.e. firewalls, application proxies, IDS, IPS, and DLP) all require the ability to read the content of the payload to determine if something is malicious or not. Therefore the tool of choice for many attackers is encryption. By setting up an encrypted session, an attacker can literally bypass most of the security devices that are on the network and be totally stealth. While there is some encryption in use on enterprise networks, there is typically not a large number of encrypted sessions outbound, especially to unusual destination IP addresses. SSL/TLS tunnels would be an exception and those connections are relatively short, with minimal amount of information being transferred. Most people think of encryption as a way to stop attackers from reading sensitive information but encryption can stop anyone from reading the information. Therefore having the ability to track, monitor, and control encrypted traffic is critical to detecting and controlling the APT.

- *Length of the connection*—How long a single connection lasts can also be a critical attribute in determining and finding adverse behavior on a network. Typical client connections are relatively short lived. They make a connection, perform some function, and close the connection. Especially with traditional Web surfing the connections are very short because in many cases a single object or small subset of objects is sent per connection. When surfing to a Website the connections are typically under a minute, if not a few seconds. If an attacker is extracting information out of the organization the connections are typically much longer, based on the speed of the connection, but can easily be several minutes or even several hours. Long connections are typically an attribute of a command and control channel and should be tracked very closely.
- *Number of connections*—Just as the defense studies the offense to build better protective measures, the offense (especially the APT) studies the defense to try and be more stealthy and avoid detection. Since long connections are an anomaly and easy to detect, what some adversaries are doing today is using a larger number of shorter connections. Now instead of one 45 min connection, they will now make 45 one minute connections. Therefore in the theme of having the defense be as adaptive as the offense, we now also track the number of connections. If there is a high number of connections to a foreign IP address with a large amount of data being transferred, those combined patterns could be indicative of an attacker. The important point to note is that number of connections is typically not of high value by itself but can provide additional insight when combined with other attributes.

Each of the above attributes can provide value independently but with sophisticated, advanced attacks, any single security measure can be bypassed by the adversary. Therefore there is strength in numbers and it is critical to have multiple parameters working together to catch the APT. As you have seen in the above discussion, in some cases a single attribute might be conclusive on whether there is an APT, but when multiple items are combined, the level of confidence becomes very high.

It is also important to note that while host indicators can also provide value, if an attacker has total control of a host computer it is easier for them to hide and provide false information back to the operator. There are still things that can absolutely be done to analyze and look for signs of compromise on a host, this section focused on the command and control channel. Other than utilizing encryption the command and control channel is much harder for an attacker to hide. Regardless of the type of attack or level of sophistication, an attacker is going to have to make connections back to an adversaries system. While complex root kits can hide the activity on a computer, a packet is much harder to disguise. An attacker can make their traffic look like other protocols, but the general properties and parameters of what is being sent, is very difficult to make covert. This is one of many reasons why adding network APT analysis to existing host-based analysis provides a powerful combination.

UNDERSTAND WHAT YOU HAVE

If you are sick and you go to the doctor they run tests and if the tests come back negative or they are inconclusive, they run additional tests. The reason they do this is you cannot fix something if you do not understand what the problem is. In order for a doctor to identify what is wrong they need to understand what is happening inside your body. The more information they have the more accurate the diagnosis. You would not feel comfortable if you went to the doctor and without examining you or running any tests, the doctor says you are 100% healthy just by looking at you. While we would never do that in real life, why do we do that in cyber? Many organizations just by looking at their network and saying there is no visible signs of an attack, conclude that they are secure and not compromised. An organization can only make a determination of their overall security by performing detailed analysis and understanding what they have on their network. You cannot protect what you do not know.

What is interesting is that the APT preys on the fact that most organizations are not looking for signs of a compromise. They know that if they can break into a network and create an outbound encrypted channel, it will go virtually undetected for a long period of time because it is not visible. Since it is not interrupting any normal operations most organizations will not notice it and the attackers have gained a long term pivot point on their network.

Traditional countermeasures are normally not effective against the APT because they are not properly tuned based on knowledge of the network.

The reason traditional countermeasures do not work is because the adversary understands how the technology works and is able to build mechanisms to bypass and defeat them. Just as we study the adversary, the adversary studies how organizations perform cyber security and looks for ways to defeat traditional defensive measures. The APT typically is able to get around traditional defensive measures.

In the past an organization could get by with installing some security devices and not performing any thorough analysis of their network. The default configuration of traditional security devices worked fine against the common attack. Today, without a detailed understanding of an organizations network and how it is configured—using that information to customize the environment, common devices will not work.

For example, traditional traffic monitoring and content filtering looked for signatures and common patterns of attack. Since the APT blends in with existing network traffic, is constantly changing and not based off of common signatures, out of the box monitoring and filtering will completely miss the APT. However, by performing proper tuning based on anomalies built off of normal baseline of traffic monitoring can now be an effective way of detecting the APT.

IDENTIFYING APT

Technology is critical and having a robust architecture is a must in order to protect against the APT, but you cannot protect what you do not know about. Therefore one of the first and most critical things an organization needs to do is be able to identify the APT. Since the APT acts and behaves differently than the traditional threat, many organizations are missing the APT and therefore being compromised for many months. What is also scary is that in many cases the way organizations know that they have been compromised by the APT is that they are notified by a third party. This is not a good position to be in. Imagine for a second that if the third party never called the organization to notify them that they have been compromised, they might never have known and think about how much additional information would have been stolen. Organizations need to be able to perform timely detection of the APT themselves and not rely on others for detection.

A key theme is prevention is ideal and it would be great if an organization could stop all attacks. However, that is not realistic. Therefore we must be able to detect attacks in a timely manner. Based on the previous paragraphs, for some organizations it is not detection in a timely manner it is detection period. Imagine if an organization that has been compromised for 9 months was able to identify and detect the attack in 2 months, while not ideal, things would still be a lot better than 9 months. The goal with the APT is if prevention fails, to move up the timeline of detection and give organizations the ability to detect as soon as possible.

In order to do a more effective job at dealing with the APT, organizations need to better understand and analyze their environment. The general process is broken down into three general sections, with four steps for each section:

- Assessment and Discovery:
  - Asset Identification.
    - Perform full network architecture review.
    - Define critical assets.
    - Define current mitigations.

  - Develop Assessment Strategy.
    - Identify tool deployment methodology.
    - Identify current restrictions.
    - Identify data collection point.

- Conduct Initial System Review.
  - Compile tools for system deployment.
  - Execute initial system sweep.

- Identify Indicators of Compromise.

  - Perform initial data collection review.
  - Identify possible system-based and network-based indicators.

- Analysis and Remediation:
  - Conduct Targeted System Scans.
    - Deploy customized detection toolset.
    - Leverage statistical anomaly-based detection and analysis techniques.
    - Refocus detection on indicators of compromise as necessary.

  - Implement Countermeasures.
    - Execute account management processes.
    - Apply additional segmentation and access controls.
    - Identify and remove command and control (C2) channels.

  - Post Assessment and Remediation.
    - Perform offline forensic analysis and code review.
    - Develop and execute host restoration strategy.
    - Implement additional host-based protection measures.

  - Program Enhancement Strategy.

    - Conduct strategic program review.
    - Recommend APT defense and detection strategies.
    - Review user awareness and training programs.

- Program Review:
  - Business Rules Assessment.
    - Conduct gap analysis.
    - Strategic alignment review.
    - Communications assessment.
    - Review policies and procedures.

  - Capability and Roadmap Assessment.
    - Review and current capability matrix.
    - Conduct gap analysis.
    - Trending and analysis.
    - Ensure needs alignment with ROI.
    - Solution implementation.

  - Develop Threat Agent Profile.
    - Develop critical asset list.
    - Develop threat vector list.
    - Vulnerability assessment.
    - Penetration assessment.

- Implement Training and Awareness.
  - Provide onsite training.
  - Develop response matrix.
  - Design awareness initiative program.
  - Design user feedback program.

Based on their importance each of these sections will be reviewed in more detail.

Assessment and Discovery

A key theme of dealing with the APT is an organization cannot protect what they do not know about. One of the many reasons why the APT is so successful is the threat knows more about an organization than the organization does. As we know, if the offense knows more than the defense you will lose. With traditional threats, the main focus of the adversary is on exploitation or breaking in. With the advanced threat the main focus is on reconnaissance and scanning, finding out as much about the organization as possible. Therefore the first step in dealing with the APT is understanding an organization's environment which begins with asset identification. The general theme is an organization cannot protect what they do not know about. This is also the reason that the first of the 20 Critical Controls is Inventory of Authorized or Unauthorized devices. An organization must discover and validate all assets that are connected to the network, confirm that all devices are authorized and perform strict configuration control to make sure that no unauthorized devices are connected to the network. Both 802.1x and NAC (network access control) can play a part in controlling and managing all devices. While controlling and managing all devices is important, attackers typically break into software not hardware. Therefore the software that is installed and the configuration of that software must also be carefully managed with strict inventory control and configuration management.

While all of this is important the secret ingredient to make it all work is proper change control. Having a robust asset inventory tied to installed software and proper configuration is good, but it cannot be maintained and will quickly deteriorate if all changes are not carefully managed and controlled. Therefore the golden rule of configuration management is all changes must go through the change control board. The push back we receive from some clients is that minor changes do not need to go through the change control board. The problem with today's systems is that they are so complex there is no easy way to determine what is minor. We have seen small changes have a significant impact on a system and it puzzled the developers because there should have been no relationship to the code that was changed and the code that was impacted.

We had a financial institution that had an online banking portal that customers used to do a significant amount of business. The organization wanted to change the look and layout of their logon page. It was deemed to be a cosmetic change with no real impact to the site so it was approved. I happened to be working onsite for the client the morning of the change. A few hours after the change was made, they started receiving many complaints that the electronic billing paying system was not working. The first question we asked was whether any changes were made since the system stop working. The response was we changed the home page but that would not impact the electronic bill paying system. We said we recognize that but humor us and put back the original page. When they loaded the original page the bill paying worked, when they put back the new page it stopped working. We did this five times with the same results. At this point the lead developer looked at us and said he is still not convinced that is the problem. You should have seen the look on my face. I said we could do it another twenty times but clearly there is a correlation. Now I fully understand the developers point. From a logical perspective there should be no correlation between the two. However, code is so complex today it is almost impossible to understand all of the different interactions that occur at a coding level. Therefore all changes no matter how minor they seem on paper, need to be fully tested and approved by the change control board.

With today's systems, there is no way to determine the impact a change can have on a system and even three lines of code could have a major impact on the system. All changes must go through the change control board. The follow-up question is what about emergency changes? Once again all changes must go through the change control board but we did not specify the order in which it has to occur. If there is an emergency change, there should be a process in which approval can be achieved in a quick, efficient manner to make a change based on a critical need or emergency. For example, if a major vulnerability is discovered and it is being actively exploited, an organization might need to make the change within the next 24 h and cannot wait 5 days until the next change control meeting. In those cases, there should be a special approval process. However, after the change is made, it must still be presented at the next change control board, explaining why an emergency change was required and receive approval after the fact. The bottom line is if a change is made to a system, the organization needs a way to determine if it is authorized or unauthorized. If all changes go through the change control board, any change that has not been approved is unauthorized and can be investigated. If only some changes go through the change control board, there is no easy way to make this determination. Since anomaly detection is a key approach for dealing with the APT, the change control process and logs provides the critical piece of the puzzle to determine if an anomaly is legitimate or not.

Once you understand all of the devices and configuration on a network, an organization needs to tie in the physical topology or layout of the network and where the critical data is located. This information would be used to determine which tools need to be used (host vs. network) and placement of the tools on the network. In essence, after an organization understands their network they need to think like an attacker. What systems and assets would an attacker target and how would they go about compromising that information. This information is used to stay one step ahead of the attacker and make sure the correct information is gathered to be able to identify signs of an attack and detect anomalies. There are many great tools for targeting and tracking attackers but if they are not connected in the correct areas of the network, they will not gather the right information and they will be ineffective at catching the APT.

The ultimate test in assessment and discovery is to run some sample attacks that are equivalent to what an attacker would perform and see if the organization can trace back the attacker. While this step seems very straight forward very few organizations perform proper threat validation to make sure they are gathering the correct information and properly correlating it. While an organization can perform many tests across the enterprise, the only test that matters is whether you are actually catching the threats you are concerned about.

In terms of setting up an assessment and discovery process for tracking, monitoring, preventing, detecting, and reacting to the APT, it is important that an organization understand what is on their network and track information related to an organization's most critical assets. The core steps that are performed and the desired outcome that can be used as a checklist to determine all the key areas are addressed are:

- Identification of critical assets including all devices connected to the network.
- Software and configuration management for all devices (i.e. hosts, servers, routers, switches).
- Robust change control process for tracking all changes to the environment.
- Proper tracking and identification of threat vectors based on likelihood.
- Tool requirements and proper testing of all security devices and software.
- Tracking and identification of indicators of compromise.
- Validation the tool properly tracks and capture indicators of high likelihood threats.
- Identification and implementation of proper mitigating factors.

While they will be covered in more detail in chapter 12, the 20 critical controls provide a robust framework for building an infrastructure that can defend against the APT. The first three controls directly map to APT Assessment and Discovery and serve as a foundation for understanding what is connected to a network and what could be the target of the threat:

- **Critical Control 1:** *Inventory of Authorized and Unauthorized Devices*— any device that is connected to the network must be properly tracked and controlled. Ideally only authorized devices are allowed to connect to the network. Currently the APT targets known workstations so while this control is important as a foundational item, it alone wiii not be effective at dealing with the APT. However, with advanced threats no single measure is going to work. Only by putting multiple measures together will an organization be able to defend and protect against the APT. The core reason on why critical control one is included is you cannot protect what you do not know about. Ultimately to defend against the APT an organization has to monitor the system and track traffic leaving the system. While this is the goal, in order to be able to do that you need an accurate inventory of all authorized systems. If an organization is tracking behavioral patterns but does not realize there are ten new systems and they get compromised, they cannot be tracked if the tracking system does not realize they exist. A key theme with the APT is knowledge is power and accurate inventory control is the key to success.

The other reason critical control 1 is important is we not only care about how the APT works today but how the attacker will evolve with APTv2 or the next generation threat. Based on the persistent nature of the APT, it will constantly evolve. As we perform better defenses and organizations can properly deal with the threat, the threat will not go away. It will continue to morph and change. Today we are playing catch up. The APT is causing massive damage and we are trying to figure out how to deal with it in an effective manner. The ultimate goal is to be predictive and proactive, look at where the attacker is going and try to get there before they do. One area that is a likely target for APTv2 is mobile devices. With BYOD (bring your own device) to work quickly becoming a norm, organizations really do not know what is on their network or have any control over it. Therefore as these devices get targeted, if organizations do not perform critical control 1, it will be even more difficult to deal with the advanced, emerging threat. The better job organizations can do in controlling and monitoring devices, the better off they will be.

- **Critical Control 2:** *Inventory of Authorized and Unauthorized Software—* tracking, controlling, and monitoring the devices that are connected to a network is important, but ultimately attackers break into software not hardware. Treating security as an iterative process of building blocks, the next logical building block after a hardware asset inventory is created, is to add in the software inventory component. The software that is installed on a system is ultimately what an attacker goes after to break in. In many cases software and/ or features that are installed is what attackers target and use to break into a system. Once again the theme of this book is how to build effective security that defends against all attacks including the APT. The APT is a critical threat that organizations have to deal with but we have to remember that other, less advanced threats are still alive and well. A common mistake we see is that organizations focus all of their energy on the APT, but lose site of the big picture which is effective security for all threats.

  Once again, today the APT typically targets email and Web browsers which are installed on most systems. These applications are needed in order to run the business, however in many cases, the APT will install additional software in order to maintain long term access, find critical information and extract it out of the organization via a command and control channel. By tracking all software that is installed (and or respective processes that are running) can also be used to track and find suspicious behavior. In many cases it is important to point out that additional tools are often needed to do this. The traditional task manager tool will typically not be able to find covert software because the advanced malware can easily rootkit these tools to provide false information. However by used tools like WMIC (Windows Management Instrumentation Console) in Windows or Tools from SysInternals, you can often find files and process that are missed by other programs. For example, see Figure 8.3,

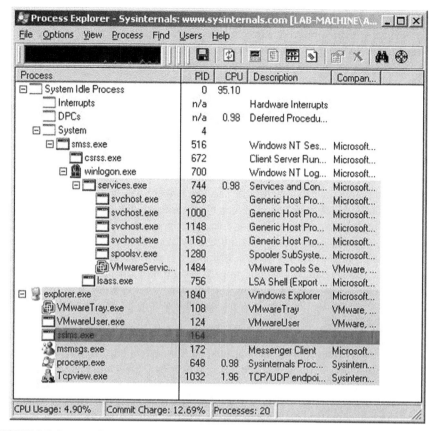

FIGURE 8.3 Process Explorer Found a Program sslms.exe that did not Show up Using the Standard Programs Built Into the Operating System

Process Explorer can often find programs and processes that do not show up with Task Manager.

In many cases the good news is that there are indicators of compromise that the system has been impacted by an APT or traditional threat. The question is are you looking in the right spot and using the right tools?

- **Critical Control 3:** *Secure Configurations for Hardware and Software on Laptops, Workstation and Servers*—While hardware and software inventory are critical foundation items and can give some indication of a compromise, ultimately the best way to track an APT is to monitor and track configurations of the systems. In many cases organizations are running extraneous components with privileged access that makes it much easier for the advanced threat to compromise a system. In many cases by hardening or limiting the exposure of the systems can make it more difficult for the system to get compromised and if it does get compromised, minimize the impact. Some examples of this include:

(1) turning off HTML embedded emails; (2) limiting attachments or flagging attachments that come from external sources; (3) running targeted applications (i.e. email clients and Web browsers) in isolated sandboxes or virtual machines; (4) configure software to run with the minimal privilege required to minimize the long term impact if a compromise does occur.

Analysis and Remediation

After discovery of compromised systems and confirmation that it is APT, there is still work to be done. One of the common mistakes that is made is after a compromised system is found, to rebuild it immediately and lose forensic evidence. We had a client that we were working with that as soon as there was an indication a system was compromised, it was pulled off the network, immediately rebuilt, and put back online. In the past, with the traditional threat the approach sometimes worked. The general premise of automatically rebuilding from a secure build is that the system that was compromised was not secure. If that is a true statement and there is proof that the system was changed without proper configuration management or was built from a standard install with default services running, that rebuilding from a secure build could have merit; however it is critical that a copy or image is taken of the compromised system.

The first problem with automatically rebuilding a compromised system is you lose the forensic evidence of what happened on this system and the level of damage or impact. Since the APT is always changing it is critical that an organization understands how the compromise occurred, learns from the information, and improves their overall security posture. The other reason is in many cases where mandatory reporting might come into play, being able to prove how much information was compromised could impact the level of disclosure, amount of the fines, and impact to the organization. This is another reason why coordinating with the legal department is so critical to make sure that everything is properly aligned across the organization.

The second reason why automatically rebuilding a compromised system is not always recommended is because today, most systems were built off of a secure build, many organizations have strict configuration control and many organizations have application white listing in place. Therefore the system that was compromised was built off of the secure build which means if an organization just puts back the original build, the same vulnerability that was exploited is still on the system and the attacker will get back in a second time. Creating a forensics image will allow an organization to understand how the compromise occurred and use it to improve the security of the so-called secure build.

After one system in the organization is found to be compromised one of the first things that is done after discovery is additional analysis. Very rarely does the APT only compromise a single system. While the initial point of compromise is often a single system, that system is used as the initial pivot point but the threat will quickly compromise other systems and create alternative channels. Just as the rule in security and IT is to have no single point of failures, attackers, especially advanced attackers, follow the same rules. If the attacker has a only a single point in and out of the organization and the system is found or taken off line, the attacker loses all access. Since one of the goals of the APT is long term access to the organization, when an organization is compromised with the APT, there are always many systems that are compromised. Therefore after a single system is found to be compromised, it is important to conduct targeted scans across the organization to look for other systems that would be compromised. Nothing is worse than having a compromise, fixing half of the systems, thinking the organization is clean but having the APT still persistent on the organization's network because they forgot to clean up all of the systems. It is important to remember that the system scanning needs to go beyond the traditional port and vulnerability scans. The focus is really on the indicators of compromise that were determined from the forensic analysis that was performed. During this scanning it is important to leverage statistical and behavioral-based anomaly detection and analysis.

Based on the advanced and persistent nature of the threat it can be very frustrating and almost feel like a game of whack a mole. As soon as you fix a problem, the threat exploits a new area. While it is important to remember that whatever you do to today to fix a problem, might not work tomorrow, it is still critical to deploy countermeasures to minimize the impact of future instances of the attacks but also perform a better job of detecting future compromises. It terms of implementing countermeasures it is important to always remember defense in depth and deploy both preventive (inbound) and detective (outbound) at both a host and network level across the enterprise. Ultimately in a perfect world, an organization should clean up all systems and prevent all future compromises from occurring. Unfortunately we do not live in a perfect world. Therefore the required countermeasures must focus on the persistent nature of the compromised system and the C2 (command and control) channels that were used to exfiltrate information from the organization. The first piece is to make sure that after the system is cleaned and rebooted that the malicious code is no longer active. One of the components of the APT is survivability or longevity. While ideally we want systems never to be compromised, being compromised for 8 h is much better than 8 months. The ultimate damage of the APT comes from the C2 which is used to steal sensitive information from the organization. It is critical to make sure that all methods of causing harm are also removed and tracked to make sure they do not reappear in the future.

The final steps in analysis and remediation is to take the information from the analysis and forensics and implement countermeasures to minimize the chances of the compromise occurring again in the future. A checklist of the key items that are done during analysis and remediation are:

- Identification and remediation of all systems.
- Better understanding of methods used to compromise the system.
- Enhance hardened configuration based on forensic analysis.
- Actionable intelligence to defend the enterprise.
- Ability to effectively implement new measures to defend and detect the advanced threat.
- Integrate APT into the overall defensive plan.

Program Review

Today one of the big trends is all of these new diets. There is the low carb diet, the high carb diet, the raw food diet, and I even saw a brownie diet. The problem with all of these diets is that they are a short term fix. People go on the diets for 3 months and lose a lot of weight. They then go back to their regular eating habits and gain it all back again. If you want to lose weight and keep the weight off, you have to make lifestyle changes that you can sustain long term. The reason this section starts with this introduction is because dealing with the APT is no different. Many organizations think that the APT is a fad and if they make temporary adjustments for several months they will be OK. Having threats that are advanced, persistent, targeted, stealthy, and data focused is the new reality. It is not going away. Fad security solutions are not going to work.

Many organizations get caught up on the name "APT" and buy solutions that address the threat and feel they are protected. What makes the APT significant is in many cases it shows us that we have not done security correctly and just like a diet, a short term fix will give you short term results. If you want to effectively protect an organization, you have to make changes to how the organization does business. The most critical change is security must be built into everything an organization does, from the beginning. Security is not an afterthought, it is not a separate discipline, it is involved in every aspect of the business.

Security is the electricity in a house not the paint on the walls. Many organizations treat security as something you do at the very end, similar to painting the walls when you build a house. When you are building a house you do not have to worry about the paint color until the very end. You can even change the color of the paint at any time with relative ease. This is how organizations treat security. Let's wait until the system is developed or the new application is purchased, we can add on some security by buying a few devices and if they do not work out, you can always add or change out the security device or add a new IDS, IPS, or firewall at a later point.

Unfortunately this does not work and is the reason why so many organizations have ineffective security. Security must be designed and built in from the beginning, similar to the electrical wiring in the house. The electricity must be designed in on the original blueprints and it is a critical part of the house. It would be extremely difficult to add it later and it is very hard to change. Therefore you think long and hard about the placement of outlets because it is much more difficult to change the electrical wiring in a house than it is to change the paint. If we want effective security, it needs to be designed in from the beginning.

The first thing that needs to be done once an organization recognizes that while they are addressing security at a high level to deal with the traditional threat, they are not dealing with it at an embedded level to deal with the APT, is assess the business rules. Many organizations have performed security over the years as a necessity but never really designed security properly. As one executive stated, "security just happened." Therefore the security posture and the way they perform the business of security is very ad hoc and not every aligned with where it needs to be to deal with the advanced, emerging threats. One of the key components of incident response is eradication and lessons learned. How did the attacker get in and what could have been done to prevent or detect the threat in a more timely manner. In essence, an organization needs to put together security requirements of all of the things they need to be doing in order to make sure the organization is protected. As bizarre as it sounds many organizations perform a gap analysis without having list of what the ideal security state should be. If you do not know where you need to be, how can you determine if you have gaps or not.

Once an organization has a detailed list of their ideal state, a gap analysis has to be done against the corporate culture. Many corporate cultures have evolved with being very user friendly with little or no concern with regards to security. Therefore an organization can look at their policies and procedures, identify gaps in security, but if the corporate culture does not support those changes, no one is going to follow them. While fixing corporate culture is critical in order to create an environment that can effectively deal with the APT, it is important to remember that only executives can change corporate culture. Very often security and/or IT will recognize that the corporate culture is not properly aligned and will try to change it themselves. That will be a long, hard, painful, and unsuccessful journey. Unless there is executive support, you cannot change the fundamental culture of the organization.

In order to change corporate culture based on security gaps, it is important that security plays the role of the honest broker. The first fundamental problem is security usually picks a side in the fight. The second fundamental problem is executives do not understand that the current way of doing business is losing money and not effective. The third problem is we have to recognize today that we might have to make decisions that could have a small negative impact on the users. Let's look at an example to illustrate this. One of the common ways of compromising a system is for the APT to send a legitimate looking attachment that ultimately infects the system. The common role of security is to pick a side in the fight and say we must block all attachments. The executives will immediately push back stating the impact it will have on the user base. The problem is that they are assuming the way they are doing business today has no negative impact and the change will have a negative impact. Actually, the way they are doing business today has a bigger impact that what is being proposed but the information is just not being presented in a proper manner.

The better way is to perform proper analysis, presenting the business case that shows the pros and cons, ultimately tracing everything back to the needs of the business. The more security can think and speak like executives, the more effective the organization will be at securing the enterprise. The really good news with security is that we have the data to justify the decisions that we want to make to secure the organization. The problem is we usually do not present it in an effective way which means everyone loses. The organization makes the wrong decision and security becomes frustrated.

One of the key themes of dealing with the APT is knowledge is power. An organization cannot protect what it does not know. Even though it was covered earlier in the book, it is worth repeating. An organization must have a single slide that shows the focus of security which includes an organization's critical data with corresponding threat and vulnerabilities. An organization must put together and create an accurate picture of where the organization is today. In order to effectively deal with the APT an organization has to understand where its exposures are today and get an accurate picture of its current landscape. Based on all of the breach data and information that is available on the APT, a separate document needs to be created on where they should be. Based on this comparison, a gap analysis should be performed which will drive what areas an organization should focus on to better protect and deal with the APT.

A big focus area that organizations overlook when it comes to dealing with the APT is the people side of the equation. In many cases the APT is less of a technical problem and more of a people problem. However, technology is easier than dealing with people so organizations would prefer to spend a lot of money on technology, thinking they are doing good, when in reality many technologies that are available today, out of the box are not very effective at dealing with the APT. The APT targets and goes after the user. Therefore a key focus area needs to be the triad that addresses the human element which is policy-training-awareness:

- *Policy*—Policies need to be clearly written and explain to the user what is expected of them. Compliance with the policy is mandatory and the document clearly lays out what someone can or cannot do. In order for a policy to be effective it needs to be SMART:
  - *Specific*—The policy needs to be very clear and concise. It should not be open to interpretation or vague. The policy should be understood and implemented in a single manner. For example, a policy statement that states "a password must be 15 characters" is specific. A password must be strong is vague and open to interpretation.
  - *Measurable*—A great way to determine if a policy is specific enough is to determine how you would measure it. If an organization cannot quickly determine if someone is or is not following the policy it is probably too vague. Specific policies are easy to measure and determine whether people are compliant with it or not.
  - *Achievable*—It is important to make sure the policy is something the user can accomplish. This is where the policy ties with training. If the person does not have the skills needed to achieve the policy, they probably need additional skills.
  - *Realistic*—While it is important that the employees can accomplish the policy, it is also important that it is realistic. For example, changing a password is achievable but having users change their password every 30 min is not realistic.
  - *Time Based*—The last piece of an effective policy is the time period in which the user needs to accomplish the task. For example, the password has to be changed every 45 days.

The key aspect of a policy is that it needs to be understandable so someone can follow it. This means there needs to be a metric that you can use to determine whether someone is following the policy or not. Policies form the foundation of an effective stance against the APT. The problem is most organizations have policies, they are just not very effective. Just because you have a document called a policy does not mean it is working. Metrics will let you track the effectiveness of the policy and see how well it is working. The most important part of the policy is that it tells the user WHAT to do:

- *Training*—While the policy tells the user what to do, training provides the user the SKILLS required to follow the policy. Very often a policy will be specific but the user does not have the knowledge, skills, or tools required in order to perform the actions required to follow the policy. We have seen cases where organizations keep re-writing their policy thinking that it is ineffective, when in reality the policy is very effective, the user just does not have the skills required to follow the policy.
- *Awareness*—In many cases users understand what has to be done (policy), they have the skills for performing it (training), but they do not feel it is important so they do not follow it. In these cases there is a BEHAVIORAL issue that needs to be addressed with proper awareness. The goal of awareness is to explain to a user why something is important so they will modify their behavior and follow the policy moving forward. Having clear metrics in the policy will allow an organization to identify areas that people are not following so awareness can focus on improving compliance. After an effective awareness campaign, the metrics should improve for the specific policy statements that were focused on.

Having effective policies that all users follow, goes a long way to building a solid foundation for dealing with the APT. The key areas of program review that organizations need to follow are:

- Create SMART policies that tie closely with training and awareness.
- Integrate security into the SDLC (software development lifecycle).
- Make security a part of all business units.
- Improve business communication to the executives by translating security initiatives into business language.
- Proper gap analysis against focus area for an organization.
- Improve overall awareness across the organization.

MINIMIZING THE PROBLEM

Based on the complexities of how the APT work and the persistent nature, it is safe to assume that at some level you will eventually be compromised and detection is critical. However a key way of dealing with the APT and minimizing the number of times an organization is compromised is by reducing the size of the attack surface. The way the systems and applications have been developed play right into the hand of the attacker. The more complex a system is the easier it is for an attacker to find a problem and the harder it is for an organization to secure. The smaller the size of code and the less complexity the harder it is for an attacker and the easier it is to secure. What is frustrating is that we continuously add complexity to code and much of the complexity is not needed. For example, embedded macros and embedded HTML with email are two common vectors of attack and are features that organizations do not need. Turning off these features takes away a key vector from the attacker.

One of the main targets of the APT is the client and utilizing the endpoint as a way to trick the user into doing something they should not. Once the system becomes compromised it becomes a pivot point for the attacker. While getting compromised is not ideal, if we can reduce the amount of time an organization is compromised it will make it much more difficult for the attacker. Today, typical endpoints can stay compromised for months and/or years without anyone noticing. Since endpoints are very rarely rebuilt except when a tech refresh occurs, which is typically 3–5 years, a system can be compromised for a long period of time. One area of focus to complement a secure network architecture is to minimize the length in time a system can be compromised. Thin clients is a great way to not only minimize the amount of time a system is compromised but to also provide better configuration management. With typical clients, overtime they slowly become different and not compliant with the original build, this not only makes it easier for an attacker to break it but also harder to detect since every system is different. Managing and making changes to a large number of systems is very difficult and hard to control. By utilizing a thin client, the configuration is managed in one spot, so changes can be made very easily. In addition, every day when the system is turned on it pulls down a new image. Now if the running image for the day is compromised it is only compromised for up to 24 h before it receives a new image. In addition to providing more robust configuration management and change control, which will make it more difficult for an attacker to break in, it also greatly limits the amount of time a system can be compromised.

While thin clients provide a nice solution, they do not scale in all environments. Based on the fact that the two most dangerous applications on the planet are Web browsers and email clients, another solution is to run those within a virtual machine. Now if they are running in a virtual machine and the user is tricked into doing something they should not, the virtual machine is compromised not the actual host operating system. Since the guest operating system closes every time the application is closed, a system is only compromised for a few minutes instead of a few months. By reducing the surface space and minimizing the time of compromise can make it much harder for the attacker to maintain long term persistence.

END TO END SOLUTION FOR THE APT

No single technology is going to make you secure or protect an enterprise. Only by integrating many solutions together in which the strength of one will offset the weakness of another, will an organization be able to properly defend against the APT. The following charts show how offense can guide the defense by building an integrated solution to the APT that maps against the steps that the threat uses to compromise an organization.

	Sample Product Protection
Step 1. Reconnaissance	Network DLP (Prevent sensitive data from leaving)
Step 2 Network Intrusion	Firewall (blocks APT connection via IP reputation)
	Web Gateway (detects/blocks obfuscated malware)
	Email Gateway (block spear-phishing emails, links to malicious sites)
	Network Threat Response (detects obfuscated malware)
	Network Security Platform (stops malicious exploit delivery)
Step 3. Establish Backdoor	Firewall (detects/blocks APT back-channel communication)
	Network Threat Response (detects APT destination IPs)
	Application Whitelisting (prevent backdoor installation)
Step 4. Install Command and Control Utilities	Web Gateway (detects/blocks access to malicious applications)
	Application Whitelisting (prevent unauthorized changes to systems)
Step 5. Data ExFiltration	Unified DLP (prevent data from leaving the network)
Step 6. Maintaining Persistence	Network User Behavioral Analysis (identifies unexpected user behavior during APT reconnaissance and data collection phases)

The critical piece of success to building a solution that defends against the APT is to make sure the solutions cover all steps that an attacker uses to compromise a network. With traditional attacks, most of the focus was on preventing and dealing with the exploitation of the systems. While that is important it is too late in the process. The attacks are too sophisticated and if you wait for them to get to the front door it will be too little too late. Mechanisms must be put in place to minimize and detect attacks so that can be tracked prior to exploitation. By tracking an attacker before compromise, allows an organization to determine if compromise was successful and deal with the threat in a timely manner. In many cases one of the reasons the APT is so devastating is that an organization has no idea of knowing when an actual compromise occurred. Since they do not know about it, you cannot detect what you do not know.

SUMMARY

Growing up there was a TV show called MacGyver. One of the things I loved about watching the show is whenever the lead character would get into trouble, he would use conventional items in a non-conventional way to solve a problem. For example, he would use a toaster as a lighter to ignite something on fire. The thing that always struck about the show was with proper creativity you could often solve a problem with what you have. You do not always have to buy something new to solve a problem, you just have to break out of the conventional mindset of how something is used, look at the capabilities it has and by re-configuring it you can solve a different problem, and utilize a device in a way that was different than how you normally use it. As we finish up this chapter, that thought comes to mind on how an organization needs to deal with and solve the APT problem. Now, please do not read more into this than what is there. There are definitely gaps in our current technology that need to be filled, but in many cases we can use existing technology, configured in a different manner to be more effective against the APT.

Many times security technology is used directly out of the box with minimal configuration or changes. That default install will often solve some problems but is typically not as effective as it could be if it was configured correctly. In addition, the default install will typically solve a single problem but does not scale well for additional problems. By looking at all of the functionality a technology has and by configuring it to work differently or utilize more of the unused components, it can often scale to other problems.

We always have to remind ourselves that there is no silver bullet when it comes to security. Not only is there no single device that will protect our enterprise, but even if there was we would not want to use it. What is the problem if we are relying on one device or technology for 85% of our security? If that device fails, we are left with minimal protection. On the other hand if we have 15 different technologies that are all providing between 10 and 20% of our security and one device fails, we are still in great shape. Organizations to protect against the APT often want the silver bullet. We often hear people say that a given technology is useless because it does not stop 100% of the APT and there are ways to bypass it. My response is of course. The real question is, does it catch any attacks. If you have a technology that catches 0% of all attacks for a several month period it is useless and I agree that is should be removed from your network. However if it catches some attacks and it is not expensive, we still need to keep it in place. One of the simple pieces of analysis we do is what you gain and what you lose by performing some action or deploying some technology. If you gain more than you lose you should probably do it. If you lose more than you gain then most likely the cost benefit does not make sense. In many cases organizations want to replace a technology instead of augmenting and complimenting it. Typically an existing technology does catch some attacks but not enough to be effective on its own. Therefore if you replace it by removing it off your network and it caught 15% of attacks, the new technology must catch all of the existing 15% plus additional attacks to be of value. Often that is not true and when you remove a technology off the network you are going backwards in security because you lose what the old technology did and the new technology does something different.

While this book is on APT, we often have to remember that the APT is not the only game in town. There are other attack vectors that we cannot forget about. Traditional worms, viruses, disgruntled employees, and hacktivists are all alive and well, trying to cause harm to your environment and they are quite different than the APT. Therefore if we say a technology is useless against the APT and we remove it off of the network, we have done a dis-service because we now lost the capability to catch other types of attacks. In building a robust defensive infrastructure we have to use many complimentary technologies to increase our security, remembering that there is a breadth of attacks we have to deal with.

In addition to saying that a technology is not of value, we also have to look at how it is configured. We perform assessments for clients and on average they utilize less than 35% of the functionality that the device is capable of. Very often security technology has a lot of functionalities and capability and many organizations do not have the devices tuned correctly or are not even aware of some of the built-in capabilities. Spend some time understanding what you have and what it is capable of and very often there is more functionality available that you are not using or taking advantage of.

Highlighting these key points, one of the statements that we often hear is a technology like AV is dead. As security professionals this is very dangerous and we have to be careful with making a general statement like this. Yes, the typical default installation of AV against an adversary that is fully aware that it is there is completely useless against the APT. Most APTs can slip by traditional AV software. However, before we say it is dead we have to ask two questions: (1) Is it catching any other attacks? and (2) Is it designed and tuned to catch the APT? Most of the AV software that we see is still catching 30% or more malicious pieces of code on a monthly basis. If we say AV is dead and we remove it off of the network, there are now 30% attacks that will now infect systems. How are those attacks going to be dealt with? Second, AV was not built to deal directly with the APT since it was built to look for viruses which operate and act quite differently. That is almost like cutting your foot and taking an aspirin and getting mad that it did not stop the bleeding, that is not what it as designed for. While AV was not typically designed to deal with the APT, it is often integrated with endpoint security solutions that if configured with application white listing, can have some impact on the APT.

When designing a building a secure network it is important to recognize that it requires many technologies and creative integration to effectively deal with all attacks, up to and including the APT. While the APT is devastating to an organization it is important that we create and deploy a secure enterprise that can defend against all attacks.

The Future and How to Win

One of the reasons why so many organizations are being compromised is because they are not proactive in predicting the next generation of attacks. Therefore, organizations are aggressively working on mitigating the impact of the APT. In defending against the APT it is important to look towards the future and the next generation of threats. One of the many reasons why APT is significant is that it has changed the rules from static attacks to dynamic attacks. The threat will continue to evolve to be successful. As soon as we create a defensive measure to protect against a specific vector of attack, the threat will create a new vector of attack. Therefore instead of trying to implement security that will just solve today's problem, we need to implement adaptive security so that it can continue to evolve and keep pace with the attacker.

In the last section of this book we will look at where threats are moving and what organizations need to do to implement security that works. The chapters in this section include:

By focusing in on the right areas of security, long term organizations can win and properly protect an organization. Remember winning does not mean it is easy and will still be difficult. In addition, just because you are effective against an attacker does not mean that you will not get bloody and some damage will not occur. An organization will be compromised but by focusing on adaptive security organizations can survive and still have a viable business even though attacks are constantly occurring.

The Changing Landscape: Cloud and Mobilization

INTRODUCTION

It often amazes me when I reflect back over the last 20 years on how much technology has changed and the impact it has had on our lives. How did we ever survive without cell phones and GPS? Imagine having to buy a map, look up a road, and write out instructions by hand. When you went out for the day, no one had any way to get a hold of you. The only option was to find a pay phone, call your home answering machine, and see if there were any messages. Gone are the days of having to write a college paper using a type writer and if you made a mistake, either have to use white out or re-type the entire page. In the words of my son, seriously, how did you get anything done?

While we always tend to look at technology from a functional perspective, if we put on our defensive cap and know the only way to be good at the defense is to understand the offense; the key question is how did attackers break into anything 20 years ago? The answer is mainly from a physical theft perspective. While it worked, it was difficult and not easy. Technology has enabled our lives in amazing ways but it also has enabled the lives of attackers.

What is really amazing is that while technology has changed dramatically over the past 20 years and helped enable attackers to break in from anywhere, the vulnerabilities that are being exploited are still very similar. If you go back to 1985, the world was completely different than it is today. Hardly anyone had computers at their home and those that did usually had the words Commodore or Atari on the front. If you had connectivity to the Internet it was through a dial-up 14.4 modem with an amber or green monitor. Very few organizations had computers on everyone's desk and most computers were stand-alone isolated systems. Most attacks took advantage of infected floppy disks that where passed around among users. You did have some limited government and research organizations connected to the Internet and attacks like the Morris worm did happen. However what is important to remember with network-based attacks like the Morris worm is what the ultimate vulnerabilities were that were exploited. The reason why worms and attacks were successful in the 1980s is because most people were unaware of the threats and unintentionally performed actions that would make it easier for the attacker; for example, most systems had a default install of the operating system, extraneous services were running and many systems were unpatched. Back in the 1980s this was not surprising since cyber security was not a top priority for many organizations.

What makes this scary is to fast forward to today. The world has changed a lot in 20 years and technology is all around us. Most individuals have at least three personal devices that they use on a regular basis, not to include work and home computers. While the technological advances are amazing, what is frightening is when we look at the advanced threats that are around us today and we explore the reasons why compromises are successful. In many cases the number one reason for compromises for organizations today is lack of user awareness and users open attachments that they shouldn't. Once the attacker has a pivot point within the network, the main reason for compromise of a server is many systems are running default installations with extraneous services that are not patched. While technology has advanced significantly over the last 20 years, the exposure that attackers are using to break in has not changed that much. The good news is if we get security correct it does scale and grow with an organization and that is even true for the APT. The main problem is that entities are so focused on functionality and increased performance, they lose sight of integrating security into the technology from the beginning. In doing so, security becomes an afterthought. With the advanced technology that we are using today, the only proper way to secure it is to design security into the software development life cycle. When someone has an initial idea for a system of any type, security and functionality needs to be balanced. With the advanced threats, complexity of systems, porous nature of our networks and the portability of our information, security needs to be designed in from the beginning.

One of the fundamental problems with security is that in some cases, it is done after the system is built. One of the problems with the traditional C&A (certification and accreditation) process is that it allows a system to be designed and built and security is engaged during the testing phase. The problem is that during the testing phase it is easy to find and identify any exposures because the system is fully operational and is the ideal time to evaluate the overall effectiveness of the security. The problem is that it is almost impossible to make any significant changes so when problems are found, minimal can be done about them. Testing must always be performed; however the point of testing the system after it is built, assumes that proper security was designed in from the beginning and to find issues that were overlooked. Testing with no integrated or built in security means that any issues have to be fixed by trying to take a band aid approach and make changes after the fact. This is not only inefficient but with major security problems that cannot be fixed in this manner, the system is vulnerable as soon as it goes into operations. The advanced threats hope and pray that this happens because it makes it easy for them to compromise and take over a system.

The idea of having a DAA (designating approving authority) sign off on a system is good, but the level of risk and exposure should be decided on and signed off during the design phase. The DAA should not be forced into a design after the system is built because they have no other options. As the APT and future threats continue to be stealthy and advanced, it is critical that new technology is not only embraced but that security is built in from the beginning.

People often claim how advanced attackers have become; honestly they have not become advanced as we have and based on how we have crafted out lives, we have made their lives a whole lot easier. If everything we do is done with paper and pencil and locked in a physical safe, regardless of the sophistication level, the adversary will never be able to be more advanced than the technology that the organization they are targeting is using. In many cases, based on how quickly technology has been embraced with minimal security, we created the problem of the APT. This is actually good news. Since we technically created the problem we can also be the ones to solve it and create the solution.

With traditional phones, answering machines, and type writers, other than physical theft or breach, there was minimal an adversary could do to cause direct harm to an organization's data. Back in the 1980s for the average organization and individual, it would have been very difficult to perform a remote compromise from China or Russia, without any Internet connectivity. As Cliff Stohl in the book the "Cuckoo's Egg" learned that if you are connected to others via a network you are a target, even back in the 1980s. Proper security can absolutely help protect an organization but we have to remember a simple fact, if there is a transmission path between two entities, there is a potential for compromise. As many organizations are learning, nothing beats a good old fashion air gap for protecting or defending against an attack.

What makes security so exciting is that it is a never-ending battle because the threats and technological vulnerabilities are always changing; once you figure out a solution to a problem, after a short period of time, it will stop working because the attackers will figure out a way around the defense measures that we deployed. This is what we often refer to as attacker leap frog. The typical approach to deal with the standard threat is allowing the attacker to find a vulnerability or way to exploit a system. Once they cause harm, the defenders react by figuring out a way to fix it. This allows an organization to be secure for a short period of time. During this time the attacker is actively working to find new ways to exploit the system and will eventually be successful and break back in, essentially leaping over the defense. The defense will react, by researching and finding ways to defend against the new threat, leaping back over the attacker. While this might seem like a hard enough game, add new technology into the equation and the game becomes even more difficult.

While this life cycle is inevitable, the APT and new technologies that are emerging changes this approach. First, the APT is so persistent that the threat is constantly looking for a variety of ways to compromise an organization. Therefore reactive security is no longer going to be effective because as soon as the defenders figure out a way to properly protect the organization, the threat has already utilized a new method of compromise. Proactive and predictive security, which requires constant evaluation of the threat is critical, with the goal of properly protecting an organization's critical information prior, during or after a compromise. In order to perform this in an effective manner it is critical that an organization properly track emerging technologies and understand how they must be deployed effectively in an organization's environment. While there are many changes occurring that impact an organization's cyber defense with regard to the APT, two critical technologies are: cloud and mobile devices.

YOU CANNOT FIGHT THE CLOUD

One area that typically stresses out security people is when you mention the cloud. Many security people say that the cloud cannot be secure and that there is no way that an organization can move to the cloud because the security risks and issues will be too insurmountable. The bottom line is whether we like it or not, organizations are going to move to the cloud. The financial justifications and increased functionality means that instead of trying to fight it, security teams need to understand the cloud, embrace it, and figure out a secure way to implement it within an organization. When you look at the cost savings that an organization can recognize by going to the cloud and the tight economic times that many organizations are facing, organizations will move to the cloud. If an organization is looking at rolling out a new application and implemenines it in-house could easily cost several hundred thousand dollars just to stand up the application, not to include testing, training, and all of the other hidden costs. However, if you move to the cloud, an organization can be up and running within a day and try out a service for minimal costs and in some cases for free. Therefore if you look at the business justifications and cost savings, the cloud is going to happen. Plus, based on the ease in which a business unit can sign up for the cloud, it can happen with relative ease. In many cases organizations are using the cloud and do not even realize it.

Many of our clients who say no cloud or that cloud is not allowed, when we start talking to other business units, quickly realize that the cloud is being utilized but no one was aware. Some cloud services can be signed up for with nothing more than a credit card and can cost around $1000 a month, which means it is easy to expense and slip through the cracks. Since the cloud does represent new risks and exposures, especially with regards to the APT, it is important to take a survey of your organization and understand what you do or do not have when it comes to the cloud. Not only is gaining an accurate picture of what cloud services are used within the organization important for security, but it is also important from a financial and legal perspective. When dealing with the cloud the CFO and chief legal counsel can be big advocates.

Very often if an organization signs up for individual cloud services there are not any discounts applied and can get expensive if every business unit is signing up separately. Instead of having individual contracts with each group within a business, having a single contract for the entire company can often allow the organization to have more cost savings, get better discounts, and have more leverage when it comes to negotiating the contract. From a legal perspective, if an individual or a business unit sign up for a cloud service they are often agreeing to the standard T&Cs (terms and conditions) which might not always be in the best interest of the organization. When an organization finds out that business units are using the cloud, legal often gets very upset and concerned because those contracts could put the organization at risk.

In addition to having better cost savings and control over an organization's liability, having a single contract with a cloud provider for an entire organization instead of individual contracts is also good for security. One of the key areas we will talk about below is that one way to secure devices that are outside of your control is to make sure there is clear contract language covering and addressing security with SLAs (service level agreements) that match the level of security that is within an organization. If an organization is signing 20, $100k contracts it is hard to be able to negotiate strict controls and security within the contracts. However, if the organization negotiates one $2 million contract, they now have a lot more leverage and control to dictate the T&Cs that will be most favorable to them.

IS THE CLOUD REALLY NEW?

Sometimes in technology, we like to create new terms for existing technology. The question that CIOs often ask is whether the cloud is really new. We will look at more formal definitions below and the security implications, but if you look at the concept of a private cloud at some level it is very similar to outsourcing of data centers or having a co-location (colo) facility to house your data center instead of running it in-house. This concept of out-sourced data centers or private cloud have been around for a long time. While there are some differences that we will discuss, the real issue with the cloud is losing control or outsourcing a specific aspect of your operations to a third party. If we break security down into its most basic components it really revolves around:

1. What is your critical information?
2. Who has access to it?
3. How is the information protected?
4. Is all access tracking, audited, and reviewed?

Whether the systems, information, and devices are in an organization's data center or controlled by someone else, the same fundamental questions still need to be answered. In addition, from an attacker's perspective, all they care about is targeting a key set of information. Whether the data is on a server in your data center or someone else's is really not important to them. For some reason organizations think that if the information is within their data centers it is more protected than if it is residing in someone else's data center; however the physical location of the servers (assuming they do not cross international boundaries) is really irrelevant in many cases, the more important question is what level of protection is being applied to protect the information.

We have seen cases where organizations are reluctant to move to the cloud because of security reasons; however after analyzing their network it turned out that by moving to the cloud would actually increase their security not decrease. There are cases where a cloud provider's security is better than the organization's security. Many organizations have very complex environments that are very dynamic and therefore configuration management is not very robust. While in many organizations all systems are configured differently and while change control is implemented it is not always enforced and all changes are not validated or audited. With many cloud providers, since they are offering a single service in a scalable manner, all systems are properly locked down, maintained, patched, and robust change control processes are implemented. Remember, one of the avenues of attack for the APT is to find one vulnerability, exploit it, and use it as a method to compromise an organization. The less configuration management, the easier it is for the attacker and the more configuration management and monitoring, the harder it is for the attacker. In many cases based on how a cloud provider is structured makes it harder for an attacker to compromise and break in. The bottom line is any security decisions should be based off of risk to your critical information based on the business your organization is in. While the calculation might be different for different organizations, in many cases when the calculation is done it turns out that in moving to the cloud, the risk is actually reduced.

The bottom line is based on the demands that are being put on an organization, the cloud is here to stay because the following drivers cannot be ignored:

- *Increase revenues and capabilities:*
    - Faster time to market, deploy products rapidly.
    - Scale (up and down) more quickly.
    - Derive actionable business intelligence from large data sets.

- *Reduce costs and increase efficiency:*
    - Reduce capital expenses and implementation and maintenance costs.
    - Pay only for "what-you-use."
    - Standardize application and infrastructure provisioning.

- *Mitigate and manage risk:*
    - Leverage best-in-class and more cost-effective security controls.
    - Improve business assurance, redundancy, and continuity.

WHAT IS THE CLOUD?

The term "cloud" has taken on a life of its own over the last several years. When talking about the cloud there are many different approaches that can be used.

When referring to the cloud the following are the essential characteristics that are needed for something to be referred to as a cloud service:

- On-demand self-service.
- Broad network access.
- Resource pooling.
- Rapid elasticity.
- Measured service.

Some of the service models that are used to deploy the cloud are:

- Software as a Service (SaaS).
- Platform as a Service (PaaS).
- Infrastructure as a Service (IaaS).

Within those service models the following are the deployment models that can be used:

- Public/vendor cloud.
- Private cloud and virtual private cloud.
- On and off-premises.
- Hybrid cloud.
- Community cloud.

While cost is definitely one valuable reason for moving to the cloud the two big drivers typically focus around IT Efficiency and Business Agility:

- IT Efficiency:
    - Enables a variable cost model for IT.
    - Minimizes overall IT costs—Shift CAPEX to OPEX.
    - Improves infrastructure resource deployment and utilization through virtualization.
    - Provides a flexible, reusable application development model.

- Business Agility and Market Competitiveness:

    - Enables quicker "time-to-market."
    - Rapid application deployment.
    - Reduced infrastructure setup/configuration.
    - Support for large-scale parallel programming.
    - Reduces switching costs associated with changing business strategies.
    - Alternatives for cost reduction efforts—allows for outsourcing segments of IT.

While this book is not about general cloud implementation, the focus is on the impact it has on security and overall APT.

One of the biggest reasons on why the cloud represents an exposure to many organizations is proper planning is not performed. If organizations actually understood the pros and cons, analyzed the exposures, and properly planned, the cloud can be an effective, cost-effective secure method for providing services to an organization.

SECURING THE CLOUD

In securing the cloud, the first thing to remember is cloud is not an all or nothing decision. One of the biggest problems organizations have with security is that they go to extremes and treat security as a binary yes or no decision. In most cases, you want to find a middle ground or a balance when it comes to security. One hundred percentage security is not good because that means 0% functionality and you go out of business. Zero percentage security is not good either because it means the organization is exposed, your data will be compromised, and you go out of business. You want to find the balance where security is optimized by providing just the services that are needed and the cloud is no exception.

Instead of thinking of cloud as a binary decision within an organization, in order to implement the cloud in a secure manner, an assessment should be performed across the organization. This assessment should be based off of risk and exposure to the organization. Instead of allowing or not allowing the cloud, organizations should break their business processes/applications into three categories:

1. *Cloud ready*—These are applications that could move to the cloud today. Based on the offering of the cloud providers and the type of data, moving to the cloud would allow them to maintain the same level of risk and not increase the overall exposure. Even though applications might be cloud ready, the ultimate decisions should still be run through finance and legal to make sure that the proper contract is negotiated from both a funding and liability perspective.
2. *Potentially cloud ready*—Applications that could be moved to the cloud if certain changes are made to the application or if certain conditions are listed within the contract. It is important to make sure that proper SLAs (service level agreements) are put into the contract to make sure the organization is properly protected.
3. *Not cloud ready*—Some applications, at least for the foreseeable future should never be moved to the cloud. These are typically applications that need to be air gapped or that the risk is too great and the organization needs to maintain control in order to make sure the organization is protected.

In order for this exercise to be successful it is important to make sure the criteria for putting business processes in the cloud is clearly laid out and there is consistency across the decision making process. It is also important to make sure that there are applications listed across all three categories. If you create the three categories but go back to the executives and say that nothing in the organization is cloud ready, clearly the criteria was too rigid and the executives will lose faith and trust in the process. It is also important to remember that security is all about managing and controlling risk to the enterprise. The acceptable level of risk should be based on the type of data that is being protected, not where it is located. We often see organizations have a very high risk tolerance if the data is on their servers connected to the Internet, but a very low risk tolerance if the data is in the cloud. If both systems have the same data and the same visibility from the Internet, we cannot have a double standard. Regardless of where the data is or where the servers are located the tolerable level of risk should be the same. By defining the acceptable risk level and overall risk for each application allows the process to be unbiased and go smoother.

When talking about securing the cloud, many organizations make it a technical discussion on how to secure the cloud. If you step back securing a server has not changed. If an attacker is going to break into a server they are going to find visible IPs, open ports, and vulnerabilities in the services. This same method of attacking a system is the same regardless of who owns the server. When protecting servers in the cloud, especially with regards to the APT, it is critical to take a holistic approach.

In securing an enterprise it is critical to provide proper protection of the data, appropriate security controls and compliance with all regulations. These areas need to be addressed regardless of whether the servers are located in a private data center or in the cloud. The big difference in moving towards the cloud is that an organization cannot directly validate all of the security in the same manner they could if it was in a private data center. The irony is that while a company in theory would have more control in a private data center, the applications are so diverse and complex, many private data centers do not perform comprehensive, holistic validation.

No matter where the data is but especially with the cloud, strong governance needs to be put in place to make sure all appropriate security is implemented and performed correctly. The last item that is unique to the cloud is the multi-tenancy aspect of the cloud. Depending on implementation, potentially multiple organizations are all running on the same systems or infrastructure, which means a breach in one organization could allow another organization to be compromised.

Governance and multi-tenancy are the two big issues to focus on with the cloud when it comes to protecting against the APT. The APT is persistent and will continue to probe an organization to find a vulnerability or exposure. Having proper governance to make sure all security is properly addressed and if an item is neglected, it is addressed in a timely manner, is one of the keys to security of the cloud. Remember our theme of dealing with the APT, prevention is ideal but detection is a must. Many organizations focus solely on prevention. It is critical that a cloud provider properly addresses the detection aspect of security. Since the APT will always use the simplest, easiest, most effective way into an organization it is important that organizations not only look at today's vulnerabilities but look at where the APT will evolve to make sure security can stay ahead of the curve. As users are made more aware that they are the target and it is more difficult to exploit the user, the APT will continue to focus on the cloud. By targeting a weaker organization that is housed at the same cloud provider that the APT is targeting, could be used as a potential foothold into the organization and the adversary could use the weaker organization as a pivot point to compromise the APT's ultimate target.

While it is important to make sure that proper security is in place, as we have talked about, securing a server is a pretty mature process whether an organization owns the server or a third party. The real question is whether the proper process is being followed.

The parts that are often overlooked when it comes to securing the cloud are proper contract language and SLAs (service level agreements) to control and manage the information. The two most critical pieces to make sure are addressed are liability of compromise and ownership of the data. With most traditional, standard cloud agreements the cloud provider takes control and has potential ownership of the information but the organization still has full liability if proper security is not managed. While cloud providers want to keep your business and controlling information is a critical way of doing that, it is important to make sure that the organization still has access to information so if they ever need to switch cloud providers or if something happens to the cloud provider, they still have accessibility to their information. Having access to full backups of the information and potential third-party escrow are critical steps to make sure that organizations does not lose control and loose ownership of its information.

While ownership is concerning, the other area that needs attention is liability. In many cloud agreements, if the cloud provider does not provide proper security and there is a breach of critical information or regulatory data, the company, not the cloud provider is liable. For example, if an organization is storing client's personal information at a cloud provider and there is a breach, the organization would get the reputational damage and be liable for an exposure of information. In moving to the cloud, an organization is never going to be able to maintain 100% ownership and 0% liability, however via proper contract language a more proper balance has to be achieved and maintained. In this day and age if you work in security, having a very close relationship with legal is definitely recommended. With the cloud it is an absolute requirement. While legal should always review all contracts, it is important to make sure legal understands the security concerns and provides proper contract language to make sure they are enforceable.

One of the themes of this chapter is that we need to take a data centric approach to security. Policies should be written to protect an organization's data. Whether the data resides at your data center or a cloud provider, the same policies should be put in place. It makes no sense to have one set of policies for data at your location and a completely different set of policies if the same exact data resides at a cloud provider. Create a single policy and enforce it with SLAs, regardless of where the data actually resides.

Today, the APT is mainly focused in on the client and has not directly targeted the cloud, at least publicly. At time of publication or shortly after this book is released, the author predicts that there will be publicly released cases of cloud providers compromised by the APT. There are many theories but remember that A in APT is referring to the advanced nature of the adversary and they are going to always use the easiest, most straightforward way of breaking into the system. Today it is the client. As organizations continue to secure the client against the current APT, APTv2 will target the cloud. One of the big weaknesses of the cloud is that if an attacker can find a way into a server, they would have access to a large amount of clients, not just one. Since the APT is targeted to attacks, some say the cloud is too broad and less of a concern but our prediction is that APTv2 will be targeted but at a larger scale and if the government or a certain industry has all of their data in one location, this can be the prime target. The reason we have a section on cloud computing, even though that is not the primary target today is that you always want to be prepared for the future. The more an organization can get in front of the attacker, the more effective their security will be overall.

REDUCING CLOUD COMPUTING RISKS

With proper planning, an organization can reduce the risk of moving to the cloud to an acceptable level. It is important to remember that the cloud must not be an all or nothing decision.

When moving to the cloud, in order to properly protect the information and reduce it to an appropriate level of risk, it is important to perform the same level of security that is implemented in your current environment. A checklist of items that is often forgotten about when moving to the cloud are:

- Robust configuration control.
- Proper change management.
- Host hardening.
- Service removal or patching.
- Constant user awareness and training.

The bottom line is to recognize that the cloud can and will be targeted by the APT. To minimize the exposure and to make sure that an organization has a proper handle on both the advantages and dangers of the cloud, it is critical that organizations take an incremental approach. Instead of all or nothing, it is critical to slowly migrate servers to the cloud in a logical, cost-effective and risk-based manner.

MOBILIZATION—BYOD (BRING YOUR OWN DEVICE)

While cloud is one piece of the puzzle, for the realization of being able to access information from anywhere and any location, the second piece of the puzzle is mobilization or mobile devices. Typically in the past, organizations would purchase the equipment that was needed in order to allow employees to be productive. However with the consumerization of IT and a large array of expensive tablets being available, more organizations are moving towards allowing individuals to bring their own device to work. Now employees are responsible for purchasing, maintaining, and replacing the devices which removes a significant burden from the organization. However, the big risk is that corporate data now resides on personal devices. What is interesting is that while both the cloud and mobilization are going to occur, cloud is driven more by cost savings and the business units. Mobilization is driven by the users and the need for advanced functionality and instant access to information from any location. Since the APT today is currently targeting users and mobile devices are directly purchased and controlled by the users, there is a direct tie into the mobile device being targeting by the adversary. What makes it more scary is many of these devices were designed for consumers, not businesses and since they are controlled by the user, not only could they have minimal security configured, there is minimal security built into some of these devices by default.

Many of these devices were built for consumer grade use which means functionality is king. If you are playing games and downloading apps, who needs security? If you are storing critical information on the devices, it is a completely different story. Since these devices are typically not locked down to the level of other devices (i.e. laptops and desktops), they offer a prime target for advanced threats. Once again since targeting a user with a directed email that contains a legitimate looking, but infected attachment is still one of the easier targets, it is still the prime focus of APT.

Since the user is what is being targeted, moving from a desktop/laptop to a mobile device is a natural transformation for the attacker.

Many mobile devices are not very secure but by understanding the vulnerabilities and by adding in additional third-party software, many of these devices can have their security raised to an acceptable level.

While mobile devices are often the focus of conversation, the APT is not after the device, they are after the data. Therefore it is important to always look at the complete architecture in which the mobile device is going to be deployed and use it to assess the overall security. Ultimately what drives the associated risks and overall security is the data that the device is going to access and the overall deployment architecture.

One of the areas that catches an organization off guard is that they focus on the device. We hear organizations all of the time ask us what they can do to secure this device or that device. The first question we always ask is what information is going to reside on the device. By taking a data centric approach to security, allows organizations to develop scalable security policies that work today and into the future. By developing device specific security, allows the solution to work today but as soon as new technology comes out, it will no longer scale into the future. Today we have to recognize that there will always be mobile devices and remote access to our network. The key focus to defend against the APT is by focusing in on the who, what, when, and where of an organization's critical information.

One of the fundamental problems with how we look at security is that the game is rigged against us and in favor of the attacker. If the APT is focused on long term control of an organization and ultimately access to its critical information and we are focusing in on securing every new device, we will lose. The reason is simple. What we have to secure changes with a much higher frequency than what the attacker has to compromise. We are already starting behind the eight ball because the attacker has to find only one way in and we have to find all of the critical exposures. If that is not hard enough, add to the equation the devices we are focusing in on are always changing and it quickly becomes a losing game. We need to change the rules, to give ourselves a fighting chance. By focusing in on the data and continuing to provide training and awareness that tracks against policies that have measurable metrics, we can continue to minimize and reduce the vector that attackers are using to break in.

DEALING WITH FUTURE TECHNOLOGIES

It is always important in any organization to constantly assess, analyze, and prioritize the risk across an organization based on the likelihood and impact of threats and vulnerabilities. We must always remember that the A in advanced does not refer to the advanced nature of the attack but the advanced nature of the adversary. An advanced adversary is always going to use the simplest, most effective way into an organization. Currently it is the end user that is the biggest target of the APT, but over time this will change. As we continue to lock down, re-engineer applications, and educate users, this will become a harder point of compromise. Typically the easiest way to exploit an organization is new technology. Organizations often deploy new technologies based solely on functionality with security as a minimal or no concern until there is a problem. This mentality is based on the fact that attacks are visible and reactive security is effective. Today, based on the stealthy nature of the attack, new technologies are the prime breeding ground for new points of attack.

The main focus of this chapter was on cloud and mobilization, two very common emerging technologies that will be exploited by the APT. However, there will be a point in time when this technology is no longer new and the next great technology will be upon us. It is important that while we cannot say no to technology, we need to make sure executives understand the associated risks and impact to an organization whenever a decision is made on implementing a new technology within an enterprise. The bottom line is new technology will be focused on easier access and manipulation of critical information—access to information on any device from any location. Since this is also the goal of the attacker, we have our work cut out for us. The exact reasons on why organizations are rolling out new technology are the same goals of the attacker. Definitely not a helpless situation, but one that will continue to require a lot of creativity and planning. The more we plan the better off we will be.

It is always important to remember that one way to look at new technology is that it is a potential medium to perform a compromise. The ultimate target is not the technology but the data or information. In dealing with the APT, organizations must embrace and shift to a data centric approach to security. Policies, acceptable risk, and mitigation measures need to be tied to the type of data that resides on the device, not the device itself. We often have clients in which we have developed robust security policies for their desktop and laptop systems. Several months later we receive a call that they would like us to write a policy for their mobile devices. We often reply that you already have a policy that can be used with mobile devices, it is your laptop policy. Since the same data is going to reside on both, the relative risk is the same and therefore the protection needs to be the same. They often reply back that there is no way they can have 12 character passwords and full disk encryption on their mobile devices. The next question is on whether the executives have fully signed off on this exposure and recognize that this is the same level of risk as having no security on their laptops.

When it comes to security we fully recognize that businesses need to operate and sometimes decisions are made based on enabling the business instead of security. This is acceptable, as long as the decision is made with full awareness and accurate information of the risk and ultimate exposure. We have to stop fooling ourselves thinking that if we forget about security it will go away. It doesn't, you just get compromised by the APT and do not realize it until it is too late. By focusing in on data centric policies and controls, an organization can easily scale and handle any new technologies that will be developed in the future. By taking a device centric approach, which many organizations do today, they will continue to struggle to protect new devices and by the time they figure out how to secure them, the attacker will have already compromised the information.

SUMMARY

Just over the last 40 years, it is amazing how technology has changed our lives and continues to evolve. When the TV was invented, people were amazed and could not imagine how anything could be more revolutionary. When cable TV arrived I remember how amazed my dad was on how many channels we could receive and we did not need to worry about the antenna in our attic in order to get reception. Add in the microwave and most people in the 1970s would have said things are perfect. Many people never imagined a world with laptops, wireless, Internet access anywhere, and the range of mobile devices that are available. When we look at technology it is important to remember two important points: (1) the adversary evolves as quickly as new technology evolves and (2) no matter how amazing we think things are, there will always be new technologies and new advances. Regardless of how awesome we think the world is today, it will be different in 10 years.

It is easy to sit back and be amazed of the mobile devices and the ability to access information from anywhere in the world. What is important to remember is that anything that can be used for good can be used for evil. Any new technological advance that increases our overall productivity also increases the capability of the adversary to exploit and compromise a system. While challenging, we always have to look at ways to secure and protect our information, regardless of the new capabilities that are available to an organization. Gone are the days when security could say no to a new technology and people would listen. Based on the ease in which cloud services can be purchased and the cost-effective nature of mobile devices, it is almost a guarantee that they will be used within an enterprise. As security professionals and as the APT evolves, we have to constantly look at creative ways to protect and secure our critical information.

The APT has shown us that gone are the days of reactive security. In the past we could wait for the attacker to take some action and react to what they did in a way to properly protect our organization. Today with attacks more stealthy and targeted, proactive security is the only effective way to protect an organization. We also have to remember that while there are new technologies that we have not even thought of, there are also new attacker vectors that will be used to compromise an enterprise. With reactive security, we had to worry about the future. With proactive security, if we have an effective way to protect our organization today, it will also work against the new threats that will come out in 5–10 years.

It is important to understand that any new technology creates new innovative ways to do business, but they also create new innovative ways for attackers to break into our organization. Going back to the basics is how you win. If an organization clearly defines its critical assets, high likelihood threats, and biggest impact vulnerabilities, organizations can continue to win and protect their organization, regardless of what the changing landscape looks like.

Proactive Security and Reputational Ranking

10

INTRODUCTION

Organizations are focusing resources on cyber security and still getting compromised. What organizations are doing today to secure systems is not completely working. It is important to point out that it is not because the technology does not work; it is because the technology does not work against the APT the way it is configured within most organizations. Let's clarify. First, many technologies are built to solve a certain problem. If you purchased a hammer to hang up a picture, you should not be mad because it is not effective a cutting a board in half. While you could argue that the hammer is ineffective at breaking the board in half, that would not be fair. It was not designed or built for that purpose. That does not mean that we should throw out all of our hammers, it just means that we need to have other tools in our toolbox. The theme of this chapter is not just what you need to add to your toolbox, but what configuration changes need to be made to your existing tools. The second important point is many security tools are pre-configured to solve a certain problem. The way they are currently configured will do minimal to catch the APT. However, if an organization just reconfigures the devices they can more effectively defend against the advanced threat.

Bottom line is we are no longer in the amateur league. The APT has raised the stakes and we are now playing against professionals. A professional knows that if they try something and it does not work, you have to adapt on the fly. The APT is very adaptive which means if we study and find out how they operate and prevent the threat from causing harm, they will adapt and find a new way into our enterprise. Therefore whatever we do today to deal with the APT will not work tomorrow. That is why this book focuses a lot more on strategies than very specific solutions. If we gave an organization very specific things to do, the book would be good for 3 months because the threat would quickly adapt. By focusing in on effective strategies allows the solutions to scale and be as adaptive as the threat. Just like the defense studies the offense. The offense will study our defenses very closely and find weaknesses and ways to exploit them. If an attacker found a weakness in our defense, we need to change our defensive approach in order to protect our systems. We often joke that the APT stands for the *Adaptive* Persistent Threat instead of the Advanced Persistent Threat.

In 1906, St. Louis University's football team was the first to make use of the forward pass. That year they had an 11–0 season and outscored their opponents by a combined score of 407 to 11. The reason? The defenses that they were facing were defending against the run since that is all they had ever dealt with previously—the defense was totally unprepared for the forward pass and the consequences were pretty devastating. The problem is this did not last very long. The first season St. Louis used the forward pass it was very effective because no defense was prepared. What do you think happened the second and the third year? It became less and less effective because the defense learned how to protect against it. What did the offense do, they came up with new plays. This is the same strategy that is taking place today in cyber security.

Today, attackers have introduced the equivalent of a cyber-forward pass with the APT. Our defenses and much of the technology that organizations have purchased were designed to stop the cyber equivalent of the run because that was the threat we had to deal with. Unfortunately, the method of attack has changed. Our defenses must change to deal with this, just as football defenses had to change to deal with the forward pass. However what is important to remember is that change is the new constant in cyber security. The APT is so significant and the reason there is an entire book written on it is because it changes the rules. Over the years worms and viruses adapted and changed but the fundamental way they worked was the same. The APT is no longer software (i.e. virus or worm that was programmed to perform a certain function), it is a person, group, and/or nation—it is an organized adversary that will not give up until they obtain what they want. Therefore, our mindset has to change. We are not looking for a product that we can buy that will protect our organization. We are looking to develop a strategy that implements a variety of solutions that can be adaptive and constantly keep pace or stay ahead of the threat.

In order to do this in addition to being very adaptive, organizations also have to be more proactive and risk based in how they approach security. The APT is very stealthy and very hard to detect, therefore traditional reactive security is not going to scale. Reactive security is based off of the simple premise that if an attacker breaks in, an organization will look for a visible sign, and take action which will control and limit the overall damage. With visible attacks, this method did scale but the problem is it assumed something visible that would allow for timely detection. In lieu of nothing visible, the attack would go undetected and significant damage would occur. Therefore as we look at solutions, methods, and strategies for dealing with the APT we need to be more proactive. We no longer can wait for the attacker to make the first move and we react to their activity by making the second move. With the current threats and reactive security, the game is over before we have a chance to do that. We need to plan that we are under attack and constantly take action to proactively deal with the threat, hopefully before or as it is occurring.

In being proactive, we have to recognize that we are no longer able to make binary decisions of good or bad, allowed or denied. We have to recognize that in the current environment that we operate in with mobilization, BYOD (bring your own device), and cloud that there will be different levels of trust and access that is required. Therefore, access has to be based on overall risk, not static rules. Essentially, if someone exhibits good behavior we give them additional access and if someone exhibits bad behavior we remove their access. Access and overall security is based on reputational ranking, not predetermined rules. If an entity is doing something that would not be harmful or cause damage, we allow them to continue their actions. If someone is doing something bad or something that could have a negative impact to the organization, the security devices would reduce or remove their access. With proactive reputational ranking, organizations can better protect and secure their enterprise from attack.

FACING REALITY

Fifteen plus years ago, organizations could debate on whether they were going to be attacked and by whom. The world of cyber security was a dark mysterious place that many people did not have a lot of details about. It was as if some organizations were facing the boogie man, knowing that there was a threat but not knowing who it was or what they were going to do. It was definitely an interesting time because there were a large number of unknowns and organizations were not sure what they were up against.

While today there are still some unknowns, there are definitely more knowns than there were in the past. Bottom line today is that you are going to be attacked. Let's remove that unknown from the table. Whether you are an individual, small company, university, or research organization, you are going to be targeted and attacked. Now remember with the APT you might not be the target but you could be a pivot point that is used as a method for ultimately exploiting the target. For example, we have heard small organizations say why would the APT or Chinese target us, we have minimal amounts of information compared to larger organizations. However, if your organization is a subcontractor and has connections to those larger organizations, the smaller organization might be the easiest way into the larger organization. The smaller organization might be the means to the end, not the ultimate target. In addition, while this book is primarily focused on the APT, it is really a book on implementing proper cyber security defenses to protect an organization from all attacks, up to and including the current APT and the next generation of threats. While understanding and dealing with the APT is important, what good is a network infrastructure that could properly defend against APT attacks but get compromised with viruses and worms on a regular basis. Cyber security is all about having a comprehensive plan of attack and focus.

The reality of today is that we always have to be in battle ready positions. If the waters look calm you are looking in the wrong direction. Not to pick on anyone but we often hear organizations today say that they have a proper level of security and they receive reports on a regular basis and everything looks fine. Their organization is secure and there are no attacks or compromised systems. While that might make a nice story that is not the reality of the situation. If you do not see any problems or find any compromised systems, you are not looking in the right spot. Almost all organizations are compromised and thinking that your organization is an exception is naïve. The message of this section is look harder and/or look in a different location. We have performed analysis for many organizations and have never found an organization that does not have some compromised systems.

The example I always like to use is many years ago while teaching in Hawaii, a few of us decided to take a whale watching boat tour. It was a beautiful day and I was looking out over the left side of the boat, enjoying the sun but not seeing any whales. A few of my colleagues were looking out over the right side of the boat and getting all excited and jumping up and down. I asked why they were so excited and they said that the whales were amazing. My response was what whales. One of my friends grabbed my head, turned it, and I started seeing all of these magnificent whales. Prior to my friend helping me, I did not see any whales. However, it would have been very shortsighted for me to make the statement that there are no whales in the ocean. Clearly there are whales in the ocean, if you do not see them it does not mean they do not exist, it just means you are not looking in the correct area. The rule I learned that day was that if you do not find what you are looking for, you need to change your vantage point. This is a message we tell many of our clients. The reality is that your organization is being attacked and most likely compromised. If you do not see signs of attacks or compromise, you need to change your vantage point so you can more effectively deal with the threat at hand.

PREDICTING ATTACKS TO BECOME PROACTIVE

While the APT is constantly changing the general techniques and methods used to target and exploit, an organization has some predictability. Most importantly the APT is mainly going to target an individual in the organization. By watching and monitoring public or open source information and monitoring social media sites, organizations can get an idea of who might be targeted by the adversary. Open source intelligence and monitoring services has moved from being a nice to have and is now a necessity in terms of dealing with the advanced threat. In many cases there are indicators and warnings that an individual and ultimately an organization are going to be targeted. The more we can understand and know what is going to happen, we can begin to predict ways an organization is going to be compromised and use that information to be more proactive.

Even though the individuals that are targeted and the specific techniques of how the APT breaks in are always going to be changing, the general methodology that is used is fairly consistent. By focusing in on the general game plan and approach of the APT, organizations can be more proactive by predicting how and when the attacker is going to strike.

The term APT is based off of the unique attributes that are used by the threat for targeting, compromising, and exfiltrating information out of an organization.

By understanding these attributes an organization can build more proactive solutions and minimize the amount of damage the APT will cause.

Advanced

The adversary understands security and knows how to defeat or get around most traditional security measures. Not to depress anyone but if an organization has security devices that have been purchased more than 3 years ago and have a standard/default configuration, in most cases it will be ineffective against the APT. The reason is that these devices were not built or configured to deal with this level of a threat. They were meant to deal with traditional worms and viruses that had distinct signatures that could be tracked and detected on a network. Now the good news is that the standard configuration for older security devices was set to look for the standard threat. With proper tuning many of these devices, in coordination with other devices, can be used as part of the solution. The second important point is that security devices that are focused on data, data flow, and anomaly analysis are much more effective at dealing with the APT than anything that is based on signatures or specific instances of an attack.

It is important when we talk about the advanced nature of the attack, we still have to remember that the attacker has to follow the general principles of finding a weakness and exploiting them. Yes, the APT is good but it is not super human or something that no matter what you do, it will still break in and go undetected. The mistake that is often made is many organizations give the APT more credit than it deserves and says no matter what you do it is unstoppable and undetectable. That statement is just not true. An attack has to take advantage of a weakness in a system and make modifications to a system once it is compromised. Based on those two factors means that the APT can be prevented and detected, if we know what vulnerabilities to close down and where to look. The correct phrase to use when talking about the APT is that it is unstoppable and undetectable using traditional security and normal remediation methods. However, if we change how we approach security, in much the same way that the APT changed how systems were compromised, organizations do have a chance of properly dealing with the threat. It is also important to remember that based on the persistent nature, an organization might not be able to prevent all attacks, some will break in and the reason for detection is so important.

Now the main problem with the APT is that it takes advantage of vulnerabilities that are needed in order for the organization to function. This makes it very difficult to track and close down the attack vector. With traditional attacks, the vulnerability that was exploited was an extraneous service or an unpatched system which meant if an organization focused in on the correct area they could remediate the threat and cause minimal impact to the enterprise. Today, the APT is taking advantage of email attachments and employees within the organization. An organization can only remediate this 100% by shutting down email and firing all employees. While they might be tempting, that is not practical. Therefore, organizations have to be very creative in how they deal with the threat.

Persistent

We often forget that we live in an imperfect world. We have to recognize that there is no such thing as perfect security and 100% security does not exist. If we compare this to the human body it can be a little calming because no one is 100% healthy, but we can still live long lives being imperfect. Every human has some unhealthy bacteria and some weakness or deficiencies but the trick is to understand our strengths and weakness and live a life that minimizes the weaknesses and plays off of our strength. Today, with the APT an organization's networks are no different. They have holes and weaknesses and we are going to be compromised, the trick is building a plan for survival not perfection.

When you understand the advanced persistent threat and how it works, it can be concerning. The threat will continue until it gets in and any attempt to block the adversary is just postponing the inevitable, the threat will eventually compromise your organization. Any reasonable size organization today has been targeted and in many cases compromised. Denial delays progress and the sooner we can accept it the quicker we can focus on minimizing the impact. Think of the attacker today as a 7-year-old that wants ice cream. They will continue to ask you, bug you, annoy you, and try every possible angle until you give in. They are going to get their ice cream, the real focus should not be on delaying the inevitable but being proactive and figuring out the when, where, and how.

With the persistent nature of the attacker it is important to understand that proper prevention is still the key. Since we know in many cases that the attacker will get in, forensic hunting has become a very popular area with regard to the APT. While this is critical, it is still important to have a robust scalable, defensive architecture not only to minimize the damage and impact, but to allow an organization to have the ability to perform more timely detection. The APT is one of the many threats that you have to defend against. There are various debates over the definition of the APT and on whether people are using it in to broaden or to tighten a fashion. The bottom line is an organization that has sensitive data has to be prepared for all threats. Let's focus our energy on defending and detecting against the adversary because they are ruthless and not focus energy and effort on arguing about definitions, that while important, is not as important as not being headline news for having a major breach. If your organization has its critical information stolen that is the definition of having a bad day. The reason for this book is because organizations have been focusing all of the energy on the traditional threat and getting compromised by the APT. The goal of this book is to enable an organization to increase its defensive posture to be better prepared to be more proactive for dealing with the threat. A key proactive aspect of the persistent nature is to actively find the threat as close to real time not 3 months later. Forensics will always play a critical role in our defensive arsenal and we must always invest proper energy and effort towards it, but we should also try to minimize the damage and the sooner we can get the attacker the better.

The Persistence in APT indicates that the attacker is out there causing harm and if we do not see the APT, we are not looking in the right area. There are cyber whales on the Internet and if you are not seeing them you are not looking in the right area. Many of the traditional devices are configured for the non-APT threat which means in many cases they are not effective at preventing and detecting the attacks. Therefore, an organization will be missing what is important, get compromised, and not detect it in a timely manner. APT emphasizes that detection is critical but it also tells us that one of two things is happening as you read this book: (1) an organization is being attacked and the adversary will not stop until they get in; or (2) the organization is already compromised. Essentially the question is on whether you are looking in the right area. Inbound traffic is the focus if you are trying to find signs of someone trying to break in. Outbound traffic is what needs to be examined to find signs of compromised systems and data exfiltration. While spending some time on the inbound is OK, in many cases it is extremely difficult to detect. The outbound is where the action is and has the best chance of success. The problem is that most organizations are spending most of their time looking at the inbound and minimal if any time examining the outbound traffic. While inbound should not be forgotten about for prevention, the more time spent on building profiles of normalcy and looking for anomalies, the more proactive an organization will be at dealing with the APT.

Threat

Threat is the potential for harm. In the past one could argue that some of the things we called threats were really annoyances or nuisances but not really causing major damage to the enterprise. Today the threat can be devastating from both a short-term profitability or goal of the enterprise to devastating, impacting the long-term success of the organization. The good news about the APT is that we know what they are after, critical data and information. In some cases the traditional threat was harder to protect against because we did not always know what they were after. It changed on a regular basis, so the best we could do was look for signs of attack and prevent them, but fortunately there were clear indicators and warnings that could be blocked.

Today with the APT it is much more stealthy but the threat is more predictable on what it is after: the data. Therefore, we might not know how they are going to break in, what methods and where they might be on the network, but we surely know what to protect, what they are after and where we should circle the wagons. In many cases an organization's network was not designed to deal with the APT. The design of many networks was based off of protecting against server-based attacks. Therefore, any system visible from the Internet is on a DMZ with no sensitive data installed and proper isolation and protection provided. Since the internal network was segmented and most components not directly accessible, the internal network was pretty flat with very strong preventive measures and inbound detective measures. We never realized how good an advanced adversary really would be. They targeted the users that were on the internal network with direct access to all of the data, slipping right into the network bypassing all of the security an organization spent years building.

While it is not an easy solution, difficult times require difficult measures. Just as an organization had to build out a data center when everything started moving to electronic records in the late 1990s, we are at a point in time where based on the sophisticated nature of the threat, organizations have to rebuild/redesign their networks to be able to handle and deal with the current APT and the next generation of APT that is just around the corner. The APT is going to adapt as organizations get better at handling them, but they are not going to go away. All critical information and data must be properly segmented and the location of the data must be controlled on the endpoint. One method of doing this is with thin clients. With thin clients, whenever a computer is started it will download a clean image from a server and run the image on the local desktop. Whenever the system is turned off, the current running image goes away and nothing is stored on the local client. No data is stored on the local computer and information can now be controlled at several server's. By thinking like the attacker and understanding the threat, new scalable defenses can be built and deployed.

CHANGING HOW YOU THINK ABOUT SECURITY

We have been hinting about it for a while but the bottom line is that the APT and next generation of threats require that we completely re-think how we do security. What has worked in the past will not work against an adversary that has changed the rules. This is evident based on the fact that organizations keep spending more money on security and are still getting broken into. Essentially many organizations keep doing more of the wrong things which will just increase an organization's frustration, not actually solve any problems. The concern we have with many clients is that if the executives keep increasing the security budget but they do not see a measurable reduction in the APT incidents, this could impact the ability of security to be an effective business enabler across the enterprise.

Some problems require small adjustments and some problems require large adjustments. The APT and the new way the adversary is operating requires large adjustments to how we implement and roll out security across an organization. The main reason is that with the APT, the adversary studied how organizations implement security and have found fundamental weaknesses in how the defenses work. The only way to start winning is by fixing the weaknesses to make it harder for the attacker. This is analogous to how someone might rob a bank. If the location of the safe is not very secure and the safe has a weakness that would allow it to be opened by someone without the combination this is a concern. However, if the main threat is someone walking into the front of the bank, pulling a gun on a teller, and stealing the money, the fundamental architecture of the bank does not have to change. By adding in more video cameras, armed guards and alarms could mitigate the threat to an acceptable level either by deterring or controlling the amount of damage a robber could cause. This is equivalent to the threats of the past that involved web site defacement, large scale worms and, denial of service attacks. By adding in more of the traditional security that is already in place would allow an organization to more effectively react and deal with the problem. Adding more or better traditional defenses worked very well against standard attackers.

Today the threat has shifted from a low-tech bank robber that walks in the front door with a gun and performed minimal planning, to an organized criminal element that would spend months planning the attack with very well-trained people. Continuing with our bank example, if a criminal element obtained the blueprints for the bank and found out the make/model of the safe and it turned out that there were fundamental flaws which were successfully exploited, this would cause major concern for the bank. After this attack, even if they installed more video cameras and better alarm system it would not help if there was a fundamental flaw in the design. The only solution would be to re-design the bank, implementing an architecture that was more robust to withstand these advanced attacks.

Today, we are in a similar situation. Organizations built a robust network (typically in the 1990s) based on necessity and over the years have enhanced it based on functional requirements. Security was added on as needed basis, but not part of the original design. As new threats evolved additional security devices were added to the existing network. If you are adding something to an existing entity, you are limited in what you could do. Adding a traditional wired alarm system to a house that is completely built is difficult to do based on how costly it is. Adding an alarm system integrated into the house when it is being built is not only more cost effective, but also more scalable. What is important to remember in these discussions is we are not stating that the current technologies that many organizations are using are useless against the APT. We are stating that the current technologies added on to an existing network that was not designed correctly are not as effective as they could be against the APT. Many of these technologies if they were configured differently and had the ability to be more integrated into the existing infrastructure could play a much larger role in dealing with the APT.

Whether we like it or not the attackers have obtained the blueprints to our networks and they are exploiting weakness in our design. The reason why adding security devices into our existing networks were effective against the traditional threat is because the traditional threat took advantage of configuration issues. Things like weak passwords, unpatched systems, misconfigured servers, and extraneous services are all configuration problems that the attacker exploited. By adding on additional devices that could filter, monitor, and/or control rogue packets or information would help protect our environments. The problem with the APT is it exploits a fundamentally different problem—it goes after flaws in the design not the configuration. Now that the rules have changed, the approach we take with security has to be adapted and changed. What worked in the past will not work in the future. The good news is most organizations recognize that nothing lasts forever and most critical items have to be replaced every 12–15 years. Since many networks and data centers were initially designed in the mid 1990s this is a perfect opportunity, to re-design the network to have integrated security as opposed to adding security on after the fact.

In re-designing our security to fix the fundamental flaws in our architecture, we need to make sure that our security devices can see the information that is needed in order to make the right decisions. While inbound traffic is important, most organizations have that covered fairly well. Between firewalls, IDS, and IPS systems there is a lot of blocking and tackling being done on the inbound traffic. The problem is the inbound traffic that is being used by the APT is normal looking traffic. The threat has done a really good job of understanding how each of these devices work, what specifically they look for, and making sure the attackers traffic is allowed through and does not fit any of the indicators that are being tracked. While rules get updated and signatures can be modified, the traditional installation of many of the common security devices is going to be somewhat predictable in terms of how they work. If you give someone who has advanced skills a somewhat static problem and ask them to find a way around it, the only question is how long is it going to take, not if it is possible. Once again it is critical not to misread any of this information or think that we are implying that these measures are not effective and should be removed off the network. They are critical components for success, but clearly not enough to deal with the APT. It is also important to note that this is not a criticism since the technology was never built to deal with this problem. This is like saying an NFL quarterback is not a good basketball player. That is not a criticism because that is not the skill set that they have trained and have expertise in.

Most devices were not built to deal with preventing the APT. While it is still important to look at inbound traffic, the real value in the inbound traffic comes on the correlation side. The firewall might not be able to block the traffic but if it is correlated with all of the other perspectives that come from the different devices that are on a network, it is usually much easier to see the needle in the haystack. The trick in finding a needle in the haystack is to reduce the amount of hay and/or make the needle bigger. By performing event correlation allows the size of the needle to grow, making it easier to find unusual or strange patterns on the network.

The key area to look for is what is leaving an organization. Many entities have traditional not invested significant time and many vendors have not built products for tracking and watching outbound traffic. The main reason is they have relied on proper blocking as the main level of protection. Now that prevention will not be 100% against the APT, timely detection is no longer a nice to have but a requirement. It must be done. While looking at the outbound traffic is important, the other really big paradigm shift is in what we are looking at. Many security devices focus in on examining the payload looking for anything strange or suspicious. The problem is that a tool of the APT for being stealthy on a network is encryption. By encrypting the payload they have changed the game in such a way that most of the security that you rely on is no longer effective. Instead of looking at payload we have to look at the properties of the packet and the relationship to other packets. Length of the connection, size of the packet, and general content (plaintext vs. encryption) are really key indicators of normal vs. malicious traffic.

The interesting part is what we need to look at and examine is not that difficult but the fact that it is straightforward is irrelevant if organizations are not looking at it. The big paradigm shift that has to occur is from examining inbound payloads to outbound packets.

The good news is that organizations are capturing the APT, they are just not doing it quick enough. If the APT was 100% stealthy and was never caught, we would have no idea that organizations were even being compromised and there would be nothing to talk about. The reason why there is so much focus on the APT, is because the attacks are becoming public and the damage is significant. One of the main reasons why the damage is so significant is that we are taking too long to detect the attacks. Finding out that you are compromised is important but finding out you are compromised 6 months after an attack and after all an organization's information has been stolen is unacceptable. Organizations need to continue doing what they are doing but quicker, faster, and better.

THE PROBLEM HAS CHANGED

In building a network that has integrated security and designed from scratch is important to properly deal with the APT, it is important that we understand the problem we are facing and the reason that proactive security and reputational ranking is the solution. One of the worse things an organization can do is rebuild a network from the ground up but do it in such a way that it solved the same problems and does not properly address the APT. The reason an organization approach to security has to change is because the fundamental problem has changed.

The most significant change with the APT is the target for initial compromise or vector has changed. With the traditional threat the vector of attack is the computer. With the APT the initial target or vector of compromise is the human. Understanding this significant shift from attackers exploiting weaknesses in computers to exploiting weaknesses in the human is critical to building solutions that properly scale. Computers can be patched, computers can be locked down, and most importantly computers only do what you tell them to do which means they can be monitored very closely. While many of us might wish that we could patch or change people's brains, it is not possible. Therefore, the new approach for dealing with the APT has to take into account methods and means for training and teaching the human how to behave correctly.

Security is a very challenging game because the attacker will always focus in on the weakest link. As soon as an organization takes their eye off of the ball, the attacker will exploit it very quickly. The point we are trying to make is that more focus needs to be put on securing the human, but if we are not careful and spend less time on securing the computer, in a few years the attacker with shift gears back to the easier form of exploitation. The trick is to augment existing security in such a way as to not reduce any of the current security measures that are in place, recognizing that this has to be done without additional resources. As we will cover later in this chapter, automation and continuous auditing is critical to make sure proper security is maintained.

THE APT DEFENDABLE NETWORK

Whether we like it or not or whether we want to admit it in public or not, we need to fix the fundamental flaws in how networks have been designed, since these flaws are what the APT is taking advantage of. The core problem is that most organization's networks were built to defend against server-based attacks with a focus on isolating critical high-risk servers on separate DMZs. While this strategy is still an important one, isolate what is being attacked and minimize any critical information that might be on the server, what we focus on has to change. The focus of creating a defendable APT network needs to be on the internal network. Most networks today are too flat, too porous which means as soon as an attacker can compromise an internal system, all bets are off.

While an organization still needs to keep focus on protecting the servers, attackers are now targeting the clients. Since the clients are directly plugged into the private network, from an APT perspective the traditional perimeter is not going to provide proper protection since the attackers have figured out how to penetrate it. The best way to think about building an APT grade network is to assume that the attackers have control of a device plugged into the private network. With that context in mind, the private network where the clients reside is the new Internet. Based on the fact that humans can always be compromised and is the target of the APT, we have to assume that the advanced threat will always be able to gain control of a client system. This means that the attackers will be coming from the client network instead of the Internet—translation—the client/private network is the new untrusted network.

Just like in the 1990s when organizations realized that the Internet was completely untrusted, what did they do? Organizations built proper segmentation and isolation, minimizing what systems and services were exposed to the attacker and through a multi-tiered network, they were able to properly defend against the attacker. So far history has shown us that we unfortunately need to assume that the attacker will be able to compromise the clients on our private network with relative ease. If that is the case, we have to re-design and architect our internal network so high-risk clients are properly segmented with no direct access to sensitive data. Just as DMZ systems are segmented and controlled, this is the new approach that has to be taken. Flat private networks will not get the job done and is one of the top reasons why organizations are compromised.

In any battle there is going to be unfortunate loss of life. A country can still win a war even though there are causalities. We have to recognize that the APT is not a government or US problem, it is an international problem. While it looks and acts differently than a traditional war, we are in the midst of a Cyber World War. This is no longer just teenagers or people wanting to prove how smart they are, organizations are under attack. Therefore instead of trying to protect all data, we have to recognize that there is going to be data loss or causalities. The important piece is to focus and prioritize and make sure critical information is not lost.

In order to build a security plan that properly protects an enterprise, the following are the core requirements:

- *Thin clients*—One of the main problems with organizations is that they have too many endpoints and everyone is configured with different settings. While application white listing can help, organizations are usually too dynamic with exceptions becoming the norm. The end result is poor configuration management and control across the enterprise. If a network was being built from scratch, configuration control could be managed from the beginning, but trying to add it in to an existing complex network in which all systems are configured differently is very difficult. Plus the hard part with configuration management is not necessarily rolling out a standard configuration but managing change across the enterprise. When a critical business need comes up it seems harmless to give an end user administrator rights allowing them to install software, but before long all systems are configured differently. The reason why configuration control is so important is not only can you not secure what you do not know, but if you do not know what the configuration is supposed to be, how do you know if you have been compromised. This issue leads to a big problem with the APT. Many organizations are compromised in a persistent way that it survives a reboot and since there is no way to detect it, it goes unnoticed from several months if not longer. Getting compromised is bad but remember it is going to happen. It is OK to get sick once in a while as long as you recover quickly. If every time you get sick you are put in the hospital, that is a bigger concern. Many organizations, based on the inability to detect a compromise quickly, have sick systems for a long time and by the time they notice, they are in a critical condition and the damage to the organization is very large. In an ideal state no one wants to be compromised but if it does happen, shorter is better. While detection is the best way to deal with a compromised system, the next best way is to control and minimize the length of time a system is compromised. Part of the solution: thin clients. The general concept of a thin client is that the OS and its associated configuration are managed at a central server that is carefully controlled and managed. Every time the system starts up it goes to the central server and pulls down the configuration and runs off of it for the day. When the system is shut off all of the associated changes go away. The next time the system boots up it goes to the server and pulls down a clean version of the operating system. With thin clients an organization gets a two for one deal. First, all configuration changes are controlled in a central location. Now if an organization has 30,000 clients they do not have to touch 30,000 clients, they just have to touch the server that maintains the configuration and the next time the client boots, they receive the updated configuration. The second benefit is any threat will only have a small window of opportunity, typically 12 hours. If an attacker breaks in to a client, when the system is shutdown any and all changes that were made by the attacker go away. Now when the system gets sick, it is only for a short period of time. Once again it is important to point out that an organization still needs to have strong robust configuration control of the operating system for thin clients to be an effective tool against the APT.

- *Cloud*—Contrary to what many security people think the cloud is not pure evil. It is important to remember that any technology can be used in a good way or used in a non-secure way. This section is not meant to say that the cloud is perfect but it is meant to show one way the cloud can be used as part of an APT solution. One of the weaknesses that the APT takes advantage of is the fact that the clients and the data are typically very close together with minimal security separating them. Therefore if the threat can target a user, compromise a client, it is fairly easy and straightforward to compromise the critical data that the adversary is after. One of the themes of dealing with the APT is to provide more separation/segmentation of the critical data in an organization making it harder for a compromised system to steal large amounts of information quickly. A method for separating and isolating an organization's critical information is via the cloud. With the cloud, information is now segmented from the clients. Any communication not only has to get, past the organization's security on the client end but it also has to get past the server's security on the cloud provider's side. With any solution, especially one that involves outsourcing a word of caution is in order. Be very careful with any solution in which another organization is managing or controlling an organization's security. In many cases, the right cloud provider actually has better configuration control and security that the organization whose data they are housing, but it is not always true. While the cloud is often not thought about as part of the APT solution, with proper planning it can be used as another method for isolating and controlling information. In order to more effectively deal with the APT, we have to do a better job of separating out the clients and the data. The more strictly we can control access the less overall damage the adversary can cause.
- *Isolated data segments*—Stepping back at how organization's networks have evolved, it is extremely clever on how the APT adversary works. Organizations recognized that in the 1990s attackers were targeting and compromising servers. All of the major worms targeted servers as the main entry point into a network. Therefore, the main area of focus was to isolate and control servers that were visible from the Internet. Any system accessible from the Internet went on the DMZ with no sensitive data residing on it and proper segmentation with various security devices. Those devices were locked down with proper configuration control. Based on the focused attention organizations paid to the main point of exposure, it became more difficult to attack and break in to an organization via the server. Since all attention was paid to the servers, organization tended to put minimal focus on the client and private network. Over the years these networks evolved, the clients became complex, and the private network was very flat making it easy for users to access the

data they needed to perform their job. In walks the APT. In looking at what they wanted, the data, the point of compromise was very evident for the adversary, focus on the client. Just as an organized criminal element would take the blueprint of a bank and carefully examine it before they rob the bank, the cyber adversary performs similar analysis. Can't you just see the foreign adversary with the blueprints on the wall of an organization circling the database servers saying that is the information we want. Trying to figure out what to compromise it seems obvious, since the clients have almost direct access to the data and many networks are very flat, that would be a good point of compromise. In addition, clients can make outbound connections which would make it an ideal pivot point for the adversary. Next question is how to gain control of the adversary. In walks social media and the ability to compromise the client via the user by social engineering seems like the next best step. They give it a try and success is an understatement. Based on the logic and the points of exploitation, in dealing with the APT it is critical to try and break the model, making it much harder for the adversary. An important area of focus would be the private network. Instead of making it flat and easy to move and access information, why not make it highly segmented. By properly segmenting the private network isolating clients and data and carefully controlling access, makes it much more difficult for the adversary to cause harm. What is really interesting about internally segmentation is if it is done correctly it has minimal to no impact on the end user. Most of the access the APT takes advantage of is not needed by the client. We have given the user extra access and the only entities using it are the adversaries. Removing the visibility of systems and access to data is transparent to the user and hurts the attacker. In order for a highly segmented private network to work, it has to be based off of trust levels. Not only should client and servers be isolated but client systems can only access servers that are of equal trust in which there is a need to know. With many APT compromises the client that is compromised as a pivot point, after analysis, there was no reason at all on why that client needed access to the data that was stolen. Therefore carefully controlling information with proper isolation can control/minimize the impact of the threat.

- *Dynamic access control*—If an organization's security is static but the adversary's method of compromise is dynamic, who do you think is going to win? The answer is pretty obvious if you look around at how many organizations have had data stolen by the APT. The problem with static security is once an adversary figures out a way around it, they win. Firewalls have value and should definitely be used as part of the security solution within an enterprise. However, firewalls are fairly static binary devices. They have a ruleset and either drop or allow packets. Once an adversary realized that email was allowed into an organization, it became an easy method to target the end users and cause harm. Therefore, the access control needs to be based on the behavioral patterns of the system it is protecting. A private network needs to have many separate VLANS based on trust. If a client's activity in terms of what it is doing, the information it is accessing, and the data flow is normal, the client is given the access they need. If the client exhibits bad behavior the client is given less access. Now the network is dynamic and self-correcting. As a normal user tries to do their job, they have the access they need and they are successful. As a system becomes compromised and without the user knowing it, their system starts doing harmful activity, access is taken away, and the attacker is limited in what they can do. What is interesting with this approach is we are hurting the attacker and helping the user. For example, most users' connections to the Internet are to a set number of IPs or areas of the world, are not very long, and do not contain a large amount of data. If a system starts to have an anomalous connection in which they are connecting to an area of the world in which the organization does not do business, it is a long connection and/or large amounts of data are leaving the organization, this activity would need to be stopped by dropping to a lower trust level with the activity generating an alert. What is interesting is the attacker's covert connection would be stopped but since the user activity is still allowed, there would be minimal impact to the client.

- *Continuous monitoring*—In the real world there are sunny days and there are cloudy days. From an APT perspective there is nothing but cloudy days. An organization is going to be under constant attack. This is the theme of the "P" in APT. Worms would target a large number of systems looking for a specific, bounded set of exploits. An organization's system would be hit for several hours or days and if the systems were secure, the storm surge would go back to normal and the attack would stop. If an organization carefully monitored activity, they could be prepared for these occurrences. The traditional threat was like a hurricane. Hurricanes do not catch you by surprise. You know they are coming and you are given time to respond and take action. The APT is like a tornado. With a tornado you do not have days or week's notice, you have hours and in many cases minutes. A hurricane, you can wait for the weather service to issue a warning and you can start to prepare for it. With a tornado you have to be more proactive. However, unlike a tornado the APT is non-stop. If the adversary targets an organization, they will not stop until they get in. Since the APT can strike at any time and will continue to attack until they achieve their goal, there is no rest for the weary. Security cannot monitor or track activity once or twice a week. It needs to be continuous. Continuous monitoring is the key to early detection and containing/controlling the damage to an organization. The best way to do this is with continuous auditing against a known baseline. All threats will make some changes to both the end point that is compromised and the traffic flow on the network. If this information is carefully monitored, looking for deviations, compromised systems can be quickly detected, controlled, and quarantined.
- *Anomaly detection*—While the APT has become the primary focus of many organizations, the traditional threat has not gone away. An organization has to be careful that it does not put all of its focus on the APT, that it forgets about the other threats. Signature detection is going to do minimal against the APT,

but it is still important to protect against the other threats that are still present on a network. If an organization properly protects against the APT but gets compromised by an old school worm or virus and critical data is stolen, reputational damage is still reputational damage regardless of what caused it. It is important to think, enhance, and not replace as organization's place aggressive focus on the APT. The trick with the APT is to establish a baseline and through continuous, monitoring look for anomalies across the host and the network traffic. If there is a strange occurrence, it needs to be researched and explained. There could be a valid reason for it but in many cases it most likely is the sign of a compromise.

- *Log management and event correlation*—The bad news is the goal of the APT is to slip past the existing security devices based on how they are configured. The good news is no matter how good the adversary is there is no such thing as an invisible attack. Whenever a system is compromised, there are always signs of the attack on the network. It is also important to note that when an attack slips past a security device, the information is still captured in the logs. The main question is whether you are looking in the right areas. Based on how the APT works there is a really good chance that looking at the logs from a single device will not give a lot of insight into the problem and what is happening. However, correlation is king (or queen) when it comes to tracking and finding the APT. Not only is it important to be able to capture the logs but correlation allows organizations to put all of the pieces together, look at the bigger picture, and really understand what is happening on a network.

- *User awareness*—Most of this book is focused on how to use technology effectively to deal with the APT. However, since the APT is targeting users not computers, spending some time educating users and how they are being targeted can also help. Trying to change user's behavior will never be 100% effective. However, the effort required to make users aware and change behavior is very cost effective compared to other measures. User awareness is not very expensive and even if it cuts down on 15% less compromises with an average compromise costing millions of dollars, there is still an effective return on investment. What is also interesting is that while the adversary is very dynamic, the fact that they are targeting users means there is predictability to how they are operating. By looking at what users have public information available that ties them to the company could make them a higher chance of being a target. By performing open source searching and monitoring social media sites would allow an organization to create a short list of employees that are publicly visible. While global awareness across the entire organization is important, focusing additional energy on high priority targets can also provide effective returns on minimizing the impact of the APT.

It is important to remember when looking at this list that there is no perfect solution. Some people who work in security like to find weaknesses and poke holes in every solution. It is always important to understand that there are weaknesses in any solution but it is just as important to understand the strengths. One of the simple but effective forms of analysis is to always ask what do you gain and what do you lose. If an organization gains more than it loses it should probably perform the solution. The trick with many of these solutions is that they reduce risk, they do not completely eliminate risk.

The other important piece of the puzzle is that these solutions work best when they are integrated together into a holistic solution. There is no perfect solution when it comes to security but by implementing many measures together, an organization can achieve a high level of security. What is important about these solutions is that the strength of each solution plays off of each other. A weakness in one solution is fixed by a strength in another. By putting all of the pieces together one can start to achieve true reputational ranking.

Reputational ranking changes the paradigm. Instead of allowing or denying access to a single network, reputation ranking is constantly changing the amount of access an entity has based on its behavioral patterns. An entity starts off with mid-level access. As the user/computer combo starts displaying good behavior that is not indicative of anything maliciou's the entity is given additional access. As the entity displays bad behavior, the entity is given less access. Now the access changes based on the activity of the user. If a system becomes compromised, the system will automatically self-correct by taking away access and making it that much harder for the attacker to cause harm. The only way the system can get more access is by stopping the malicious behavior. While this is not an unstoppable defense, it gives an organization more time to react and proper time to protect the critical information with the organization.

SUMMARY

Change is inevitable. If the attackers change and an organization does not, they are going to lose and unfortunately that is what has been happening today and the reason the APT is so devastating. Yes, the adversary is very advanced which means they will adapt very quickly but if you really look at how they are breaking in and what they are doing once they are in a network, it is not insurmountable. Organizations are losing because they have not changed and are not focusing in on the right areas; organizations are not losing because the problem is impossible. The trick is to not just change an organization's tactics but change the entire strategy of how we deal with cyber security and attacks.

If an organization just changes their tactics, they will be able to properly defend against the current APT and control overall damage. However, once we do that the APT will evolve and the organization will be back to where they are today. They would have gone one step forward but two steps back. To continue proper forward motion involves changing the general strategy that is used for protecting an organization and implementing tactics against the strategy. The first critical strategy is to focus energy on protecting data not the device. Devices will change and where the data is stored will change, but attackers will keep following the data. While a specific tactic that will be encompassed in the strategy is to secure tablets, that should not be the only thing that is done. For example, if an organization creates an approach for securing a specific brand of tablets, they are protected today; however, when a new device comes out they are back to square one. If an organization develops a strategy for protecting portable data, whatever device that data exists on will still be protected.

The target and point of exploitation is no longer the computer it is the operator or the human behind the computer. Therefore host hardening and configuration management is important, training the user and looking for anomalies is critical to success. Based on the diversity in which an adversary can attack an employee, organizations need to move beyond binary devices that either block or allow certain packets. Today we have to move towards an integrated approach that ties into a core network design. Networks need to have many levels of protection, control, and separation. They also need to be modular to allow reconfiguration with changes occurring on the fly. Now as new threats evolve, devices that contain different levels of sensitive data can be moved farther away from the attacker and ultimately harder to attack. Also, as systems that might have been compromised exhibit bad behavior, they are given less trust and access on the network and as computers exhibit good behavior, they are given more trust. Since the attacker is dynamic, the security that an organization deploys must also be dynamic in adapting and dealing with the threats that they are facing.

In implementing an approach that is more focused on proactively protecting an enterprise prior to compromise, it is important to remember that removing access is not necessarily the right solution. The way many organizations deal with new emerging threats is to reduce access and make it more difficult for someone to perform a job function. In essence, they hurt the users and employees by making it much more difficult to do their jobs. What is ironic is this approach will ultimately backfire. If an organization makes it harder for their employees to perform their jobs they will find ways around the security. The attacker will then use those workarounds for their advantage and all the security did was hurt the organization and help the attacker. It is critical to figure out what the attacker is going to do, how they are going to do it, and make it more difficult for the attacker.

Ultimately, an organization needs to control the damage points that will be used by an attacker by understanding how they operate and how they work. Knowing that the attacker is hyper-focused on the data and will target a human in order to get the information they need enables an organization to focus their energy in the correct areas. If you look at a bank's security most of the focus and protection is on the safe, where the money is located. It would be much easier to steal a stapler off of someone's desk in a bank than steal money. The stapler is not important to the bank but the money is. An organization needs to take the same approach as the bank. Information will get stolen but it is really not that important to the organization if it is not critical. Focus in on the critical data and information and build scalable security measures that properly adapt to the advanced threat.

Focusing in on the Right Security

11

INTRODUCTION

Effort does not always lead to desired results. Most of us do not need to attend a motivational seminar to understand that concept since we have witnessed it first hand in our lives. We can spend considerable amount of time, energy, and money, but if we are not focused in on the right areas we might not get the results we desire. While some of us might like to try throwing only money at a problem, usually that does not work. With a proper plan that has been validated and tested, money used in the right area to build a solution could definitely be needed but money alone does not solve problems. This concept seems simple and is well understood in our lives, but organizations tend to forget about it when it comes to security.

After an incident, breach or APT compromise, what is the number one question that executives ask? How much and what do we need to buy? Instantly when there is a problem many organizations want to pull out the check book to arrive at a solution. Typically some lucky vendor will be at the right place at the right time and sell them a solution. The executives feel good because they took some action and in their minds they now claim that they have fixed the problem, APT crossed off the list and they move on to focusing in on a new problem. It is important to point out that there are some very solid vendors with associated products that can significantly help with solving the APT challenge. The important piece of the puzzle is it must be part of a solution and it must be configured with proper integration into the environment. Just buying a product with no resources trained and no one with the skills needed to configure it correctly will not lead to a viable solution that scales.

Let us compare this to someone wanting to build a deck in their backyard. On Saturday morning they drive to the home repair store and buy wood, nails, and all of the supplies needed. They go home and stack up all of the lumber and supplies in the backyard, plug in the nail gun and saw, and go to their friend's house for several hours to watch a game. As they are leaving their friend's house they are so excited to see their new deck. They walk in the backyard and they are angry because there is no deck, the lumber is sitting exactly where they left it. Most people reading this book are puzzled at this point, saying but they did not buy a deck. They bought the supplies that in the hands of a skilled craftsperson could build a deck, but they did not buy a deck.

This example is very similar to what many organizations do. They buy a product which is the supplies needed to implement a secure solution and think they are secure. We have heard so many executives after they have been infected multiple times by the APT say how could this happen, we purchased product XYZ. Buying a product and thinking you will be secure is as naïve as buying lumber and thinking you have a deck. Products are a good thing to do and needed but implementing an integrated solution that is embedded into your environment is the right thing to do. Right things will keep you out of the headline news, good things might still cause reputational damage.

WHAT IS THE PROBLEM THAT IS BEING SOLVED?

Growing up one of the jokes that people would make is that every Miss America candidate when asked what her dream goals are would state "to solve world hunger" or "bring peace to the world." These are high-level goals but in order to solve them you have to identify what the problem is that is trying to be solved. Every great journey begins with the first step. An organization cannot identify the first step, if they do not know what the problem is they are trying to address. We have worked with many clients and when asked what they are trying to accomplish they would state "to be 100% secure" or "to never be compromised by the APT." While these are notable goals, they are as nebulous as solving world hunger. The million dollar question is where do you start? What are the problems and associated project plans that need to be developed to ultimately maintain forward progress toward the goal? Goals are hard to achieve by themselves but problems can be solved with the right focus.

Every organization should always perform an assessment within their environment to identify the main problems that need to be solved in order to do the right thing in terms of defending against the APT. The good news is the high-risk problems for many organizations typically are similar. In shifting from doing good to doing right things, the following are typical problems that organizations are ignoring but need to solve to make forward progress in dealing with the APT:

- *The ability to detect compromised systems*—One of the number one problems today is that organizations have most of their focus and attention on inbound prevention. Trying to stop attacks is important and should continue. Even though the APT is very stealthy, if an organization can prevent 20% initial attacks, that is still better than nothing and is 20% less attacks that have to be detected after the fact. However, the APT is persistent and will continue to target an organization until they accomplish their goal. Bottom line is regardless of what number of attacks can be prevented with inbound traffic, it is not going to be 100%. Organizations must be examining outbound traffic looking for signs of a compromised system. One of the million dollar questions is if an organization had a compromised system, would they be able to detect it and how long would it take. In some cases organization can take 6–8 months in order to detect a compromised system. Think about how much information is leaving the organization every day. Even if it was detected within 3 months instead of 6 months, that would still be a lot less damage and exposure to the organization. Any skill including security takes time. Ideally you want to be able to detect attacks as soon as they occur and contain/control immediately or within a short period of time like 12 h; however the most basic question is regardless of time, would your organization have any chance at all of being able to detect a compromised system? The immediate response is of course, but step back for a second. If a system was currently compromised on your network today, leaking information how would you know? It is critical in combatting the APT that organizations solve the problem of being able to detect compromised systems. Once an organization has the capability to do so, they need to continually decrease the amount of time it would take to detect the attack. Every minute a compromised system goes undetected is an increased damage and exposure to the organization.

- *Being able to identify anomalies from known baselines*—anomaly detection is critical to dealing with and detecting the APT, but the fundamental question is how can something be an anomaly if you do not know what is normal. An organization must track usage, network patterns, connectivity, and bandwidth to understand and build a profile of what is normal and expected to be seen in an organization. Depending on the type of attack it might be very visible or it might be subtle, but if someone compromises a system they are going to act differently than a normal user. If their behavior is exactly the same, then they are not an attacker or your normal users are attackers. Organizations need to figure out which activities to build baselines against, but the ones that work well against the APT are: (1) length of the connection; (2) amount of outbound data; (3) external IPs being connected to. In almost all cases that we have seen the APT creates an obvious anomaly across all three areas that is quite different than normal traffic. The powerful component of anomaly analysis is the correlation across multiple sources. While one item might give a little insight into something being an anomaly, the real value is when the results are compared across 3–5 different variables. When this is done it becomes quite obvious that something is an anomaly. Creating baselines are quite easy if you have the traffic, sniffer output, or logs, but the base analysis has to be done for it to be of value. The big problem for many organizations is that they have the data but it has never been normalized. It is like there is an oil deposit under someone's house that is worth millions but because they never checked, they never realized and therefore was not able to take advantage of the value of it.
- *Properly segmented networks*—Flat networks are easy for users to be able to access data but it is also extremely easy for attackers to also be able to access the information. What is ironic is that properly segmented networks can also be configured to be very easy for users to be able to access data but also very difficult for attackers to be able to cause harm. The question for your organization is whether you want option (1) easy for the user and easy for the attacker or

option (2) easy for the user and hard for the attacker. Life is full of adventures so when it comes to protecting information, let us stay away from excitement and pick option 2. The big problem with many organizations is that they cannot properly control who can access what systems and once a client system is compromised, it is very easy for the attacker to have full access to any information they want. Gateways and control points have been used for many years in the physical security realm to protect valuable possessions and the same concepts can be used in with electronic information to protect critical information.

- *Better correlation to prevent/detect attacks*—The APT is like a puzzle, in order to solve it you need to have all of the pieces. With a large puzzle if you only have one piece you really have no idea what the picture of the puzzle is. The more pieces you have the clearer the picture. A puzzle piece is an entry in a log file on a single device. If you just look at the logs or information on a single computer you only have a small number of pieces, the more devices you gather and correlate information against, the clearer the picture and the more useful the data. With the APT correlation is king. In many cases better detection can lead to improved prevention. Once an organization is able to detect an attack and see what they missed, that information can be used to build better defensive measures in the future. Proper detection should lead to improved metrics and better information for enhanced prevention of future attacks that are similar. Now the critical piece is to correlate the information and look for general patterns that can be blocked, not specific signatures. Since the attacker is always changing, signatures will provide minimal protection in dealing with the APT. While looking at specific log entries is good for detailed analysis, most of the energy and effort in dealing with the APT should be focused on high-level correlation, tied with anomaly analysis.

- *Proper incident response to prevent reinfection*—When an organization finds out that they have been compromised for 6–8 months and it went undetected, the response is not usually a calm and peaceful response, it is usually people freaking out. The typical response is to make the problem go away as fast as possible. Most organizations forget about the six-step process for handling an incident, skip steps and all focus is on recovery. Get the systems back up and running as quickly as possible. Since people are under stress they often forget the obvious. If the attacker compromised a system once, there is very good chance they will compromise it a second time. While catching an attacker is important, reinfection is deadly. If the first time the attacker broke in you eventually caught them, they are not happy. They will break back in but they will work even harder to be stealthy and not get caught. If it took an organization 6–8 months to detect the attacker the first time and now they are really trying to be stealthy, how long do you think it will take the organization to catch them the second time. When it comes to compromise, do it right the first time, there are no second chances. Many organizations that have not been compromised take a logical look at the problem and say the longer a system is down the more money it is going to cost the organization. Therefore the quicker we can recovery the better off the organization is. The problem is it is better to be down once, for a longer period of time and fix the problem, than recover quickly but become reinfected and have additional data loss. However, it is important to point out that there are some systems in which availability is critical. In these cases systems might need to be brought up before they are fully remediated, but this should be a business decision and all systems should be carefully monitored and controlled in these circumstances. The important lesson with an incident, but especially with a devastating attack like the APT, is do it right the first time and fix the problem. There are no second chances.

Security is very challenging and it is always important to make sure the problem you are fixing is the highest priority problem.

IF THE OFFENSE KNOWS MORE THAN THE DEFENSE YOU WILL LOOSE

A simple question that any organization should ask is whether they really understand their weaknesses and how would an attacker break in and compromise their organization. Knowing that an organization has a limited budget and recognizing that there is no such thing as 100% security, it is critical to understand where an organization's weaknesses are located so in cases where they cannot prevent attacks, they can monitor and pay more attention to those areas. In order to do the right things in terms of security an organization needs to understand the attacker's playbook. If an organization does not understand what the attacker is going to do and where their weaknesses are located, how will they ever be able to properly defend against an attack? Now the common response is that the attack is more advanced and stealthy than it used to be. While that is true it does not mean that there are still not patterns and playbooks that the attacker uses that we can better understand to build up more effective defensive measures.

This approach is no different than how most people deal with personal health. It is not good to be surprised and get very sick without realizing it. Most people who are diabetic, track and monitor their blood sugar level on a regular basis. People who are not diabetic do not perform the same monitoring because you only have to watch it closely if it is a known weakness. People who have high cholesterol and other issues know they are more prone to heart attacks and therefore are much more careful when they go out to dinner on what they eat and try to avoid stressful situations. If you know your body is more vulnerable, that area is going to be watched and monitored much more closely. This same concept needs to be applied to securing our systems. The networks at our organizations are our cyber bodies and we need to understand where exposures lie and watch those areas much more closely.

What is always very concerning is after we perform an assessment or an incident response, people at an organization are surprised or argue with the results. Very often an IT manager will turn to their engineers and say I thought we removed that system off of the network. The reply is it should have been removed, but we will go back and check and make sure. In other cases when sensitive data is found on systems that are not properly protected, we have had people argue with us stating they are positive the information no longer resides on the system. What is concerning is that we have the sensitive data in our hands that we found on the server, so either we are magicians or the data is still there. One of the sayings we jokingly have is computers do not lie, people do. They are well intentioned but we should not be assuming or guessing at what the state of our organizations' security is, we should be validating it on a regular basis. If an organization does not understand what is on their network, how can they protect it?

Making sure that the defense understands and knows their network is all about three critical pieces: configuration management, change control, and continuous monitoring/auditing. If systems are not built off of a known build, changes are properly controlled and scanned to make sure they have not been changed, it is almost impossible to win at security. First, an organization must understand and know the state of a system from the beginning. Starting off with a secure configuration for a server is critical to success. The day a new system goes on a network, an organization must understand how it is configured to be able to carefully monitor it. If every system is configured differently, an organization is going to lose. Having robust configuration management across all systems is important to make sure that it can be managed, controlled, and deviations identified quickly. Second, a static organization is a dead organization. An organization needs to continue to grow, change and being dynamic is a requirement for organizations today. Recognizing that systems are going to have to change and be updated means that all changes have to be carefully controlled and managed. If systems can change without any approval, the change could have had an adverse effect on security. Since there is no way to determine if a change will have a negative impact on security without testing, all changes must be carefully controlled. In addition, if a list of authorized changes is not maintained and through monitoring a change is detected, how would an organization know if it is authorized or unauthorized? Change control is the glue that holds configuration management together and allows an organization to very quickly spot anomalies. Third, when attackers make changes to a system they do not submit their changes through a change control board. Therefore if an attacker is changing a system, how would an organization know unless they were performing continuous auditing/monitoring? Every single tool that is used to secure a system should be run in an automated, continuous manner to be able to identify changes in the environment. As soon as a change is detected and deemed to be unapproved, immediate action needs to be taken. One of the best indicators of a compromised system is change; therefore tracking changes closely can provide a robust, early detection warning system.

What is interesting is that with the APT the attackers have a really well thought out game plan. They understand an organization very well, they have a thorough plan and execute against it very well. Even if the defense had a well thought out game plan, the game would still be very difficult today, but we would have a chance. The problem is we are going up against a well-versed adversary and the defense has a weak or no game plan. Organizations need to go back to the basics and focus energy on understanding their environment and knowing what the offense knows. Many organizations have spent a lot of energy and effort into security. The frustrating part is if the foundational items are not in place and an organization does not understand what they have, effort does not always lead to results and organizations will get compromised.

Surprises are never a good thing except for proposals and birthdays. Take the mystery out of the APT and start fully documenting and understanding your organization's environment. At a minimum, from an understanding perspective an organization must have an accurate up-to-date network diagram and a network visibility map. If an organization does not know how all of the pieces fit together, how can they identify exposures or weaknesses? Based on how efficient the attacker is and how quickly they can identify the sensitive information they are after and extract it, shows that the attackers understand an organization's network layout better than the organization.

In terms of doing the right thing and understanding an organization's environment, after an accurate network diagram is produced and all systems are fully accounted for, the next critical step is data discovery. While knowing how the systems are connected together and understanding what systems are connected to the network are important, we have to remember that security has been and will always be about the data. The next question is not only where does your data primarily reside but in how many other locations is the data stored? Most organizations do a pretty good job with knowing the primary storage location of their information. In order for applications and general business processes to function this information is required. However, where things get really scary is identifying not just the primary, but how many other locations does an organization's data reside? In many cases the data is primarily stored in one location, but there are literally hundreds of copies on servers all around the enterprise. Remember, if an attacker wants to acquire a piece of information they do not have to go to the primary database, any copy on any system in the enterprise will do. The reason this is so important is in many cases an organization will focus significant energy on securing the database. The database server, which is the primary storage location for critical data is properly locked down and hardened. Application aware firewalls are in place and all traffics are properly filtered. The problem is the attacker never touches or even tries to break into the database server since they know it is too hard. Instead, they find another system that has a copy of the information and has minimal security and all of their energy and effort is focused on that server.

Unfortunately in security an organization is only as strong as the weakest link. Therefore, in order to be successful an organization needs to understand where the weakest links are and either fix them or monitor them very closely. The more time, energy, and effort an organization can invest in understanding their environment, knowing their weaknesses and mapping them against the attacker's game plan, the more successful they will be. An organization cannot fix a problem that they do not know about and therefore knowledge is power. Focusing energy on understanding one's environment is critical because one of the key rules for dealing with the APT is know their system.

ENHANCING USER AWARENESS

In order to protect an organization it is important that all users know what they need to do (policy), they have the skills for doing it (training) and they understand the importance so they will follow what they are supposed to do (awareness). Since many users do not understand the importance of security and typically do not think security is important, awareness is a critical part of any security program. The main goal of awareness is to clearly explain to a user why something is important, giving them examples they can understand with the goal of having them change their behavior so they follow the policy correctly. The goal of awareness is to change behavior to increase the security of an organization.

Training users on spear-phishing attacks and explaining to them how to identify obvious attempts is very important and should be done. The fundamental problem with the APT is that the attackers have done their research and the attacker's emails look just like real emails. Therefore, in order for the user to perform their job, they will have to click on APT emails. From a user perspective, there is not a difference between a legitimate looking email and an advanced spearphishing attack. Therefore, the user would delete malicious emails but since these emails look legitimate, they would also in the process be deleting legitimate emails. While user awareness is a critical foundation to any security program, it is not going to be sufficient against high-tech attacks. For example, imagine if you are working and you receive an email that there has been an accident at your child's school. You pull up the local news and there is actually an accident at the school. Is there a single parent that would not click on the link that claims to have a list of students who were involved in the accident? Remember, this is no longer business, this is your family and we know that 99% of all parents would click on the link to make sure their child is OK. This is the level of sophistication of the attacker. They perform their research and they make sure that the email looks so legitimate to the casual observer that there is no way to differentiate between a good or bad email.

As simple as it sounds, three areas that can complement awareness to make them more effective in the enterprise are: virtualized sandboxing, patching, and white listing. This builds off of the principles of defense in depth. By properly protecting or isolating the damage that an attacker could do would help increase the effectiveness of user awareness.

VIRTUALIZED SANDBOXING

The ultimate goal of compromise of the APT is to gain a beach head that can be used to cause harm to an organization over a long period of time. The goal of the initial exploit is to compromise a system to create, maintain, and set up this pivot point that can be used to start propagating across the network and gathering the desired information. If a system is exploited but the pivot point cannot be controlled and maintained the attacker's house will fall apart. The critical component is long-term access to a system which means the core host operating system has to be exploited, typically at a kernel level so it is hard to remove and will automatically start every time the system is booted. If this cannot be maintained it becomes much harder for the attacker to cause damage.

Minimizing what runs on the host operating system and the access available to the code that is running on behalf of the user is important to control the damage caused by the APT. The bottom line is the general premise of an operating system and how we use it today was never designed for security or thought out properly. A desktop or laptop computer typically has a single hard drive, a single partition in which the operating system is installed with all applications having direct access to the operating system. From both a security and logical perspective, that does not sound like a great plan. The problem is the core components of the operating system should be used to startup the system, not be easy to change, and absolutely not be changed by the user during the normal running of the system. What is interesting is following these general rules would have zero impact on the user. They do not need to do any of these requirements anyway in order to do their job. During maintenance, system administrators would need this access, but during the normal running of the system, users do not need this access. The only thing that needs to perform these functions is the APT. Emphasizing one of the many themes of this book, we need to stop making things easier for the attacker by implementing functionality that only they use. Some organizations are getting so fed up with the APT that they are willing to remove functionality that users need. The philosophy is that drastic times require drastic measures. While I completely agree, we need to do this in a logical order and let's fix the items that will not hurt the user first and if that does not work we can try something additional.

Ideally all applications should run in a separate virtual machine but at a minimum, any code that is not a part of the secure build protected with application white listing, should always run in a separate guest operating system. Containing and controlling the APT is key. If we cannot prevent the APT, which in some cases is extremely difficult, we need to contain it to a separate environment that is only infected for a few minutes not several months. In addition, not only is the infection contained, but it will not survive a reboot. Not only does it not survive a reboot but as soon as the virtual machine is closed or the application stops running, all remnants of the malicious code disappear and most importantly nothing touches the core host operating system. Isolating potential dangerous code with virtualization is a key tool that needs to be added to the anti-APT arsenal that we are building.

While this next step is completely a bonus step and not needed for isolated, virtualized sandboxes to work, it will add an extra level of protection. In addition to sandboxing, a bonus is to install the core operating system on a separate partition on the hard drive and boot it read only during the normal running of the system. Now even if all things go wrong and the malicious code can escape out of the guest, since the core OS components are read-only, it is much more difficult for the attacker to gain a foothold and maintain long-term access.

Now anyone who works in penetration testing can put this in a lab and figure out ways to break it or get around the security. It is important to point that any security can be broken or bypassed but we have to step back and look at two things. First, any solution by itself is always weaker than when it is integrated into a larger solution. The sum of the parts is always greater than the individual pieces. Picking of a single solution and showing weaknesses is important and critical to make sure we understand, as we create larger solutions. However, what is extremely dangerous is to make the leap of faith and conclude that just because something has a weakness it is useless. Yes, some things are but not all solutions fit under this category. Second, we must always step back and always look at both the strengths and weaknesses together to see if the benefits outweigh the losses. We cannot just hyper fixate on the weakness, ignoring anything good that is also brought to the equation. If this was done in real life, no one would be married. There is no perfect person. Therefore, if all someone did was look at the bad, people would give up. Whenever someone makes a mistake, we always compare it with the good and make a proper decision. The same balance of looking at both the good and the bad has to be made with security solutions.

PATCHING

The most basic definition of a patch is it is the vendor telling everyone that there is a vulnerability or mistake in their code and the patch is the way to fix it. Now that is not a glorious definition but it fundamentally is true. A patch is an accident waiting to happen because it is an exposure in the system that all attackers know about, and it is just a matter of time before it gets compromised. Many organizations know this and focus significant energy on patching Internet visible systems or devices located on the DMZ. This is important and should continue but what is important to understand is that the APT changes the rules. Typically the APT does not target an unpatched system as the initial point of compromise, they target a user. Based on this information alone people typically conclude that patching is not important with regards to the APT; however it is. While an unpatched system is not the initial point of compromise, a targeted attack against an individual is, we have to look at what the attacker does after they compromise a client system. After the attacker established a beach head on a network, the system that was compromised typically does not contain sensitive information or data. Now the threat has to find the system with the sensitive data, break in and compromise the system. What is one of the ways they compromise those servers, through known vulnerabilities or unpatched systems. Based on how the APT works, patching internal systems is just as important as external systems.

The general (flawed) logic in the past has always been that the more visible the system, the more critical it is to patch. Therefore, systems on the private network are not visible to the Internet and therefore do not need to be patched as much. However, with the attacks now technically coming from the private network and therefore the client private network is the new untrusted Internet, unpatched private systems are easy picking for the attacker. As we focus more attention on the private network systems and patch them in a timely manner, an organization must still make sure that they continue to patch the DMZ systems. One of the problems with security is that if an organization starts focusing all of their energy in a new area and stops addressing a previous area, the previous area will become the weakest link and be used as a point of compromise for the attacker. What we have to be really careful with is that as we make the internal servers harder and harder to break into since more attention is being paid to configuration management and patching, is to make sure that the DMZ servers do not become neglected. If an organization stops maintaining and patching DMZ servers, we all know what is going to happen in 1–2 years. The APT will now focus in on breaking into the DMZ servers because they are now the easiest way into a network.

WHITE LISTING

There is no perfect solution but carefully controlling, monitoring, and allowing what can run on a system is an effective way to minimize an attacker from running extraneous code and causing harm. White listing switches the paradigm. In the past most security devices would look for evil on a network and block the known evil. This worked in the 1990s when the amount of evil was known, detectable and somewhat controllable. Today with the stealthy nature of the attacker, looking for evil no longer works. An approach to effectively control evil is to create a list of known good applications and only allow those applications to run. Everything else is blocked. As we talked about earlier in the book, one of the complaints of white listing is that it is harder to do in more complex environments. The reason why it is harder to do is because it forces an organization to do their homework.

With past attacks organizations could get away with not knowing what was on their network and not doing their homework. Today, if an organization does not do its homework which is carefully understand, know, track, and monitor one's environment, they will not be effective against the APT. What is nice about white listing is not only does it increase an organization's security by carefully controlling and monitoring what can or cannot run, but it also forces an organization to do the work that is needed to understand their environment.

It is important to note that there is no single solution or silver bullet that is going to make an organization secure. In addition, every organization is different and unique. Any decisions that are made in an organization should be based off of risk and tailored to the critical intellectual property that an organization is trying to protect. However, the key three areas are provided as a starting point for implementing effective security that works. While these solutions will not block all APT all the time, no solution will. Thus the key phrase of prevention is ideal but detection is a must. Dealing with the APT is a continuous process but an organization cannot make forward progress, if core foundational items are not in place and performed correctly.

SUMMARY

My children are taking piano lessons and if you had to overhear the conversations we have about getting them to practice, you would think we were torturing them or making them do something really evil like eat spinach. One of the mistakes I made was I told my son he had to practice for 30 min each evening. We noticed that while he was "practicing" he was not getting any better. We quickly realized that he would stare at the piano for 30 min each night. Based on this we changed the approach that he had to play 15 songs each evening. The moral of the story is just because you put time into something does not mean you will get the results that you want. Time, energy, effort, and results are not necessarily the same. Even if my son actually tried and banged on the keyboard for 30 min every night, if no one told him what to do, he would still not get the desired results. Doing good things and trying is not good enough if you want results, you must understand, focus, and do the right things.

There are some organizations that when post mortem analysis is done after a compromise, you are amazed that they lasted as long as they did. Their security is a mess and there is no unified effort. However there are some organizations that really, honestly, and earnestly try to implement security but they are all over the place, they are not focused and they do not have a unified plan. In security sometimes less is more. It is better to focus on a few areas and do it right, than try to do everything and have sub-par results. In making decisions on what needs to be focused on for properly dealing with the APT, focus in on the right areas by:

- Involving other people from across the organization. Security has a limited view of how all business units operate. Coordinating with other business units will help give additional insight into the business problems and challenges across the entire organization. It is also critical to make sure all of the executives are on board. If you walk around an organization and ask high-level questions on security and critical assets, you should receive similar answers.
- Proper planning is critical. Do not rush into the latest trend or buzz word. There is so much movement in IT and security, it is easy to lose sight of what is important and to chase after the next best thing. In focusing on the APT, it is critical to put together a plan, fully validate the plan, and only change the plan if there is a valid reason and buy-in across the enterprise.
- Let risk not emotion drive security decisions. People have different reasons for making decisions but the only logic that matters is the one that maps back to risk. Risk is the gospel when it comes to security and needs to guide decisions to make sure the right resources are used in the right areas.

Implementing Adaptive Security

12

INTRODUCTION

It is amazing how quick and fast technology changes. Almost overnight technology has taken over and has become a key part of our lives. Since the beginning of time there has always been a constant battle between good and evil. The second that new technology is invented there are entities that are looking at ways to exploit it and take advantage of it. Technology that makes employees lives easier can also make an attacker's life easier. Technology that allows an organization to streamline its operation, increasing overall productivity, will also allow an adversary to more easily attack an organization in a streamlined manner. The APT was an evolution of how adversaries used advanced technologies to increase their ability to exploit information in a more efficient manner. Regardless of what we did, the APT was inevitable.

The reason we have advanced persistent threats, is because we have advanced persistent technologies that must be available 24/7/365 to allow employees to be as productive as possible. With paper-based systems locked in offices, the primary tool available to the attacker was physical theft of the information. It would be very difficult for someone to steal information, bypassing international boundaries and perform the attack anywhere in the world. Thirty years ago things were much harder for the attacker, however, things were much harder for the user. It was difficult to access information remotely and if someone was working on the weekend and needed access to data, their primary option was to drive into the office. The APT is a constant reminder that there is a price to pay for technology—functionality that makes an organization life easier will often make an attacker's life easier.

What is very interesting about the APT is that while it uses technology to be more efficient, the general methods of attack are actually very old school techniques. During the cold world and before the massive use of the Internet and technology, what was the main weakness and main method of foreign governments extracting information from their adversary? Human targeting, manipulation, or social engineering was the main method of data extraction. While physically breaking into an intelligence organization was an option, it was too difficult and too hard to perform. After detailed analysis it was deemed to be much more efficient to target an employee or trusted insider and convince them to steal information. Today even with the ability to access computers from anyone in the world, the adversary realized it was much easier to target an individual to give them access. While directly breaking into a system is always an option it is much harder and more difficult than targeting a human.

In many cases today, compromising a human is much easier than compromising a computer. Humans can be manipulated, tricked, and deceived; computers cannot. As technology has changed and the methods of doing business have evolved at an amazing rate, the weakest link in an organization has and will be the human. What is interesting is that while the human is the target, today they could be helping an adversary and not even realize it. In the days of paper, it would be very hard to have someone steal information without realizing. Typically an adversary would have to pay them money and tell them what they wanted access today. There was little way to do this covertly. Today, in many attacks, the insider is tricked into giving the adversary access to the network and in many cases they do not even realize it. The accidental insider is a very scary concept because now well-intentioned individuals could be targeted. One of the many reasons on why this is so concerning is not only is it easier to have someone help an adversary covertly but now there are minimal moral issues that the person is actually doing something wrong. The other concerning aspect is that there is a much larger number of people that could be targeted. If an adversary was going to convince someone to steal, there are moral and ethical boundaries that have to be crossed and some people would not cross them. Plus it is high risk because if the person being approached gets concerned, they could notify the organization and put them on alert. If anyone in the organization could be a target and they will not even know they are being a target, it becomes much easier and simpler for them to cause harm.

I often sit back and look at the technology that we have available at our finger tips and it is downright amazing. It is easy from a security perspective to get caught up on all of the technology and trying to figure out how to secure it. We often get questions on how do you secure an iPad, an android, the cloud and the list goes on and on. While it is important to understand the technology, the focus should not be on the technology, the focus should be on the data and the human. Technology changes too quickly and if you focus on it, it is similar to a dog chasing its tail. In addition, the technology is the medium of the attack it is not the source or the target of the attack. In many cases with regard to the APT, the source of the exploitation is the human and the target of the attack is an organization's data. While technology might change, those two aspects of the attack will not. The more organizations put energy and effort into controlling the human and protecting the data, the better they will be at protecting against the APT today and the next generation of the APT in the future.

As you read the last chapter of this book, it is important to note that many of these concepts have been mentioned in various pieces throughout the book, since the general themes of all chapters are the same—properly dealing with and defending against the APT. Some of the concepts you have read in previous chapters, but this chapter ties all of the pieces together and shows how an organization must adapt to changing security requirements. What worked yesterday, will not work tomorrow. By constantly enhancing and improving an organization's security posture through constant adoption, will allow organizations to implement security that works.

FOCUSING ON THE HUMAN

In dealing with any threat including the APT it is important to always take a risk-based approach to security. The quickest way for an organization to get into trouble and waste resources is by focusing in on something other than risk for making critical security decisions. While risk should also drive the decision, the biggest risk in many organizations with regard to being compromised by the APT is the human. In many cases the APT is actually compromising a human not the computer or the technology they are using as their endpoint. The more energy and effort an organization can put in place to protect the human or minimize the damage the human can cause, the better.

It is important to point out that when dealing with the human there are two key pieces: (1) protecting the human and (2) minimizing the damage the human can cause. Many organizations put significant amount of energy and effort in protecting the human. Awareness programs are critical and without them things would be a lot worse and organizations would be in a lot more trouble. However, as with any security methodology, there is no silver bullet. There is no single technology that will make an organization secure. Awareness is important but the problem is with many of the high-tech APT attacks utilizing advanced social engineering techniques, awareness will not help because from a human perspective there is no way to differentiate between an attacker's email and a legitimate looking email. For APT targeting spear phishing attacks, either the user is not going to be able to perform their jobs because they will have to be so cautious in deleting emails that in filtering out APT emails, they would also be filtering out legitimate emails. Clearly this method would be unproductive. The second approach is the problem we have today. If the user opens and processes legitimate looking emails, they will also click on APT emails and be infected. The APT has done their research and the emails look so good, awareness alone will not be able to protect against the attack.

What is so scary about these techniques is that with proper planning, the act of actually compromising an organization and gaining a foothold is relatively straightforward. It is not terribly advanced or sophisticated but it is very hard to defend against and mitigate. Just by monitoring open source information it is amazing how much information an adversary can gain. Let's look at a brief example. An APT attacker would scan social media sites looking for a list of people who work at a target organization. They would also go to the organization's website and see who is listed on the webpage. Press releases, job vacancy sites, and other open source information are all used to obtain a list of employees. Subcontractors would also be targeted as a potential access point. Once a list of employees is gained, Google alerts are set up on those individuals tracking all postings and any information that is publicly available about those people. Correlation analysis is done to try and find out the bosses including the overall structure of the organization. Once a threat actor finds out about a person's job, their interest, and co-workers, they begin to put together a plan. It can be as simple as tracking postings that the individual likes to compete in triathlons and is actively looking for a certain brand bike. The analysis shows that they are part of several groups on the topic. A spoofed email from the group address is sent to the individual with details about the bike they are looking for and it is signed by a trusted source. It is almost a guarantee that they will open the attachment or click on the link. While some of the attacks can be more advanced, with an advanced adversary, simpler is better. What is so interesting is the more work and analysis that is done the easier it is for the attacker to be successful. Training and awareness is always critical but with this style of attack, it is almost impossible to block the system from being compromised. In cases where you cannot stop the attacker, containing or control the damage is critical.

One of the core goals of security is to fix the problem not the symptom. However, the APT is typically taking advantage of a tried and true weakness, the human, that in many cases it is very difficult to fix the problem. Since the weakness and the nature of what is needed to run a business is so closely tied, if you remove the weakness of an organization it hurts their business. Since being so secure that an organization goes out of business is silly, an organization in these cases has no choice but to accept the weakness to allow the business to function. While directed spear phishing seems so simple, it is actually brilliant that this is the component the APT chose to go after since the adversary knows that it cannot be completely shut down or eliminated. However, all is not lost and hope is not gone. In these cases, an organization can still recognize that while the actual emails look so similar between a legitimate and adversary, they both must be allowed and ultimately opened; the associated activity that occurs after the user action is quite different.

Now instead of focusing on the action, do not open any email that could be suspicious, which with really advanced attacks does not work; we now switch to focusing on the activity that is performed and controlling and minimizing damage. The good news is that there are many ways to control and limit damage, but they often require some change of behavior or inconvenience for the user. The following are many ways to minimize and control the damage with the APT:

- *Run the email client or attachment in a virtual machine*—the goal of the attacker is twofold: (1) compromise a system to maintain long-term access to the network; and (2) extract out critical information from the organization. Minimizing where potential dangerous applications or malware can run is focused on item 1, reducing or minimizing the chance of the attacker getting a foothold on the network. If the attacker cannot get a pivot point and have the access for long term, essentially survive a reboot, it is going to be much harder for the attacker to do long-term damage. The ultimate goal with any attack is not to get compromised and no damage. Since that is not always possible, the next best option is if an organization does not get compromised, minimize the length of time the system is compromised which will ultimately control the amount of damage that can be caused. When an attacker breaks into a system, they want to gain control of the host OS kernel, modify startup files, and run a reboot. If they are not able to accomplish those goals, the next time the system is rebooted, the attacker loses control of the beachhead and essentially has to start over again. Therefore taking a systematic approach for dealing with the APT, the trick is to limit the exposure of any applications that are used by the adversary or that they hope the user would run on their behalf. Having email and web browsers run in virtual machines and any applications that are going to auto-launch when an attachment is opening also be isolated, the amount of damage is contained. Isolation and virtual sandboxing is a scalable solution that can greatly minimize and reduce the amount of damage.

- *Explicitly indicate whether the email is from internal or external*—The trick with helping users make the right decisions with regard to security is to provide information to them that is simple but effective. In addition, it needs to be easy for them to use and integrate as part of their job. One of the problems with the APT is that the emails look like legitimate emails and in many cases they look like legitimate emails from co-workers or bosses. Looking at the from address, subject, and body of the message it is almost impossible to differentiate or determine whether the email is from an adversary; therefore because it looks legitimate employees assume that it is and open the attachment. From a user perspective there is no difference. However, in cases where the APT is impersonating internal users, there is a technical difference. The email that is legitimate from employees originates from within the network and is received by the mail server over the internal network. Attacker emails that are not valid are actually coming in from the Internet or the external mail relay. The good news is looking at the logs there is a technical difference. The bad news is there is so much email it is not practical to perform this check manually at a centralized level. The only way for this to scale is to push the analysis to each user and have them perform the check. The problem is users are not going to pull up the technical details of the email and analyze the source and run a trace. While there is a solution, we need to figure out how to make it scale so it will be easy for the user. The solution is for any email coming from the Internet or outside network to append [EXTERNAL] to the beginning of the subject line and for any email that originated from the private network, append [INTERNAL]. What is interesting is that this is highly effective. If someone is always used to receiving emails from their boss with [INTERNAL] on the subject line and now they see an email with [EXTERNAL], they will immediately be concerned and take action. The trick with security is simpler is better. While many really smart people love creating high-tech and often complicated solutions, it is the simply solutions that work and scale. Also, while it sounds counterintuitive, it is much harder to create a simple solution to a hard problem that works. Anyone can create a complicated solution but if it is too hard, has too many steps, and subject to mistakes, it will eventually fail and not work as planned.

- *Convert attachments for clients to review prior to opening*—Names can be very confusing, misleading, and incorrectly interpreted, especially when it comes to files or names of a website. It is easy to name an attachment AlphaTechProjectPlan051512ppt or have a URL look legitimate. However, once the attachment is opened or the link is clicked, the damage is already done. We often receive calls from clients saying that they received a suspicious attachment or URL and they want to do know what to do. The suggestion is to delete the email and do not open or click the link. The response is usually, well what if we already opened the attachment or clicked on the link. My initial thought process originally was why in the world did you click on the link if you knew it was suspicious? What I realized is the only way to recognize that it was suspicious was after they opened the attachment or clicked on the link. Hindsight is 20/20. Looking at the email it looks legitimate, only by taking action do you review the content and very quickly realize that there is a problem. Therefore, another method of dealing with the APT is giving the user the ability to preview the content of an attachment or other content to a safe format, allowing them to review before they actually open it in the real application. In many cases content can be converted to a safe format or run in a sandbox to isolate the user from any damage but give them a chance to analyze the content and make sure everything is OK. Essentially we are giving the user a try before you buy option. While there is some really clever code that can bypass and get around this trick, remember security is a numbers game. Even if we can catch 50% of all attacks using this method, that is a lot better than zero. The idea in dealing with the APT is knowledge is power. The more information the user has, the better a decision they can make. By giving them some insight into what the content of an otherwise mysterious file contains, can help in giving the users the right tools to make the correct decisions.

• *Remove all executable content and/or html encoding*—Functionality drives technology and innovation. In any area of our life if we are looking to buy something, functionality usually drives our decision. If you are looking at any technology and try to determine which product you should purchase, a common question is what features does it have? Features are great for allowing someone to get the full value out of a purchase or piece of software but functionality is also what an adversary targets as a point of compromise. The more features, the more complexity, the greater the chance of mistakes and the more opportunity for exploitation. One way to control or minimize the ease in which an adversary can compromise an organization is to reduce or limit the amount of functionality. The simpler something is the easier it is to secure and the harder it is for someone to break in. What is ironic is, in many cases, the main functionality that an attacker uses to break into a system is often not utilized for legitimate purposes. This means if we remove that functionality it would have a big impact on the attacker and minimal to no impact on the user. It almost seems that sometimes we have gone out of our ways to make things easier for an attacker. One of those areas is allowing executable content in applications, files, and other content. Very often this functionality is enabled by default but has a very small amount of use by legitimate users. Therefore a key approach to minimizing the impact of the APT is to disable, turn off, or remove any executable content from any files received from the Internet. One could argue that there might be a few cases where this could break legitimate functionality; however taking a risk-based approach of looking at what do you gain and what do you lose, the positive definitely wins. Turning off any executable content from files coming from the Internet would stop or make it much harder for an advanced threat to cause harm and overall would have minimal if any impact to the organization. Any negative impact would be small compared to the big benefits that are achieved by doing this.

- *Force all external users to register and create an internal email*—In a perfect world, an organization would like to create security measures that are completely transparent to the user but very effective at stopping the attacker. However, in some cases an organization has to make a decision between a little extra work in order to get increased security or status quo with a high risk of compromise. One of the fundamental problems with how the APT works is it targets email from untrusted sources to impersonate and act like a trusted source. One method of dealing with this is to have any external parties that want to send email or send email with attachments, register, and receive a guest account that they used for sending any email or any email with attachments into the organization. Now all entities would have to register and use a separate web interface in order to communicate with anyone inside the organization. This extra step makes it harder for automated style attacks and adds an extra step of having to be verified and validated. While not perfect, it adds an extra level of trust than one would have if they just sent email from the Internet. An organization could configure it for all emails but in many organizations this would be too time consuming. Instead regular emails are allowed through but any emails with links or attachments, would have them removed and the sender would receive notification that this occurred and tell the sender where they would have to go to register and get an authorized account in order to upload the attachment. This is definitely not a preferred solution but the reason it is covered last.

Remember with security it is not about building a single level of protection, it is all about defense in depth. Organizations that want to properly deal with the APT need to have a comprehensive set of measures that are all integrated together, that compliment and provide robust protection. If any single measure fails, other measures will take over and minimize the impact.

Looking at the news and talking with organizations the APT could seem like an insurmountable beast that no matter what you will do you will lose. This is based off of observations of organizations spending millions of dollars and still getting compromised. What we have to recognize is that while dealing with the APT is difficult, it can be managed. Just because organizations have not been successful in the past, is an indication that they have not been focusing in on the correct areas. By focusing energy and effort on controlling the damage an accidental insider could do to an organization, will also control the damage and impact of the APT.

FOCUSING ON THE DATA

When defending against something, it is always important to look at the basics of the attack and ask what the ultimate goal is. Bank robbers are after the money and advanced threats are after the data. It is really that simple. Therefore if we know what the attacker is after we should have an easier time of controlling the information. Overall, the APT is compromising a significant number of organizations and stealing large amounts of data, therefore if we want to do a better job of dealing with the APT, let's go back to the basics. Focus on an organization's critical information and data. Focusing on the data sounds so simple, but many organizations do not even really know where their data is or the overall sensitivity.

If someone is really struggling in a particular area and you are a consultant, tutor, advisory, etc. you are going to find the one foundational area that will give them the best return and help them the most. If your organization is struggling with the APT, let's keep it simple. There are many things you could be doing but the one thing you must be doing is taking a more data-centric view of your organization. Therefore, the foundational plan for more effectively dealing with the APT is to focus on the following:

- *Data prioritization*—The first step is to determine what information or type of information is the most critical to an organization's current and future success. This typically is not a single item but a list of different types of data in priority order. Most organizations do not have the resources to protect all information with the highest level of security. Even if they did, it would not be very cost effective and would not be recommended. An organization needs to prioritize its resources and put the highest level of protection on the most critical pieces of data. The next level of data would receive slightly less security based on the business need and overall exposure. So many decisions within an organization that impact security are often made without having complete information and not focusing in on the correct areas. Ultimately what the attacker is after is an organization's data, that is what is going to cause the most damage and that needs to be the focus of attention. However, data cannot be the focus if an organization does not understand the different types of data that it has and which ones are the highest priorities. What is very interesting when we perform assessments is that there is often minimal or no alignment between where an organization focuses their resources and what is important to the organization. We often create a list of all of the different types of data the organization deals with, prioritizing it based on the business focus and mission. We thrn take the security budget and show what percent of the budget is used to protect which type of information. Very often the highest priority data is receiving less than 10% of the focus in terms of the security resources and very low priority items are receiving a much higher percent of the budget. Many people are confused on why organization would do this. The simple answer, they did not know. They never performed this mapping and therefore had a false view of reality and were not properly aligning the organization's resources correctly.

- *Data classification*—Once an organization identifies its critical information, it has to determine the criticality of that information to the business and what the overall risk or exposure to the organization would be if it was compromised. Based on the impact to the organization, a data classification scheme needs to be created and applied to the information. Identifying what information is critical to an organization is important but it will not have tremendous value if there is no way electronically to be able to identify or filter this information. Not only does a data classification scheme need to be developed to be able to label information of various sensitivity labels, but the classification also needs to be able to be embedded within the data. Having all data proper classified is critical, but there needs to be an equivalent of a physical marking of paper documents done at an electronic level. This often falls under the area of DRM or digital rights management, but involves labeling all of the information in a way so it can be identified and tracked at an electronic level across the organization. Digital watermarking and other technologies can be utilized to better track and control the flow of information. This is an area that is often overlooked in protecting against the APT. If the adversary is ultimately after the data, if an organization better classified, marked, tracked, and controlled the information, the organization would have an easier time of finding, controlling, and minimizing the damage of the APT. When you look at APT breaches in which terabytes of information are stolen, it is evident that organizations are not doing a good job at tracking and controlling the sensitive information within their networks.
- *Data discovery*—While the term data theft is used a lot, it is really an inaccurate term. Theft implies the taking of an item so the person who owns the item no longer has it in their possession. With data theft, an attacker is not taking an organization's information so they no longer have it, they are merely making a copy of it. The organization whose information was stolen, still has the information and can still use it. The problem is the adversary also has a copy and can use it against them. This is meant to illustrate the difficulty in protecting and controlling information. If someone had a piece of gold and wanted to protect it, they would lock the gold in a safe and properly guard it. There would be no way to make a copy of the gold and there would only be one instance of the gold that would have to be kept protected. With data, it can easily be copied, backed up, and exist in many different locations. Now when someone wants to protect a critical piece of information or a file, it is not a single instance of a file, it can exist in many locations and any user who has access to it can make additional copies. Therefore once critical information is identified, an organization needs to find all of the locations where it exists and either securely remove the extra copies or properly protect all of the locations that contain the information. The APT is very opportunistic and is ultimately after critical pieces of information. It does not matter to the adversary which data store or location they copy the information from. In some cases the primary database that contained the information was kept secure but the

adversary found a copy on a development server that was an exact copy of the information, but it was not properly protected. Unless an organization is 100% confident that the only copy of a piece of information is on a single server, performing data discovery is a critical part of understanding what needs to be protected and the scope of the problem. Many organizations have no clue of all of the places their information resides and is often shocked when data discovery is performed. As we always tell our clients, if you do not perform data discovery and properly protect your information, the adversary will, but at that point it will be too late.

- *Data reduction*—When it comes to securing and protecting an enterprise, less is more. The more information an organization has, the more expensive it is to store and the harder it is to track, control, and monitor. What is ironic is organizations often store a lot more information that what they actually need to run a business. Extra information often makes extra work and organizations can end up spending energy trying to protect information that does not need protecting because it currently has no value to the organization. Reducing the size of the attack surface is a theme of this book and reducing the amount of data that has to be protected is a key part of this puzzle. If the adversary is ultimately after the data, the more data that exists, the easier it is for the attacker and the harder it is for an organization. The less data the less work. Understanding all of the servers that reside on a network, what data they contain and mapping that against business function will identify the information that is important to the business and the information that is not very important. Removing the information that is not needed, will reduce the amount of effort that has to be put into protecting the organization. The use of expiration dates is a good practice to put in place when data is classified. With expiration dates, not only is an organization classifying the information but they are also giving a date when the information is no longer needed. This allows an organization to better manage and control their information.
- *Data isolation*—The best way to protect critical information is physical isolation or an air gap. It is hard for an attacker over the Internet to compromise information that they cannot access. Data isolation is useful in cases where very sensitive information needs to reside at an organization but it is only used by a small number of systems on a closed network. Ideally all critical information should be isolated or segmented into separate networks or enclaves. The problem is that while physical isolation makes it very hard for an attacker, it also makes it very difficult for legitimate users to perform their job. If physically isolation cannot be achieved, virtual isolation would also work. With virtual isolation, the information is still accessible on the network, it is just not directly accessible and there are additional control gates or security measures that provide an extra level of protection. Once again the balance is always between functionality and security. This provides additional security but also makes it harder for the legitimate user to access the information and perform their job.

- *Data protection*—Ultimately in order to minimize or reduce the impact of an APT, an organization has to provide proper protection of their information. The issue is that many organizations jump right to this step, implement various security devices but without performing all of the previous steps, the data protection will not work effectively. Taking shortcuts rarely works out and with an advanced adversary, shortcuts only provide you a false sense of security. An organization needs to know what information is critical, the classification and where it is located in order to be able to provide a proper level of protection. The level of protection that is provided should be based off of the criticality of the information to the enterprise and the amount of damage that would be caused if it was compromised. Data protection should also have a series of both preventive and detective measures covering the host and the network. Now by having four levels of protection (preventive-host, detective-host, preventive-network, detective-network) an organization can properly protect and track who is accessing key information and for what purpose.

There are many risks that organizations face but all of the critical risks focused on the APT involve controlling and protecting the organization's information. Spending time today to focusing on a better understanding of the data landscape will reap dividends in protecting against the advanced, emerging threats.

GAME PLAN

Anytime we are engaged in an activity, what makes it frustrating and difficult is if we do not know what the adversary is thinking or how they are going to operate. If you have played an opponent before and you understand their strengths and weaknesses, there are less surprises and overall less stress because you know what to expect. Most importantly if you understand how they are going to operate, it allows you to be better prepared, focusing on your weaknesses that there is a high likelihood that they will exploit. Understanding an adversary's game plan gives you an upper hand because you know how to plan, operate, and the steps that need to be taken to proper deal with the threat.

The bad news is that the APT attacks are increasing in number and overall the adversary has been very successful in causing damage to organizations. The good news is that there have been enough attacks that we have a good understanding and idea of how they operate, what they exploit, and what they are after. Essentially we have the attacker's game plan. We know that the adversary has switched from "computer attacking computer" to "human attacking human." Worms that would scan IP addresses, find an unpatched server, and compromise it was a computer breaking into a computer. The worm was programmed to perform certain actions, it was deterministic and static in terms of the actions that would be taken. We could reverse engineer the worm, determine how it operates, apply the patches to the computer, and be protected. Even though today the attacker will use software and exploits to break in, it is a human making the decisions not a piece of code like with a worm. Therefore, it will perform detailed reconnaissance, identify a high likelihood attack, and be very adaptive at trying to break into an organization. Essentially the adversary will keep changing targets, adapting methods until it is successful. The good news is because most organizations show fairly predictability, the adversary while it has the ability to be very adaptive, today does not have to adapt that often because their current methods are very successful and work extremely well.

Regardless of how adaptive they are the one item that is static is that the adversary is ultimately after your data or information. While their means and methods might change, they are targeting an organization to access and extract critical information. If an organization is going to be targeted it is because they have critical information that the adversary is after. An organization needs to figure out what that information is. What business is your organization in that would make you a target of the APT. Based on this information what data are they ultimately after and just as important, what information that if compromised would cause significant harm or reputational damage to your organization. Understanding what information an adversary might want to target might take some work. Knowing what information if compromised would cause significant damage to your organization should be much easier to identify. The bottom line is if information is stolen from your organization, but there is no criticality to the information and no damage to your organization if it is stolen, than at a most basic level who cares. We know that no organization ever wants to be compromised, but if they take information that is essentially public with minimal value, that there is no really a big issue or need for concern. Looking at the game plan for the APT, they are obsessed and hyperfocused on an organization's critical information. The more an organization can focus on the data, the more successful they will be at dealing with the APT.

The next part of the game plan is they are focused on exploiting and compromising people. Employees, contractors, and other entities within your organization are what they are ultimately targeting. The APT as the initial point of entry is not looking for a weakness in the OS to directly compromise, they are looking for a weakness in an individual with the hope that they will trick a human into taking some action that would give them access to an organization's network. The good news is most of the entry points APT exploits rely on the fact that a human will take some action. The more an organization can do to limit executable content, contain any actions the user performs, and limit the amount of access they have, will also make it harder for the adversary to cause harm. It is important to note that currently today the human is the weakest link. As organizations become more aware and better protect against the APT, the adversary might change what they are targeting and adapt, so it is important to understand that this might change over time. However, the human has always been the weakest link in any enterprise. Insider threat has long been recognized as a major concern and area that organizations need to focus on. Security professionals have been saying for years that the insider is the biggest exposure and biggest source of compromise. Since many organizations operate in a reactive not proactive manner, they did not follow this advice. All the APT did was bring this weakness to the forefront and show what happens if you do not deal with the insider threat.

Another key difference of the APT game plan is they focus on compromising a system on the private network instead of the DMZ. Traditional attacks were always focused on visible IPs on the DMZ as the initial point of compromise. The reason is simple. If a computer is breaking into a computer, you can only break into a system you can see. Therefore, the only systems that were visible were DMZ systems. However, since organizations have spent considerable time in securing these systems, they are actually a pretty difficult way to enter an organization. The APT learned that by focusing in on computers as the target, they were limited to what they could attack. By focusing in on humans, they could now get behind the iron curtain of security, directly target and compromise a system on the private network and now have an easier job at extracting critical information from the enterprise. Organizations were always under the assumption that private network systems could not be attacked from the Internet, put up a strong cyber security iron curtain, and felt they had proper security. From traditional worms these assumptions were true. From an adversary that changed the rules, most of the investment on security did not do a great job against the APT because they figured out a way to bypass it by directly targeting the human on the private network. The rules have changed and if the adversary is focusing all of their energy on compromising an organization from within the private network, additional security needs to be put in place. A private network needs to be highly segmented and since the adversary is targeting the clients, client system need to follow the same rules as DMZ systems, since clients are the new DMZ. All client systems need to be isolated with minimal to no sensitive data residing on the local system.

The last part of the APT game plan that is important to remember is that the adversary wants long-term access to a victim's network. While the initial point of compromise is to extract critical information, their ultimate goal is long-term access to continuously monitor the organization and extract information over the next several years. This piece is critical because it means that if an organization is compromised, there is an active command and control channel leaving the enterprise, even if the attacker is not currently stealing information. Focus on outbound traffic, looking for unusual connections—focus on finding the command and control channel and you will find the adversary that you are looking for.

PRIORITIZING RISKS

The difference between doing good and doing right is based on whether you are taking a risk-based approach to security. With the traditional threat, an organization can get away with not letting risk drive the calculation and the technologies they pick might work. With APT, an organization will only win if they focus in on the right areas tied back to risk. Every decision must be based on three questions:

1. *What is the risk?*
2. *Is it the highest priority risk?*
3. *Is it the most cost-effective way of reducing the risk?*

Putting all of the pieces together, an organization should be focused on the following:

- *Threat assessment and analysis*—In performing proper risk analysis and making sure an organization is focused in on the correct areas. The piece that drives the risk calculation is threat. Clearly the APT is a concern, otherwise you would not be reading this book, but in order to make sure an organization is properly prepared with both preventive and detective measures, the specific attributes of the threat need to be defined. It is important to clearly list the threats, how they are going to get into an organization, and the damage that they are going to do. A specific threat to address with regard to the APT is targeted spear phishing attacks that look like legitimate emails. It is important to create a prioritized list of threats based off of likelihood of occurrence, tied with the impact it would have to an environment.
- *Asset identification and valuation*—Even though it has been mentioned many times, it is important enough to mention it one more time. Security and protecting against the APT is all about managing risk against an organization's critical information or assets. An organization needs to identify, track, and control its most critical information, mapping it against key business processes and ulti-mately identifying which servers the data resides on. Only by understanding critical assets, business processes, applications, and servers can an organization know what has to be protected and controlled in the environment. This becomes the focus of our defensive position in terms of what the organization should focus on in terms of preventing and detecting the adversary. Once the critical areas of focus are identified, the next question that always gets asked is how much should an organization spend on security? My response is what are the assets worth and the general revenue/profitability of the organization. If the assets are only worth $1 million and the overall revenue of the company is only $5 million, spending $3 million on security does not make sense. However if the assets are worth $700 million and the organization's revenue is $4 billion, spending, $3 million on security might be too little. One of the mistakes that are often made is to take a cookie cutter approach to security in which the same exact security model is applied to every organization. Since every organization is different and unique, one size does not fit all when it comes to implementing effective security that works. The security must be adapted to the business structure, revenue, and importance of the digital assets to the success of the business. Only by tracking critical information and the overall value of those assets, can "effective" be defined in terms of how much should be spent and what should be done in the name of security.
- *Vulnerability analysis*—In order for a threat to be considered a high-risk item, it needs to map against a vulnerability that exists on a system that contains critical information. Threat drives the risk calculation so after high likelihood threats are identified and the value of critical assets has been performed, the next step is to identify vulnerabilities that would allow a threat to cause damage to a critical asset. These are called high impact vulnerabilities. Organizations often

like to fix random vulnerabilities, but when it comes to advanced attacks, we only care about the vulnerabilities that would expose critical information and cause a high impact to the success of an organization. The trick to dealing with the APT is prioritization and focus. Do not try to do everything. As we talked about we know the attacker's game plan and we have to mimic our approach to minimize the impact of what the adversary is going to do. Since the adversary is very much focused on the easiest way into an organization, we have to be very focused to make sure we are doing the right things, not just good things when it comes to security. Having a list of prioritized vulnerabilities based on attack vectors will allow an organization to either minimize or monitor the areas of attack that would have the highest impact to the organization.

- *Risk evaluation*—Once an organization has the high likelihood threats, the critical assets, and the highest impact vulnerabilities, they have all of the ingredients needed to calculate risk. They need to mix them all together and create the risks to the organization that have the highest chance of occurring and would cause the most damage to the enterprise. If this is done correctly this should map very closely to how the APT plans on successfully attacking an organization, ultimately compromising critical information. The bottom line is the more the defense can think and act like the offense, the better of they will be. The APT focuses on the easiest, most effective way of gaining long-term access and extracting out critical information. The APT focuses in on the high risk items. The reason why the threat is so successful is because the adversary has done a better job of identifying the high risk areas and exploiting them. At the same time many organizations are not taking a risk-based approach, spending money on lower risk items, which are good, but not effective at stopping the attacker. Dealing with the APT is not easy but it is not impossible. Having a clearly focused plan that is as good as the adversaries plan, would allow an organization to properly deal with and control the damage of the APT.

- *Interim security roadmap*—Taking a risk-based approach to security proves to be very effective but it turns out to be a lot of work. It is important to recognize that there are two main steps that have to be performed in analyzing risk across an organization for any type of threat, including the APT: (1) calculating the risk and (2) determining the countermeasures. Both steps are very time consuming and require executive buy-in. Therefore instead of doing all of the work on figuring out the risk and identifying all of the countermeasures, only to find out that the executives did not agree with your risk calculation, it is a good idea to put together an interim report. Even though the executives should be involved during the entire process, it is not a bad idea to put together a formal report to just confirm agreement. Nothing is worse than spending time on the second step of figuring out the appropriate countermeasures, if the risks that the analysis is based on are not correct. When it comes to being successful with security there is always a balance but it is better to error on overcommunicating, than undercommunicating. However, there is one caveat. It is critical to make sure any communication with the executives is in an easy-to-understand language (i.e. money) and is information that is important to them. One of the number 1 complaints that we hear from executives is that the security team is a black hole. They give them money and receive very little "useful" feedback or information on how effective the organization's security is. In the past where the number of attacks was contained and not very damaging, while not ideal this approach was tolerated. Today where organizations are losing significant amount of money, not providing the executives useful information they can understand can be very limiting to one's career. Putting together a clear, accurate snapshot of the state of the organization in terms of risks, likelihood, and impact of compromise to an organization's most critical asset is important to make sure the executives understand their exposure and can spend the correct resources on the problem. The interim report should contain: what is the risk, what is the likelihood of occurring, what is the cost if it occurs, and estimated cost to fix it.

- *Establish risk acceptance criteria*—An organization will not be able to fix every vulnerability. Being 100% secure does not exist if an organization wants to stay in business. Based on the type of business, revenue, assets and goals of the organization a determination has to be made on what the risk criteria are so a decision can be made of what is above the line and needs to get addressed and what is below the line and will be accepted. One of the frustrations that many security people have is they want to make that determination and if the executives do not agree with their recommendation, they get upset. In most reasonable size organizations, the focus of security is to make recommendations and provide accurate information to the executives. The goal of the executives is to balance all of the criteria and determine what the proper level of risk is, based on the goals and growth plan for the organization. Some organizations are aggressive and might take more risk than a more conservative organization. It is important to remember that the role of security is not to determine the risk criteria, it is to provide accurate information and recommendations and as long as the executives understand the information that is being presented to them, it is ultimately the executive's role to determine what the acceptable level of risk is. Security needs to focus on a simple rule: no surprises. If the organization is compromised and the executives are surprised because they were not aware of the associated risk and given a chance to remediate it, they have a right to be upset with the security team. However, if security made them aware of the risk, gave them accurate information on the potential of it occurring including estimated damages and it occurs, security did their job. Being an executive of an organization is all about balancing priorities and making choices. The result of a choice is never guaranteed and with security there is not an unlimited budget, so some bad decisions might be made to not mitigate a risk that ended up causing damage. As long as security clearly presented the information to the executives and there were no surprises, security performed their role as the honest broker.
- *Safeguard (countermeasure) selection with risk mitigation analysis*—After an organization agrees to the interim report and the executives determine the risk criteria, any risk above the line needs to be mitigated with an appropriate

countermeasure. The second big area of focus after risk determination is what is the most appropriate way to mitigate or reduce the risk. In order to determine what the appropriate countermeasure is an organization needs to understand what the goal of the risk is. Normally eliminating a risk is too expensive, so most organizations will decide to reduce the risk to an acceptable level. That acceptable level needs to be determined. If security does not understand how much the risk needs to be reduced by, they will not be able to pick an effective countermeasure. They might spend too little and not reduce the risk enough or they might spend too much and spend money on one risk, that could have been used more effectively to deal with another risk. In selecting countermeasures, it is always important to create a list of requirements that the solution must meet in order to effectively reduce the risk. Otherwise an organization can be buying random solutions that sound good but do not address the areas of concern that could be exploited by an attacker. Carefully tracking requirements is an effective way to make sure the right countermeasure is deployed.

- *Cost benefit analysis*—When implementing effective security it is important to remember the opportunity loss any time resources are used or money is spent. Every time a dollar is spent in one area, it is a dollar that cannot be spent in another area. Therefore, it is important to always perform a careful cost benefit analysis on any countermeasure to make sure that an organization is spending the least amount of money to achieve the desired result of reducing the risk below an acceptable level. In performing cost benefit analysis it is always important to remember two important acronyms ARO (annualize rate of occurrence) and TCO (total cost of ownership). Often organizations will underestimate the true cost of a risk and not fix the risks that they should or they will underestimate the cost of a countermeasure and not be able to properly implement it because it is more expensive than they thought. When it comes to risk the SLE (single loss expectancy) is the cost if the risk happens once. Depending on the type of risk this could be a relatively small number, seem inconsequential, and be ignored. The problem is the cost of a single occurrence might be low but if the number of times a year or the annualized rate of occurrence is high, the cost can be very significant. For example, there might be low end spear phishing attacks that only cost the enterprise $20,000 when it occurs. Based on this number it would not make sense to spend $100,000 to mitigate the risk. However, in a large organization a minimum of 2 people a week fall victim to this threat, the annual rate of occurrence is now around 100. Multiplying the single loss times the ARO now gives a value of $2 million for that threat per year. Now spending $100,000 might make more sense as a way to mitigate the risk. It is always important to make sure the ARO is used in calculating the risk so the total cost is recognized and proper decisions can be made. Just as underestimating the risk can be dangerous, underestimating the countermeasure can also have a devastating result. For example, an organization decides to implement a DLP (data loss prevention) solution to better manage and control the flow of data. They pick a vendor and receive a quote for $200k for the solution, since it is a high risk, they put $200k in the budget. The problem is the cost of $200k is for the delivery service to place the box on the loading dock. As soon as an employee picks up the box it is more than $200k. After installing, configuring, tuning, training, and maintenance, the total cost of ownership might be $550k. The problem is that only $200k was allocated in the budget. This means that either the solution will not get implemented correctly or some other important item in the budget will not get done because you over-spent on the DLP solution. The other important reason to always include TCO is to fully recognize the cost of the countermeasure. It might make sense to spend $200k to reduce the risk but spending $550k no longer provides a good return on investment. Therefore to make sure you are successful always remember to include the ARO when calculating the risk and the TCO when identifying countermeasures to make sure there are no surprises in the budget.

- *Final security roadmap*—Once all of the calculations, analysis, and approval have been done it is time to put together the final security roadmap. This is the interim report with countermeasures added in to the analysis. The final report should contain the following: what is the risk, what is the likelihood of occurrence, what is the cost if it occurs, what is the cost to remediate, and what is the countermeasure that will be implemented. Since the security roadmap was based off of a thorough risk analysis, it will now always map to risk and pass the test when you ask the three questions about any security decision.

It is always important to prioritize every decision we make, even if the decision is based off of risk. It is always important to make sure that based on the environments and threat, the risk that is being focused on is the highest priority risk. Even a risk-based approach can take an organization down the wrong road if it is not focused in on the highest priority area. While focusing in on high priority items is critical for effectively dealing with the APT, the trick is to know when to let go. Many security professionals will find a high priority risk and not let it go until it is completely elimi-nated. There are a few cases where eliminating a risk might be good but in most cases reducing a risk to an acceptable level is much better. To look at it from a different angle, the general approach is to find the highest risk and reduce it until it is no longer the highest risk. At the point attention should be given to the current highest risk and it should be reduced in a similar manner. The main reason this approach works is the APT typically utilized the highest priority risk as a point of compromise. The more high priority risks that can be eliminated the better.

KEY EMERGING TECHNOLOGIES

This book laid out an approach for effectively dealing with the APT. The methods in this book will scale, providing effectively security today and into the future because they focus in on fixing the problem and not on treating the symptoms. However, the threat will effectively evolve and it is important to not just focus on the current concern, the APT, it is also important to focus on all next generation threats. As organizations continue to focus on effectively dealing with the APT, the APT is not going to go away, it is going to evolve. As the defense gets more effective, the offense will change and adapt. In addition to focusing in on properly protecting data and mitigating risk, it is also important to look out on the horizon and track the emerging trends that are needed to effectively scale security into the future. Some of the key emerging trends that effective organizations are focusing on are:

1. *More focus on data correlation*—Instead of adding more devices to a network, perform data correlation across the existing devices first. Networks are becoming so complex that no single device will be able to give enough insight into what is happening across an organization. To better understand both normal and anomalous traffic, data correlation has to be performed across all critical devices. Each device/server has a piece of the puzzle and only by putting all of the pieces together, can organizations understand what is really happening.

2. *Threat intelligence analysis will become more important*—Many of the products in the security industry are becoming more commoditized. Many consoles and network devices are very similar in how they work and operate. The key differentiator is having accurate and up-to-date threat data. Organizations cannot fix every single risk. Therefore as the risks grow, more focus has to be put against the real attack vectors. A growing theme is the defense must learn from the offense. Threat must drive the risk calculation so that the proper vulnerabilities can be addressed. Only with proper threat data, can the avenues of exploitation be fixed.

3. *Endpoint security becomes more important*—As more and more devices become portable, the importance of the endpoint becomes more critical. In terms of the data it contains, there is little difference between a server and a laptop. A server might have more data but laptops typically still have a significant amount of critical information. However, the server is on a well-protected network and the laptop is usually directed connected to untrusted networks, including wireless. Therefore, we need to move beyond traditional endpoint protection and focus on controlling, monitoring and protecting the data on the end points.

4. *Focusing in on proactive forensics instead of being reactive*—Attacks are so damaging that once an attacker gets in it is too late. In addition, with technologies like virtualization and SCADA controllers, performing reactive forensics is more difficult and sometimes not possible. Therefore, more energy and effort needs to be put against proactively identifying problems and avenues of compromise before major impact is caused to an organization. With the amount of intellectual property that is being stolen and the reputational damage, proactive is the only way to go.

5. *Moving beyond signature detection*—Signature detection works because the malicious code did not change and it took a while for large-scale exploitation

to occur. While signature detection is still effective at catching some attacks, it does not scale to the advanced persistent threat (APT) that continues to occur. Therefore, signature detection must be coupled with behavioral analysis to effectively prevent and detect the emerging threats that will continue to occur. Since the new threats are always changing and persistent, only behavior analysis has a chance of being able to deal with the malicious attacks in an effective way.

6. *Users will continue to be the target of attack*—Everyone likes to focus on the technical nature of recent attacks, but when you perform root cause analysis the entry point with most of these sophisticated APT attacks is a user opening an attachment, clicking on a link, or performing some action they are not supposed to. After an initial control point is gained on the private networks, the attacks became very sophisticated and advanced but the entry point with many attacks is traditional social engineering. Advanced spear phishing attacks will trick the user into performing some action they are not supposed to. While you will never get 100% compliance from employees, organizations need to put energy against it because they will get short and long term benefit.

7. *Shifting from focusing on data encryption to key management*—Crypto is the solution of choice for many organizations, however they fail to realize that crypto does not do any good, if the keys are not properly managed and protected. Crypto has quickly become painkiller security because organizations are focused on the algorithms and not the keys. The most robust algorithms in the world are not any good without proper management of the keys. Most data that is stolen is from encrypted databases because the keys are stored directly with the encrypted data.

8. *Cloud computing will continue regardless of the security concerns*—Even though there are numerous concerns and security issues with cloud, you cannot argue with free. As companies continue to watch the bottom line, more companies are wondering why they are in the data center business. By moving to both public and private clouds can lower costs and overhead; however as with most items, security will not be considered until after there are major problems. Attackers will always focus on high payoff targets. As more companies move to the cloud, the attack methods and vectors will also increase at an exponential rate including an APT focused on the cloud.

9. *New Internet protocols with increased exposure*—As the Internet continues to grow and be used for everything, new protocols will continue to emerge. The problem is the traditional model of deploying new protocols, no longer works. In the past, a new protocol was developed and would take a long term to achieve mainstream usage. This allowed the problems to be worked out and security to be properly implemented. Today when a new protocol comes out it is used so quickly, the problems are only identified after there is wide spread use, which quickly leads to wide spread attacks.

10. *Integrated/embedded security devices*—Not only is technology becoming integrated into almost every component, more functionality is being moved to

the hardware level. Beyond the obvious implication of having more targets to go over, embedded devices create a bigger problem. It is much harder to patch hardware than it is software. If software has a problem, you can run a patch. If hardware has a vulnerability, it will take longer to fix and increase the attack surface. Smart grid is a good example of items 9 and 10 combined together.

THE CRITICAL CONTROLS

One of the questions that often gets asked is where should an organization get started and what are the areas that will give the best overall return on the security investment? The correct answer is that it should be based off of the high risk areas to an organization's most critical assets. While that is the proper way of approaching security, it is not actionable and organizations need a roadmap to start with so they can jump start their approach with securing against the APT. A comment that is often received is we are getting compromised today by the APT and cannot wait to build a plan from scratch, we need a list of the top attack vectors that are in general causing the most damage to organizations across the Internet. A great starting point for implementing APT effective security is the Critical Controls from SANS. These controls are based off of a consensus project in which a simple guiding principle was used, offense informs the defense. The question that was asked a field of experts is what are the root cause problems that the advanced threats often use to exploit an organization? Based off of the threat information the critical controls were created as a way to fix the root cause problem that is often taken advantage of by an adversary to cause harm to an enterprise.

The Critical Security Controls have already begun to transform security in government agencies and other large enterprises by focusing their spending on the key controls that block known attacks and find the ones that get through. These controls allow those responsible for compliance and those responsible for security to agree, for the first time, on what needs to be done to make systems safer. The key goals of the critical controls are:

1. *Offense must inform defense*—many organizations perform reactive security fixing the symptom of a problem, not the actual problem. Since the controls are based off of a consensus, an organization can now perform proactive security by learning from other people's data breaches. All of the controls are based off of actual attacks and threat that are causing harm to organizations. By using the threat data as a guide, the controls focus in fixing the actual problems that allowed attacks to be successful.

2. *Agreeable metrics across all business units*—The controls give an organization a way to measure the effectiveness of a control because each control has different sub-controls broken into different levels of sophistication. In many organizations a fundamental problem with security in IT is doing one thing, auditors are measuring something different, security is creating a standard, and the executives have no clue on what is happening. By creating clear metrics,

all entities in the business can have a common language and work together. Security can define the metrics, IT can implement the metrics, auditors can validate against the metrics, and executives can understand and track progress across the metrics.

3. *Automation*—Even though the APT is human against human, one of the reasons the threat is so effective is that many attacks are automated to be efficient and be performed very quickly. With many organizations detection is still heavily based on manual methods. It does not matter how smart someone is and how much training they have, manual methods against automation will always lose. Fifteen of the controls were designed to be automated to take away the unfair advantage that attackers have.

Each of the controls is broken down into categories to allow organizations to have a more scalable roadmap for implementing the controls. The four main categories of subcontrols are:

- *Quick wins*—These fundamental aspects of information security can help an organization rapidly improve its security stance generally without major procedural, architectural, or technical changes to its environment. It should be noted, however, that these subcontrols do not necessarily provide comprehensive protection against all attacks. The intent of identifying "quick wins" is to highlight where security can be improved rapidly.
- *Improved visibility and attribution*—These subcontrols focus on improving the process, architecture, and technical capabilities of organizations so that they can monitor their networks and computer systems and better visualize their own IT operations. Attribution is associated with determining which computer systems, and potentially which users, are generating specific events. Such improved visibility and attribution helps organizations detect attack attempts, locate the points of entry for successful attacks, identify already-compromised machines, interrupt infiltrated attackers' activities, and gain information about the sources of an attack. In other words, these controls improve an organization's situational awareness of its environment.
- *Hardened configuration and improved information security hygiene*— These subcontrols are designed to improve an organization's information security stance by reducing the number and magnitude of potential security vulnerabilities and by improving the operations of networked computer systems. They focus on protecting against poor security practices by system administrators and end-users that could give an adversary an advantage in attacking target systems. Control guidelines in this category are formulated with the understanding that a well-managed network is typically a much harder target for computer attackers to exploit.
- *Advanced*—These subcontrols are designed to further improve the security of an organization beyond the other three categories. Organizations already following all of the other subcontrols should focus on this category.

SANS (www.sans.org) maintains the most up-to-date copy of the critical controls. The following are the current controls that can be used as an effective method for fixing the root cause problem of most major attack vectors:

1. *Inventory of Authorized and Unauthorized Devices—Reduce the ability of attackers to find and exploit unauthorized and unprotected systems:* Use active monitoring and configuration management to maintain an up-to-date inventory of devices connected to the enterprise network, including servers, workstations, laptops, and remote devices.

2. *Inventory of Authorized and Unauthorized Software—Identify vulnerable or malicious software to mitigate or reduce the impact of attacks:* Devise a list of authorized software for each type of system, and deploy tools to track software installed (including type, version, and patches) and monitor for unauthorized or unnecessary software.

3. *Secure Configurations for Hardware and Software on Laptops, Workstations, and Servers—Prevent attackers from exploiting services and settings that allow easy access through networks and browsers:* Build a secure image that is used for all new systems deployed to the enterprise, host these standard images on secure storage servers, regularly validate and update these configurations, and track system images in a configuration management system.

4. *Continuous Vulnerability Assessment and Remediation—Proactively identify and repair software vulnerabilities reported by security researchers or vendors:* Regularly run automated vulnerability scanning tools against all systems and quickly remediate any vulnerabilities, with critical problems fixed within a set time period.

5. *Malware Defenses—Block malicious code from tampering with system settings or contents, capturing sensitive data, or spreading:* Use automated anti-virus and anti-spyware software to continuously monitor and protect workstations, servers, and mobile devices. Automatically update such anti-malware tools on all machines on a daily basis. Prevent network devices from using auto-run programs to access removable media.

6. *Application Software Security—Minimize vulnerabilities in application software:* Carefully test internally developed and third-party application software for security flaws, including coding errors and malware. Deploy web application firewalls that inspect all traffic, and explicitly check for errors in all user input (including by size and data type).

7. *Wireless Device Control—Protect the security perimeter against unauthorized wireless access:* Allow wireless devices to connect to the network only if it matches an authorized configuration and security profile and has a documented owner and defined business need. Ensure that all wireless access points are manageable using enterprise management tools. Configure scanning tools to detect wireless access points.

8. *Data Recovery Capability (validated manually)—Minimize the damage from an attack:* Implement a trustworthy plan for removing all traces of an attack.

Automatically back up all information required to fully restore each system, including the operating system, application software, and data. Back up all systems at least weekly; back up sensitive systems more often. Regularly test the restoration process.

9. *Security Skills Assessment and Appropriate Training to Fill Gaps (validated manually)—Find knowledge gaps, and fill them with exercises and training:* Develop a security skills assessment program, map training against the skills required for each job, and use the results to allocate resources effectively to improve security practices.

10. *Secure Configurations for Network Devices such as Firewalls, Routers, and Switches—Validate the security configurations of all critical devices, making sure they have implemented effective security:* Compare firewall, router, and switch configurations against standards for each type of network device. Ensure that any deviations from the standard configurations are documented and approved and that any temporary deviations are undone when the business need abates.

11. *Limitation and Control of Network Ports, Protocols, and Services—Institute a principle of least privilege by only running the minimal services and reducing the number of open ports into a system:* Apply host-based firewalls and port-filtering and -scanning tools to block traffic that is not explicitly allowed. Properly configure web servers, mail servers, file and print services, and domain name system (DNS) servers to limit remote access. Disable automatic installation of unnecessary software components.

12. *Controlled Use of Administrative Privileges—Protect and validate administrative accounts on desktops, laptops, and servers to prevent two common types of attack:* (1) enticing users to open a malicious email, attachment, or file, or to visit a malicious website; and (2) cracking an administrative password and thereby gaining access to a target machine. Use robust passwords or two factor authentication.

13. *Boundary Defense—Control the flow of traffic through network borders, and monitor content by looking for attacks and evidence of compromised machines:* Establish multilayered boundary defenses by relying on firewalls, proxies, demilitarized zone (DMZ) perimeter networks, and other network-based tools. Filter inbound and outbound traffic.

14. *Maintenance, Monitoring, and Analysis of Security Audit Logs—Use detailed logs to identify and uncover the details of an attack, including the location, malicious software deployed, and activity on compromised systems:* Generate standardized logs for each hardware device and the software installed on it, including date, time stamp, source addresses, destination addresses, and other information about each packet and/or transaction. Store logs on dedicated servers, and run biweekly reports to identify and document anomalies.

15. *Controlled Access Based on the Need to Know—Prevent attackers from gaining access to highly sensitive data through data classification:* Carefully identify and separate critical data from information that is readily available to

internal network users. Establish a multilevel data classification scheme based on the impact of any data exposure, and ensure that only authenticated users have access to proprietary information.

16. *Account Monitoring and Control—Control access to the network by disabling unneeded accounts and requiring strong authentication:* Review all system accounts and disable any that are not associated with a business process and owner. Immediately revoke system access for terminated employees or contractors. Disable dormant accounts and encrypt and isolate any files associated with such accounts. Use robust passwords or two factor authentication.

17. *Data Loss Prevention—Stop unauthorized transfer of sensitive data through network attacks:* Analyze the movement of data across network boundaries, both electronically and physically, to minimize the exposure to attackers. Monitor people, processes, and systems, using a centralized management framework.

18. *Incident Response Capability (validated manually)—Establish an incident response plan that can perform timely reaction to incidents:* Develop an incident response plan with clearly delineated roles and responsibilities for quickly discovering an attack and then effectively containing the damage, eradicating the attacker's presence, and restoring the integrity of the network and systems.

19. *Secure Network Engineering (validated manually)—Validating that security is embedded into the software development lifecycle (SDLC):* Use a robust, secure network engineering process to prevent security controls from being circumvented. Deploy a network architecture with at least three tiers: DMZ, middleware, private network. Allow rapid deployment of new access controls to quickly deflect attacks.

20. *Penetration Tests and Red Team Exercises (validated manually)—Use simulated attacks to improve organizational readiness and identify vulnerabilities:* Conduct regular internal and external penetration tests that mimic an attack to identify vulnerabilities and gauge the potential damage.

The best way to get started with the controls is to perform an assessment or gap analysis of the current state of an organization. It is fairly simple to do but highly effective. Create a spreadsheet with four columns. In the first column list all 20 of the controls. The second column should be the current state of your organization today. For each control give your organization a score:

- 0—means you are not implementing any part of the control
- 1—means you are implementing the Quick Win subcontrols
- 2—means you are implementing Improved Visibility and Attribution subcontrols
- 3—means you are implementing Hardened Configuration and Improved Information Security Hygiene subcontrols
- 4—means you are implementing the Advanced subcontrols.

In the third column list where your organization should be with regard to the controls in 12 months. The fourth column should be a subtraction of the second and third columns which will tell you the biggest gaps. Any control that has a 4 in the first column should be fixed first, then a 3, followed by 2 and final 1's. This brief analysis will provide your organization an effective gap analysis of areas that need a higher priority focus. Once this is done a fifth column can be added in which you would list the tools your organization currently has that can implement the control. This will allow an organization to see where they have gaps in their products.

The controls are always being update so it is important to check the SANS Institute website (www.sans.org) for the latest version of the controls and cyber security training needs. Portions of this section were taken from the controls document as an introduction to how the controls can be used as an effective way of dealing with the APT.

SUMMARY

Every journey begins with a single step. Implementing effective security that can adapt to new threat vectors can seem overwhelming but the trick is to start. Remember when dealing with the APT is to not forget about the other attack vectors. It is important to implement new security to deal with the APT but to also maintain the current security measures that dealt with the traditional attack. While the APT can cause significant damage, the traditional threats are still alive and well and must not be forgotten about. The trick is to augment an organization existing security measures not replace them.

The book covered many different methods that need to be implemented to effectively deal with the APT but some of the core themes to always keep in mind are:

- *Know thy systems*—It is very difficult to protect, secure, and defend against an attack if you do not understand what you are protecting. An organization must create accurate network diagrams and visibility maps to understand what is connected to their network and the overall exposure. Proper configuration management with robust change control will allow an organization to better monitor and control what is happening across their network.
- *It is all about the data*—Perfect security does not exist. Prioritization is critical to being successful and all focus should be on protecting, controlling, managing, and monitoring the critical digital assets within an organization. All critical information, the business processes that use that information and the servers they reside on all need to be carefully managed and controlled. Focusing in on the critical data will give you a path to victory. Focusing in on anything else will lead to pain, suffering, and heartache.
- *Manage the risk*—No one knows what the future holds and since every organization is unique, adaptive security is key. The critical controls provide a nice framework because they can be adapted to a particular organization but

the adaption and focus needs to be based on risk. Organizations that allow risk to drive business decisions are winning the fight against the APT and organizations that allow factors other than risk to drive decisions are spending significant amount of money and still being compromised. Focusing on risk is critical.

- *Prevention is ideal but detection is a must*—Gone are the days in which attacks can be prevented or stopped. No matter how good an organization security is based on the fact that offense is much easier than defense, means the offense will find vulnerabilities. Focusing energy on prevention is critical but just as important is to recognize that prevention will not always be successful and in cases where an organization cannot properly prevent an attack, detection must be there to catch the attacker quickly to minimize the impact of the compromise. To be most effective it is important to focus in on inbound prevention and outbound detection.
- *Correlation against known baselines to look for anomalies*—Describing specific characteristics of the APT is difficult because it is always changing and one of the reasons why signature-based detection is not very effective. However, describing specific characteristics of normal activity can be done knowing that no matter how good the threat is, it will still differentiate from normal user activity. By constantly correlating information from multiple sources, building profiles of normal activity and looking for anomalies can be a very effective way of dealing with and detecting the APT.
- *Continuous monitoring*—The threat is constant and the longer an attack goes undetected, the more damage to the organization. Based on how efficient the APT is means, continuously monitoring and auditing an environment is critical. Any security tool that is used to analyze or secure an organization should be run on a constant basis looking for deviations from previous results. One thing that is true of the APT is that it always makes some changes to the environment. In order to maintain long-term access to an organization changes have to made. Therefore by looking very closely at how systems are configured and traffic patterns, continuous monitoring can spot any deviations or anomalies which allows more timely response and detection of the threat.

It is important to give one last warning that there is no such thing as perfect security. In the hands of an expert, one can give reasons why each of the individual items would not work in all cases against the APT. With an advanced adversary that is true. No single measure will work 100% but the real question to ask is whether all of the measures together will increase an organization security and put them in a better position to deal with the APT. The answer is absolutely. Hunting for the APT after a compromise is always important to find compromised systems but in many cases this can be several months after an attack. The goal is to build a robust framework to allow organizations to proactively identify and deal with the APT as quickly as possible minimizing the exposure, fully recognizing that this threat is persistent and constant and will require multiple avenues to be effective. Hunting and forensics will never go away but this book is meant to complement those measures by dealing with the APT head on and building a network and organization that is more APT aware, being more proactive and adaptive to the threat.

Putting all of these themes together the most important component of dealing with the APT is to understand what is normal and properly track, identify, and look for anomalies across an organization. The threat is advanced and it is a difficult battle but through proper focus, persistence, and adherence to risk, you might lose a few battles but you will win the war!

Index

Printed and bound by CPI Group (UK) Ltd, Croydon, CR0 4YY

08/06/2025

01896868-0014